The Literary Man

The Literary Man

Essays Presented to Donald W. Hannah
Edited by Karl-Heinz Westarp

AARHUS UNIVERSITY PRESS

Copyright: Aarhus University Press, 1996
Cover design: Inga Friis
Photo facing title page: Karl-Heinz Westarp
Printed by Cambridge University Press
ISBN 87 7288 540 8

AARHUS UNIVERSITY PRESS
University of Aarhus
DK-8000 Aarhus C
Fax (+ 45) 8619 8433

73 Lime Walk
Headington, Oxford OX3 7AD
Fax (+ 44) 1865 750 079

Box 511
Oakville, Conn. 06779
Fax (+ 1) 203 945 9468

ANSI/NISO
Z39.48-1992

Cover: Edward Hopper, *People in the Sun*, oil on canvas, 1960
The National Museum of American Art, Smithsonian Institution, Washington,
gift of S.C. Johnson & Son, Inc.

Contents

The Critical Perspective

The Welcome to Denmark

For Donald Hannah

Undaunted, sitting astride his horse,
the coast-guard answered, 'Anyone with gumption
and a clear head has to consider
two things: what's said and what's done.
It's obvious to me that you are a band
our king could rely on. So come on ahead
with your arms and your gear, and I will guide you.
What's more, I'll order my own comrades
to pledge their honour and protect your boat
down there on the strand — keep her safe
in her new tar, until once again
her curved prow cavorts on the waves
and ferries this favoured man to Geatland.
May one so valiant and venturesome
come unscathed through the crush of battle.'

So they went on their way, the watched boat
floating behind them, broad-beamed
and anchored fast. Boar-shaped flanges
topped their cheek-guards, goldsmith's work,
each bright-forged bristle watching over
those stern-faced men. They marched in step,
hurrying on until the timbered hall
and its gold appointments appeared before them.
There was no other building like it on earth
or under heaven. Majesty lodged in it.
It was a luminous outpost, a light to many lands.
So their gallant escort guided them
to that dazzling stronghold and indicated
the shortest way to it; impetuously then
he wheeled on his horse and spoke these words:
'It is time for me to go. May the Almighty

Father defend you and in His goodness
watch over your exploits. I'm away to the sea,
back on alert against enemy forces.'
   (*Beowulf*, lines 286-319, translated by Seamus Heaney)

To an Admirable Teacher

> His hearers could not cough,
> or look aside from him without loss ...
> The fear of every man that heard him, was,
> lest he should make an end.
> (Raman Selden about John Oakley)

Mention Donald W. Hannah among graduates of English from Aarhus University, and they will unanimously and gladly pay tribute to their one-time teacher's well-informed and extremely entertaining perform-ance-lectures. To them Donald Hannah is the incarnation of one of G.B. Shaw's 'Maxims for Revolutionists': 'He who can, does. He who cannot, teaches'. Handled by him, all texts become what Voltaire characterized as 'eminently teachable'. His love for literature, his voracious reading and his empathic readings have a catching spill-over effect on freshmen and experienced students alike. His tone is always semi-detached, never far from irony, including self-irony, which makes his performances all the more charming. With his total presence, always conscious of the importance of the paedagogy of teaching literature, he can easily hold his audience spellbound — students and fellow-scholars alike. In the same vein, students and colleagues remember fondly his unforgettable performances as 'toast-master' in connection with the department's Christmas parties. Though tone-deaf, Donald Hannah conducted the crowd safely through a string of Christmas carols, always graciously laughing at his own inability to sing, and he could make us do whatever he wanted.

Who is this wizard with words and gestures? He was born on June 16 (1927) — he loves to refer to this date as 'Bloomsday', the famous day on which James Joyce's *Ulysses* takes place. Himself a native of coal-mining in-dustrial Nottingham, Donald Hannah chose D.H. Lawrence, one of Notting-hamshire's best-known creative minds, as the first subject of his research. Later, in keeping with his own change of residence, he chose the Danish writer Karen Blixen, *alias* Isak Dinesen, as the subject of his Ph.D. research. Donald Hannah's love for foreign parts showed itself first when in 1954 he took up a lectureship in Sarajevo, a place often fondly remembered by him in conversations, not least because of the 'otherness' of the system there, a system without respect for Voltaire's famous exhortation: 'We are not only responsible for what we do, but also for what we do not do'.

A welcome and as it turned out life-long change of system occurred with Donald Hannah's appointment on August 1, 1957 as native-speaking lecturer at the Department of English at Aarhus University, a post he held until he was appointed to an *amanuensis* post in 1961. In 1966 he became *Afdelingsleder*, in 1967 he was appointed senior lecturer, and from 1974 until his retirement in August 1996 he held the Chair of English Literature. In the spring of 1978 he served as an exchange professor at Centenary College of Louisiana, Shreveport, USA. There new friendships and scholarly contacts developed, as they did in many other ways through participation in international conferences and symposia, and Donald Hannah has always been very good at looking after those contacts.

One of Donald Hannah's colleagues and friends through many years was Erik Arne Hansen. When we planned this collection of essays Erik Arne was immediately willing to contribute. His was to be an essay on John Donne's poem 'The Ecstasy', but before he could begin writing, Erik Arne fell seriously ill and died on July 31, 1995. On the shelf next to his desk we found three volumes on Donne and a couple of notes, witnessing his work on the article. May his presence among the contributors to this volume and his memory be honoured by the last lines in Donne's poem:

> ... he shall see
> Small change when we are to bodies gone.

During his first visit to Århus and his meeting with the Tollund Man, which among other things inspired a series of bog poems, Seamus Heaney was looked after by Donald Hannah. We are glad and grateful that the now Nobel-prize honoured author found time to contribute to this volume with lines from his 'translation' of *Beowulf*, 'who was welcomed to Denmark in much the same way' as Donald Hannah was.

All the other contributors have known Donald Hannah during different phases of his period as teacher here in Århus. In the notes on contributors they briefly describe their relationship to Donald Hannah. Others had hoped to contribute, but for one reason or another have not been able to compose their essays in time for them to be included.

All essays in this volume are previously unpublished, and the editor decided to leave them in their original size and form and to restrict himself to giving them a style-sheet uniformity. The contributions lent themselves to a structure that mirrors Donald Hannah's manifold literary interests, namely British literature since Shakespeare, 20th century literature in English and critical theory. Each section is arranged chronologically according to its subjects. The first part, 'The British Tradition', contains apart from two discussions of Shakespeare an essay on Dr. Johnson, one on Fanny Burney and one on *Frankenstein*. Claus Bratt Østergaard discusses among other things the many layers of importance in Shakespeare's image of 'ambush' and in the figure of the 'deputy' in *Measure for Measure*. Michael Skovmand's essay questions Shakespeare's affirmative title *All's Well That Ends Well* and investigates the difficult task of dating the play. Lee Morgan demythologizes the scholarly notion of seeing Dr. Johnson as a bellicose man. Knud Sørensen questions the tradition of Fanny Burney's employment of many different styles as opposed to the notion of a characteristic 'style'. Inger Hunnerup Dalsgaard discusses the wide range of political and scientific implications in Mary Shelley's *Frankenstein*.

The second part, 'Modern Voices', reflects Donald Hannah's interest in modern British autors and in other literatures in English. Per Serritslev Petersen has studied the growth of D.H. Lawrence's *Women in Love* and found manuscript evidence of a new genesis of the love triangle in the novel. Niels Bugge Hansen relates the many dreams present in Graham Greene's novels to the importance Greene attributed to dreams in his own life. Michael Böss takes up Colm Toibin, a modern Irish author, and his revolt against the traditional explanations of the troubles, thus moving us right into the heart of present-day Irish issues. Jørn Carlsen has studied the archives of Danish emigration to Canada in the 1920s and found surprising evidence of deceit in luring Danish families to Canada. Earle Labor presents Jack London's understanding of art, which allows for a combination of good realistic writing and making money at the same time. Karl-Heinz Westarp's comparison between Flannery O'Connor and Eudora Welty focusses on the striking similarities between these otherwise different authors' views on mystery.

In part three, 'The Critical Perspective', Hans Hauge looks at the revolutionary development in critical theory and the understanding of aesthetics that has taken place since the 1950s. Lars Ole Sauerberg draws an all-round picture of Harold Bloom's critical career all the way up to his controversial agonistic canon.

This gift to Donald Hannah would not have been possible without the generous financial support of the Aarhus University Research Fund; without the critical eyes of Anne A. Collett and Tim Caudery, Donald's successors as native speaking lecturers at the department; without the patient technical assistance of our secretary Vibeke Kjaer and the professional advice of Tønnes Bekker-Nielsen, Director of Aarhus University Press. Thanks to all those, thanks to the contributors, who responded willingly and quickly to the editor's requests, and thanks to Hans-Jørgen Frederiksen, who helped us find a suitable cover picture for *The Literary Man*.

Looking back into the history of the Department of English, there was only one member who equalled Donald Hannah's record of 39 years of service — namely Professor Torsten Dahl, who gave as many years to the organization of the department since its beginnings in 1928. After Donald Hannah's years of active involvement may he have many years to come characterized by the last line in Milton's sonnet on his blindness, 'they also serve who only stand and wait'.

Karl-Heinz Westarp
Århus, January 1, 1996.

The British Tradition

In the Ambush of My Name:
A Discussion of *Measure for Measure*

Claus Bratt Østergaard

The objective correlative and the excess of disgust

T.S. Eliot's 'Hamlet and His Problems' is surely one of the most enduring short essays on Shakespeare of all time. The essay gave rise to considerable controversy on its appearance in 1920, when Eliot pointed to 'some intractable material' in *Hamlet* which Shakespeare had failed to represent in any acceptable form. In addition, Eliot introduced his own, equally enduring notion of the objective correlative — since, in fact, this valued feature was what he saw as lacking in *Hamlet*. Simply, the play suffered from a combination of too much and too little. Gertrude, as dramatically conceived by Shakespeare, was too little in the sense that she formed an inadequate target of too much emotion in her son. Too much emotion and too little in terms of objective correlative. Eliot would often state his preference for Dante over Shakespeare. Dante was classical. Shakespeare, however great, was either too much or too little, intractable and recalcitrant — like *Hamlet*. However, Eliot does, ambiguously, temper his disaffection with the play, calling it 'interesting'.

In 'Hamlet and his Problems' Eliot also mentions *Measure for Measure* and the *Sonnets* as interesting in this sense. Although he restricts his analysis to *Hamlet*, it is clear that in all three cases, the problem is too much and too little. Too much and too little demands interpretation; however, '*Qua* work of art, the work of art cannot be interpreted'; there is nothing to interpret; classical works are self-explanatory. Eliot stresses that he cannot say what is wrong since *Hamlet* does not inform him. The play remains opaque, baffling the reader because it fails to provide its own interpretation. Nevertheless, Eliot does come up with several hints: the problem is an excess of disgust on the part of the son and a representation of the mother on the part of the poet which, somehow, is not up to it. He further guesses that this is due to Shakespeare's insufficient handling of his sources, the presence of some unfashioned revenge thematics from previous *Hamlet* dramas that 'hibernate' in Shakespeare's text, preventing the poet from finishing his job; Shakespeare translated the motive of revenge into 'some stuff' that remained unexplained in his play, refractory and frustrating.

We are surely justified in attributing the play, with that other profoundly inter-esting play of 'intractable' material and astonishing versification, *Measure for Measure*, to a period of crisis ...

But Eliot's biographical hint is not much use either. I shall term his intract-ability the problem of the remainder. He clearly saw that this problem runs through Hamlet's entire drama and, baffling the reader of 'Hamlet and his Problems', he called the play a failure; indeed, not a work of art. If few readers and critics have agreed with Eliot's denunciation of the play, many have admitted its final intractability. Nevertheless, I think Eliot's analysis heightens our understanding of the play rather than discredits it and that he is much closer to its central concerns than many contemporary inter-pretations that sought coherence at all costs, such as John Dover Wilson's *What Happens in* Hamlet?[1] However, with the advent of post-structuralism aesthetic criteria have changed dramatically since Dover Wilson and Eliot; in particular, what Eliot views as defective in *Hamlet* may now be seen as the source of its rich dramatic and symbolic structure. Whatever his intentions, Eliot has helped pave the way for this new interpretation. I suggest in this essay that we may even recover his objective correlative at a point beyond the current post-structuralist onslaught on any form of order, textual or metaphysical.

What remains is Hamlet's disgust for Gertrude, according to Eliot. But there is no reason to stop here since, indeed, a pervasive feeling of disgust enshrouds any body mentioned in this play — from Claudius and his excessive drinking, Gertrude and her obscene hunger for sex, to Ophelia and her female pretence as well as the dead men's fingers grappling her on her way to the grave, all of which is summed up in Yorick's emblematic skull and the curiously innocent reminiscence it triggers in Hamlet. The right body of the father disappears, the wrong body of the uncle stands in the way; too much and too little: the father's unremitting urgency as Ghost is coupled to his shadowy lack of physical substance; flamboyant potency in the uncle versus ineffectualness in son and father, etc. The body in *Hamlet*, one way or the other, is always putrid, spectral, lascivious, dead or dying. For some reason or other it becomes a topos of desecration, deceit, lust and truth. Truth will out. But something, some thing or some body, stands in the way or remains to be accounted for — like Polonius alive behind the arras or Polonius dead behind the staircase. If Hamlet doesn't want to account for this dead body to Rosencrantz is that not similar, on some level, to his inability to dispose of Claudius' living body? The remainder, it seems, must be related to the direct and indirect preoccupation with cleansing, ablation, removal, purgation (Purgatory), sin and guilt, and it resounds throughout the play in the ambiguous echoes of these ideas. From another perspective, it is also linked to the play's preoccupation with theatrical representation. Thus, the dumbshow and its relation to the Gonzago-play, Hamlet's 'some sixteen lines', his instructions to First Player and several other significant points, big and small, may be seen as various instances of what remains, the residue, the surplus, the addition, what is in excess and what lacks or what must be discounted or deducted in terms of representation.

In the final analysis, the question includes the discord between what Hamlet has to say at a semantic level, where he desires one-to-one representation between speech and (f)act, and his propensity for speech as performance where he indulges freely in wordplay, rhetorical tricks and other forms of poetic licence. As speech act his language is 'pregnant' — in a somatic metaphor of some symbolic residual — with too much meaning to Polonius, while this surplus correlates to a lack of knowledge in Hamlet respecting the object of this same meaning. When Hamlet speech-acts he invariably adds something to what he says — his own put-on, his uncalled-for presence and un-self-fashioned desire, which he cannot disentangle from what he has to say at a semantic level; once added, his comments on everything and everybody stick and can no more be retracted than the steady increase in dead bodies, beginning with Polonius and ending with Hamlet himself. A steady increase also in T.S. Eliot's 'intractable matter'.

Something remains to be accounted for. Hamlet identifies it in his uncle, his mother, his girl-friend — in the world as such, but only to remain dissatisfied. This combined identification plus displacement implicates his own being in a complicated way which appears to operate on the borderline of what he is conscious of and what remains in the dark because only manifest in his fellow beings in terms of excess or lack. Hamlet's subjective addition emerges as a form of deceit; but what he adds, as subject of speech and other signs, is also central to the idea of truth, and the play abounds in translations from lack of truth to a surplus of signs and *vice versa*. What remains is manifest in various elusive emblems of dead bodies, skulls, graves, spectres, politic worms and dead politicians; truth remains also, in a linguistic sense, in the interspace between saying something and speaking otherwise, it governs the relation between words and deeds, and it is related, via metaphor or other devices, to Hamlet's central concern. All these symbolic transactions are relentlessly spotted by Hamlet in his search for truth and invariably denounced as sinful in his next of kin who are enveloped in a cloud of disgust.

When Eliot criticizes *Hamlet* and *Measure for Measure* because of a surplus of material and a defective presentation of it, he also defines an implicit ideal that whatever is seen must submit to the full control of the author's intention. And when, in particular, he denounces these works for not displaying full control over the sources he states the related ideal that every aspect of the drama must be transparent and self-contained. Eliot will have no traffic with excess or lack, addition or subtraction — he desires perfect form where no matter remains to be accounted for. Nevertheless, it is precisely because he insists on clarity and the classical ideal that he so lucidly perceives what remains when all is said and done.

On the whole Eliot is consistent, if embattled, but he is no doubt bordering on contradiction when, in a short passage in the essay, he also admits that things could hardly have been otherwise in *Hamlet* than they in fact are. Thus he acknowledges a kind of feeling in Hamlet which could only be stated precisely in that imprecise form in which Shakespeare failed to provide Gertrude and her act as an objective correlative to her son:

And it must be noted that this very nature of the *données* of the problem precludes objective equivalence. To have heightened the criminality of Gertrude would have been to provide the formula for a totally different emotion in Hamlet; it is just *because* her character is so negative and insignificant that she arouses in Hamlet the feeling which she is incapable of representing.[2]

The wrong words are the only right words, according to Eliot. That is Eliot's problem. But isn't it also Hamlet's problem? Isn't Eliot repeating both the problem and the emotional disgust which correlates with it? Whatever the case, we may assume that this is the heart of what Eliot finds interesting, the play's basic enigma; the point where *Hamlet* fails coincides exactly with the point where it becomes interesting.

Saying something and speaking otherwise

As for *Measure for Measure* (and the *Sonnets*) Eliot equates them with *Hamlet* in terms of intractability, but otherwise remains silent. I suggest in this essay that we may follow his hint and see the remainder as what is left to account for when measure meets measure and something still persists; as in *Hamlet*, the remainder may be identified thematically in a number of ways in *Measure for Measure*, directly and indirectly. I also discuss how, as in *Hamlet*, the question appears to influence the dramatic staging itself in a complicated and multilayered way. In addition, I propose that, as in *Hamlet*, this relates to an excessive development of disgust and I discuss what happens to Eliot's objective correlative in the process.

Measure for Measure, not surprisingly, has been variously classified. The play has a complicated source history and Shakespeare's version represents a rescription of several other plays and stories, mixing traditionally (and semiotically) separate narratives — the Corrupt Magistrate, the Disguised Ruler, the Substituted Bedmate — in a way which forces unity on difference. No doubt Eliot's idea that various heterogeneous strata enter into the final combination of *Measure for Measure* in an unresolved form may be as relevant to this play as to *Hamlet. Measure for Measure* contains distinctly allegorical elements and it mixes comic and serious matter on many levels; it is not a tragedy, but it contains the promise of one; it is not a comedy, but somehow comic features enter into the heart of the play's serious ideas. Thus Northrop Frye notices that when the disguised Duke steps forward to speak to Isabella (III, ii), the rhythm changes abruptly from blank verse to prose: 'The play breaks in two here ... from now on it is a different kind of play'.[3] Surprising details abound; thus, according to Mary Lascelles,

It is surely odd that the whole resources of authority in the prison should be engaged in obtaining /Barnardine's/ compliance; odder still that it should prove unattainable, and that a character called into being only to die, should survive.[4]

Measure for Measure even stages a romance, albeit in the inverted form of Angelo's and Isabella's encounter and the seemingly unrelated development of a final marriage between the Duke and Isabella. Admittedly, there is a didactic lesson spelled out in clear letters and merciful terms in the end, and 'problem play' would perhaps seem a fitting term. Yet once you start identifying the problem, its firm outline quickly disintegrates in the quicksand of the play's mixed generic attributes, and the final judgement-*cum*-atonement allotted to Angelo seems an inadequate summary of the events that lead up to it.

'The true significance of the whole is the triumph of mercy over strict justice', according to A.W. Schlegel.[5] This is the traditional reading, accepted until recently even by critics who dislike the play. Yet it is also true, as Terry Eagleton has it, that 'the mercy which is officially 'supplementary' to that justice threatens to erode it from the inside'.[6] When strict law is replaced by mercy in the end, the matter is brought to rest at an arbitrary point; indeed, we may begin all over again, since, as we are informed by the Duke himself, tempering the law with mercy leads to mercy in excess of the law — which was what started it all; on some significant level, the problem is circular. At a more personal level, a new state of affairs is corroborated in terms of love on the part of the Duke to replace Angelo's lust. However, the Duke's is a curious form of love, not only because the girl is claimed rather than asked, but because the Duke, as lover, seems motivated neither by desire nor by any romantic impulse; in fact not even the ethical position he perceives in Isabella appears to be what invites him to suggest that they marry. Apparently, love is not inherently motivated in either duke or nun. In the context, love, as marriage, is transformed into something other than love. Bradley thought it 'a scandalous proceeding'. As a solution to a problem, it is awash in political considerations; yet the idea of marriage in the end is also that it closes the gap between law and life, arguing a final symmetry which the play otherwise shows to come to bits and pieces everywhere.

Following Eliot, I shall address the intractability of *Measure for Measure* in relation to various issues that spring from the play's three separate narrative sources.

First, The Disguised Ruler as focused on the curious nature of the substitution of the Duke with Angelo, his deputy; Angelo is corrupt, but somehow that is not the only problem; the narrative of The Disguised Ruler disguises something which the unravelling of the disguise does not reveal.

Secondly, Isabella's confrontation with Angelo in The Corrupt Magistrate where his blunt directness answers a language in her which has alerted critics because of its ambiguousness. Angelo and Isabella, it seems, share with each other a kind of experience which is unrelated to their character to the point of being anonymous, an experience which they consequently fail to incorporate, but which is nevertheless made possible precisely in that impersonal and improper form which their unforeseen encounter engenders. The play accounts explicitly for his lust, but only in inadequately moral terms and the final arbitrary judgment. With respect to Isabella's involvement, as seen in the duplicity of her language, the critics are divided: seemingly her moral status depends on the final undecidability of her eroticism *versus* her purity of mind — and, discounting the Duke's motives for proposing to her, her final position remains in the dark.

Isabella bargains for death — *in nomine fratris et virtutis*; but diverting from tragedy in the nick of time, the plot sidetracks, adding Mariana and The Substituted Bedmate, upon which the heroine is paid by marrying the Duke. This happy outcome, as several critics have pointed out, seems a poor answer to her passionate apology for virtue in the face of Angelo's lust; in consequence, any idea of romantic love or tragic death becomes untenable. If the play is a problem play this is surely also in the sense of the problem that persists when everything else is measured out in the end.

Angelo, at one point, admits that 'I can speak/ Against the thing I say' (II, iv, 59-60). However, saying something and speaking otherwise is in no way limited to Angelo, but covers large tracts of uttered meaning in the play, including everybody of importance on the way. The contrast is provided by Barnardine who bluntly states his preference for sleep over life. What is singular to Barnardine, as we are informed by the Duke, is that he 'apprehends no further than this world/ And squares thy life according' (V, i, 479-80). Barnardine is indifferent, beyond the reach and sway of symbols. If, by contrast, you live according to the symbolic mode, Angelo's ambiguity applies throughout. Indeed, the ambiguity informs the very structure of the play. In the two main narratives (The Disguised Ruler and The Corrupt Magistrate) the title of the play applies ironically: the Duke achieves what he wants by means that contradict the ethical and political premises of his intention, and Angelo and Isabella experience a form of joy, but only via inversion of the romantic formula or by metaphoric displacement in Mariana. In both cases something, an experience, represents something else, an intention, from which it signally deviates.

The Disguised Ruler

In a sense T.S. Eliot is engaged with the same kind of problem which faces Angelo (and Vincentio) in *Measure for Measure*. Eliot's concern is aesthetic, Angelo is concerned for morality, but both cases involve the relation between a system of representations and what is represented. Like Eliot, Angelo will admit no discrepancy. Like Eliot, he insists on the exclusive lawfulness of his own system of values. There must be law for lust, form for content, measure for measure. In both cases something remains to be accounted for.

Eliot, as we have seen, stops short before his own near admission of the existence of something in objective life — Hamlet's surplus emotion — which his (Eliot's) critical vocabulary does not correlate with. But Shakespeare couples Angelo's moral rectitude to the Duke's talent for disguise and substitution; when the Duke leaves Angelo behind in office and name and moves into the thick of things, he may examine the (un)lawfulness of the law from a point of view which differs from his previous, official position. This amounts to a change in perspective. The law, we learn, may only be perceived clearly if a non-representative point of view is added to the representative position; to get the perspective right you must supply another view askew, the Sovereign must split in official Angelo and Vincento under cover.

Choosing Angelo as his deputy, the Duke also substitutes him for Escalus, discounting the latter's seniority. But why Angelo? Because Angelo is all virtue, we learn. We also learn that Angelo's virtue consists in the circumstance of its unrelatedness to his person.

DUKE: Angelo:
                              There is a kind of character in thy life
                              That to th'observer doth thy history
                              Fully unfold. Thyself and thy belongings
                              Are not thine own so proper as to waste
                              Thyself upon thy virtues, they on thee.
                              Heaven doth with us as we with torches do,
                              Not light them for themselves; for if our virtues
                              Did not shine forth of us, 'twere all alike
                              As if we had them not.
                              (I, i, 26-35)

Angelo's character is writ all over him: he is a cipher, his virtue consists in being a nobody, he is all bureaucrat. This is the Duke's reason for choosing Angelo as deputy, and although he (the Duke) later (in I, iii) supplements his official declaration with some ambiguous remarks to Friar Thomas (which are commented on below), he never explicitly detracts from the above considerations. Notably, his remarks are determined by the occasion of the first scene and phrased in official rhetoric. Yet the formality of his language cannot veil his dilemma: he wants to remove himself from the political scene while he also, at the same time, wants to remain. So he remains as someone who both is and is not himself. Angelo's new status is that of someone representing someone else as both the same and a different person.

As it happens, Angelo (unlike Antonio of *The Tempest*) is not, as deputy, motivated by a desire for power, and he modestly states his personal reservations:

ANGELO: Now, good my lord,
                              Let there be some more test made of my metal,
                              Before so noble and so great a figure
                              Be stamp'd upon it.
                              (I, i, 47-50)

Nobody listens to this. In particular, the Duke pays no attention, choosing, no doubt, to see Angelo's reservations as in the main rhetorically motivated — saying something and speaking otherwise (in Angelo's phrase). Yet there is every reason to relate Angelo's remarks to his poor show as deputy and unhappy fate as a private being; in context, his remarks are ironically charged. Ostensibly, he subsequently forgets his reservations whereupon he is engulfed by his official persona and only manages a breakthrough from it in exclamations of shock realization that he, as a private (proper) person, errs from his offical persona (in particular II, ii, 163-187 and II, iv, 1-17). If there is no reason to doubt the sincerity of his self-recriminations, his failure to act on this insight is nevertheless telling; he is shocked not by the content of his heinous proposal as much as by realizing that he is himself a contradiction in terms. In the end, the reader is well pleased to see him punished with due, if lenient measure.

What the Duke does apprehend in Angelo's reservation, on the contrary, is that the latter represents an ideal where, as he hopes, the deputy's private person will prove to be completely absorbed by his official persona. Angelo's reservations are conventional and therefore negligible, but his metaphors answer the Duke's demand, so this is where he chooses to listen: 'metal' means content (signified), and 'stamp' means form (signifier), the idea being that the metal is such that it will be shaped by its form with no residual. But, however conventional the idea, this is a paradox, because it invariably destroys any inherent semiotic balance between content and expression which makes the statement possible, if taken at face value. In fact, it is like saying: my person is specifically such that it is not a person and may therefore entirely be transformed into the abstract persona; I am only a mask, I wear no face beneath it, as person I am a non-person. Content absorbed in form with no residual. This makes no literal sense. The statement's only valid function, therefore, is as pure rhetoric.

We should certainly take Angelo's reservations precisely as such if they did not prove so deadly true in what follows. As it turns out, the paradox of being something by being nothing at all not only determines Angelo's fate (for which public and reader may not feel very sorry), but structures the presence of the remainder in this play and directly points to what must be termed one of its outstanding features: the imbalance between opposites impossible to reconcile on the one hand and the trust in absolute identity of representation on the other hand — the inherent discord that propels the chain of substitutions (which are discussed below).

However, let me return to the Duke's above address to Angelo (I, i, 26-35). J.W. Lever, the editor of the New Arden edition, must have felt that it stands in need of clarification for he supplies a note to lines 29-31 ('Thy-self and ... they on thee'.) in which he suggests the following paraphrase: 'Neither your personality nor your virtuous attributes are so far private property that either can be wasted in cultivating the other'. This no doubt covers the Duke's meaning, and Lever implicitly argues its unity in his paraphrase. I suggested above, however, that the speech veils a contradiction in its rhetoric which comes out in the pure semantic content of what he has to say: thus the Duke announces his step-down and the consonant choice of Angelo as deputy on the basis of two contradictory assumptions expressed in para-metaphoric language; first (l. 27-29) he says that the composition of Angelo's outside and inside is such that the outside entirely reveals the inside to the observer (in keeping with Angelo's subsequent use of the metaphor of the stamp and the metal); but then he proceeds to claim in two individual statements, which repeat each other (ll. 29-31 and 32-35), that there is indeed a difference between Angelo as person and Angelo as a man of virtue in the sense that his virtue dissociates itself from his person so that, by implication, his proper self is not represented by these same virtues.

Considering only the semantics and forgetting the rhetoric, we may conclude that Angelo, as person, is himself when he is virtuous (his outside objectively correlates with his inside); but we are also informed that Angelo's virtue is such that his person, his proper self, is not part of it; his person, therefore, is no signifier of his signified virtues — they no longer represent him, but 'shine out', arguing their own autonomous value; the virtue of virtue is therefore that it exists solely by itself, not as an extension of the person who displays it. This is a paradox, and we may reduce it to the following simple contradiction (phrased in a rhetorical chiasmus)[7]: Angelo, as person, incorporates virtue (a – b); virtue, as part of Angelo, excludes his proper self (b – a).

J.W. Lever, we saw, paraphrased the Duke's statement so that it acquired only one sense, papering over the semantic (literal) contradiction. Lever is preoccupied with straightening out the convoluted syntax of the Duke's rhetoric and forgets half of what he (the Duke) says. In a way he is justified in this since there is no reason, in the above situation, not to trust the rhetoric and forget about the semantics. However, in view of what later happens, the logic of the semantic content takes over, and the duplicity of Angelo's character — specifically, the impropriety of what the Duke refers to as his proper self — turns out to be covered by the semantic paradox; what Angelo in fact says ('I am not fit') becomes his fate, while his rhetoric turns out to be a form of conceit or delusion. While Angelo succumbs, the Duke survives, and he survives because he finds a retreat behind another name (Friar Lodowick) which provides a symbolic escape; notably, the Duke's retreat is only possible if Angelo steps in where the Duke vanishes from the scene. Angelo must therefore pay the price for what the Duke gets; Angelo does not enter the game of substitution and alienation otherwise indulged in by everybody in this play; he is stuck with the Duke's name, he has nowhere else to go and must meekly submit to his fate at a literal level of semantic truth.

On one level, the Duke is himself aware of the difference between saying something in an official capacity and speaking otherwise to gain his ends; he consciously and unswervingly practices deceit, and he explains why he must do so to Friar Thomas (in I, iii). Many critics have noted that the reasons he gives are unconvincing — that he cannot, in his proper person, both have allowed social practices to deteriorate and authorize the enforcement of the letter of the law. However, there is every reason to think that the Duke's deceit has a further reach than he is conscious of, and even if Shakepeare gives us no further direct evidence, he does provide us with the following significant metaphor, informing us that it is here, in the metaphor, the Duke performs what he could not do in his official position:

> DUKE: Therefore indeed, my father,
> I have on Angelo impos'd the office;
> Who may in the ambush of my name strike home.
> (I, iii, 39-41)

'Ambush' is undoubtedly ambiguous in several respects. First of all its negative connotation would seem to demand a further moral explication — which does not occur (at least not until much later and then indirectly, in The Corrupt Magistrate); secondly, we may wonder why the Duke chooses to have his deputy trapped in this metaphor when he otherwise refers to his absolute trust in him; finally, it is clear that even if the semantic agent of 'ambush' is overtly Angelo, it is nevertheless also Angelo who is shot down from the vantage point provided by the ambush. Who pulls the trigger? Supplying him with his proper name, the Duke, however unwittingly, has set a trap for Angelo, effectively ambushing him by reducing him to a metaphor of himself. Clearly, this is beyond anything he could have intended (although he does state his desire to see how he will perform). The proper name, we may therefore guess, is the guilty symbol. François Guizot once wrote that 'In Angelo, crime is only a vague abstraction, connected *en passant* with the proper name'.[8] Guizot does not develop

his idea, and presumably he refers to Angelo's proper name, not the
Duke's. Be that as it may, the conferment of authority is a duplicitous act
by which the Duke keeps his power and lets Angelo remain ambushed with
nothing but the name of the law, not the real exercise of it — as he later
learns. In a further perspective, I think we may also relate 'ambush' to the
ambiguity of the Duke's initial remarks — the discrepancy between the
literalness of the semantic level (where Angelo is trapped in the Duke's
name) and the metaphoricity of the rhetorical level (where the Duke
escapes by leaving his proper name to Angelo). Indeed, this is possible precisely because of the vague abstraction of the proper name, as noticed by
Guizot.

Commenting on the above lines, J.W. Lever does not discuss 'ambush'
directly but adds an explanatory note to the effect that the Duke refers to
a distinction between his name (as Body politic) and his private person:
'ducal authority as contrasted with the Duke in person'. Lever states what
is conventional Elizabethan wisdom and, to be sure, the distinction is
central to the politics of deputizing; the Sovereign, as personal Body, is consistently, if not unambiguously, seen as metaphor (deputy, copy) of the
body Politic (original). In *Measure for Measure* the discrepancy between
original and copy is not, as in many of Shakespeare's other plays, concerned
with the relation between Sovereign and Body politic but, one rung down
the symbolic ladder, between Sovereign and deputy. In the process, Angelo
comes to represent the failures of the personal Body while the Duke chooses to solve the dilemma by retreating from it, concealing under a different
name and gaining the stamp of true metal and undiluted essence of the
Body politic.

However, this does not explain 'ambush'; I don't think the metaphor
reduces to the general dialectics of the King's two bodies without a trace,
but that it specifically covers the problem of what remains between the
Duke as proper to the Body politic and Angelo as deputy: in particular, we
may see that 'ambush' is not a figure of speech referring to 'deputization'
as (f)act but a word in which the Duke literally denotes the process of
making a metaphor of someone else via his name; thus the social act of
deputizing is unveiled as metaphor in 'ambush' and Angelo is the victim
of the Duke's metaphoric license in real life (not, or only after the fact, in
language). That is Angelo's tragedy; but his sad fate only covers him in a
personal capacity — and as a personal being he counts as nothing, as we
know right form the beginning and as he indeed emphasizes himself.
Unlike Shylock, and except for his reservations which pass unnoticed in the
rhetoric of the occasion, Angelo is not really allowed a point of view; on

the contrary, he is conceived largely as someone who has no proper self. Instead the undisputed impropriety of his lust is punished in the noisy triumph with which the problem is solved in the end.

'Ambush' is ambiguous, therefore, in the specific shift it announces between literal and figurative language. In particular, it denominates the ambiguity of a literal metaphoricity in 'deputy'. The ambush of deputization allows Shakespeare a play on sameness and difference between Angelo and Vincentio where one term is continuously replaced with the other according to the dramatic development. What the Duke leaves behind when he goes into cover under a different name is the ambush of his proper name. We must ask if the metaphor is gratuitous and, if not, if it is explained in terms of the narrative of the Disguised Ruler, i. e. in what may be termed its proper semantic field. In fact, I think that is not the case. 'Ambush' remains unreclaimed as symbol in this narrative. But I suggest that it supplies a link with the narrative of the Corrupt Magistrate, building a connection which both gives sense to the metaphor and, in the process, confers some additional lurid light on the overt ethics ruling the play of substitutions and deputizations in this play.

In metaphoric terms the Duke relates to Angelo as Isabella to Mariana. In both cases the difference is concomitantly pointed out and veiled by the symbolic act of deputization. If admitted, the relation is metaphoric; if denied, it is postulated as a nominal identity. Both these possibilities are exploited at various points by the Duke in The Disguised Ruler and by Isabella in The Corrupt Magistrate. Indeed, there is a continuous subliminal shift from metaphoric displacement to nominal identity and *vice versa* in this play — in a semiotic substitution between signs which is repeated in the subtle ongoing shifts in mode between semantic literalness and rhetorical performativity.

The Corrupt Magistrate

I said that the narrative of the Corrupt Magistrate is shaped as an inverted romance. It represents a story in its own right and might conceivably have received independent dramatic treatment. When Shakespeare chose to graft it on to the narrative of the Disguised Ruler, he created the kind of heterogeneity that Eliot disclaimed along with *Hamlet*. On one level Eliot's reservations — in the shape in which I imagine them to be — seem valid enough: there is no inherent necessity in the Disguised Ruler as such which argues its continuation in the Corrupt Magistrate. The conjunction of narratives seems arbitrary, even overdone, in the sense that it imposes on the final version a non-classical surfeit of dramatic plotting merely to clear the ground of semantic surplus. However, once the two narratives merge we must ask both what links and what separates the otherwise independent stories.

I suggested above that 'ambush', although sprung from the ambiguity of replacement, did not find its explanation here, and I further suggest that we may look for it in the Corrupt Magistrate instead if we link this narrative to what I shall term the dialectics of alienability, as enacted by Angelo and Isabella. I have already classed their meeting as an inverted romance. In particular, the inversion results from a play of difference and sameness between what is proper and improper in sexual terms and in terms of what belongs to a person as properly his or her character. In other words, what takes place between Angelo and Isabella may be seen as the reciprocal substitution of propriety with impropriety in both a sexual and a moral register; their confrontation demonstrates a subtle interchange between one register and the other. Specifically, we may locate the translation from one story to the other in the relation between desire as evinced in the Corrupt Magistrate and 'ambush' as the metaphor left over from the Disguised Ruler as unexplained.

Isabella's approach to Angelo in (II, ii) is fashioned as a supplication for mercy, and she argues what we may term the overt ethics of the play. First she clarifies her own moral position by admitting the unlawfulness of her brother's act and her personal abhorrence, then she proceeds to appeal for mercy in spite of facts and law, as it were. In effect, she bases her appeal on what is basically a contradiction, and Angelo does not need to resort to legal sophistry to reject it:

ISABELLA:	I have a brother is condemned to die; I do beseech you, let it be his fault, And not my brother. ...
ANGELO:	Condemn the fault and not the actor of it? (II, ii, 34-37)

At this early point, she clearly senses the weaknesses of her position and she is on the verge of giving it all up. But Lucio prompts her to go on:

LUCIO [TO ISABELLA]:	Give not o'er so. — To him again, entreat him, Kneel down before him, hang upon his gown; You are too cold. (II, ii, 43-45)

Isabella then renews her appeal, spurred on by Lucio who repeats his objection to her coldness in l. 56, but later several times intersperses the dialogue between judge and nun with approval of her performance. Moving on from legal argument to invoking divine justice, Isabella develops her capacity for persuasion in a gradual increase until she achieves her full range. In short, she warms to her case to the extent that what started as argument is transformed, in the process, to a form of language where the discursive argument of her case has given way to rhetorical effectfulness. As her legal position dwindles, her feminine powers grow. Indeed, she exploits the full panoply of persuasion-*cum*-supplication and ends up as what Angelo later terms her: 'a woman'. This has lead Northrop Frye, among others, to wonder 'if she isn't suppressing the awareness that she is much more attracted to Angelo than she would consciously think possible'.[9] I don't think this is textually warranted. Frye notices her desire. But he fails to identify its nature and source. Lucio, in his asides, appreciates her change from coldness to heat, no doubt closely recording the effects in Angelo's attitude. It is noticeable that whatever Isabella says is throughout perfectly legitimate from the point of view of what she in fact speaks — she remains consistent in the semantics of her suit. Yet she, too, suffers from Angelo's discrepancy between speaking something and saying otherwise. What changes is the increase in rhetorical volume, and at one point the balance between rhetoric and semantics becomes so ambiguous that it correlates objectively with what Angelo now realizes that he desires:

ISABELLA:	Because authority, though it err like others,
	Hath yet a kind of medicine in itself
	That skins the vice o'th'top. Go to your bosom,
	Knock there, and ask your heart what it doth know
	That's like my brother's fault. If it confess
	A natural guiltiness, such as is his,
	Let it not sound a thought upon your tongue
	Against my brother's life.
ANGELO [ASIDE]:	She speaks, and 'tis such sense
	That my sense breeds with it. — Fare you well.
	(II, ii, 135-43)

In a comment to Angelo's use of 'sense', William Empson has it that

To Angelo the combination of meanings ... can only appear as a hideous accident ... Yet the real irony, apart from the verbal accident, is that her coldness, even her rationality, is what excited him.[10]

At this early point Empson may still be justified in speaking of Isabella's coldness and rationality; yet he does not explain why coldness and rationality may arouse the deputy.[11] However, the ambiguity of 'sense' which Angelo reacts to may be seen as a continuation of Isabella's duplicity. No doubt Eagleton, discussing what stirs Angelo, is right that 'the play makes it clear that law actually *breeds* desire as well as blocks it'.[12] Isabella, too, is motivated by a law, her virtue, as stern as his, and her case is more complicated than what may be explained as a return of the repressed (even if this is perhaps also the case). She may in fact preserve her rational coldness in the midst of her heat because she speaks with two tongues, one which is properly her own and which she would acknowledge at a literal level, and another, which rivals it, and speaks not a language of semantic sense, but a rhetoric of contextual effects and potential interpretation (in Eliot's sense of the word). Angelo reacts adequately to the rhetoric and chooses (or perhaps hopes — as at this point he still may, following Frye) to view her semantics as merely a cover-up for her rhetoric.

Between Isabella's two tongues there is a representational difference between what is said and what is spoken. In the blank in-between her semantics informs her rhetoric while her rhetoric, at the same time, kindles her argument and the purity of her intentions. As I said, she is doubtless guilty of duplicity;[13] yet there is no court of law which may define her transgression; Angelo terms her a tempter (II, ii, 164) and at various points seems not to believe in her rejection of him; but, in the main, even he finds fault especially with himself and does not accuse her of consciously practising upon him; 'The only passion which influences the story is that of Angelo', says Hazlitt;[14] Isabella's passion is in fact securely veiled to most early critics — while most modern critics notice it and proceed to harbour a psychoanalytically influenced mistrust of her.

Isabella is certainly passionate, but her heat is mixed with coldness, her sexual suggestiveness is paraphrased in the para-juridical language of ethical appeal; in short, like the Duke, she indulges in rhetoric and cashes in on its effects with nobody the wiser. If these effects prove to be different from what she expected, this does not argue her moral defect, but rather shows us that the rhetoric she indulges in reveals an anonymous layer in language over which she exercises no control.

Isabella's language, in its transfer between her proper semantics and her improper rhetoric, may be read according to the metaphorical left-over from the Disguised Ruler — 'the ambush of my name'. This is a formula for desire. Isabella goes to Angelo; but only in the name of her brother — first to defend him, later to reject him; to the extent that she may argue her case in his name, her desire will be perfectly concealed in the nominal metaphor and in the objective anonymity of her rhetoric.

Desire, in sexual terms, is strictly speaking Angelo's, of course. But as we have seen, it becomes difficult at one point to dissociate his speech from hers with the confusing result that the vocabulary of her denial merges with the gross provocation of his suggestions. Thus she manoeuvres critically between one form of desire, her own for her brother and for Christ's calling, and another, Angelo's, for her proper self. If there is no cause for doubting the sincerity of her intentions (although many critics have done so), we may nevertheless identify a level of communication between the two where they speak as of one voice:

ANGELO:	Admit no other way to save his life —
	As I subscribe not that, nor any other,
	But in the loss of question — that you, his sister,
	Whose credit with the judge, or own great place,
	Could fetch your brother from the manacles
	Of the all-binding law; and that there were
	No earthly mean to save him, but that either
	You must lay down the treasures your body
	To this suppos'd, or else to let him suffer.
	What would you do?
ISABELLA:	As much for my poor brother as for myself;
	That is were I under the terms of death,
	Th'impression of keen whips I'd wear as rubies,
	And strip myself to death as to a bed
	That longing have been sick for, ere I'd yield
	My body up to shame.
	(II, iv, 88-104)

Consciously or not, Isabella chooses not to take his meaning — we cannot know which. But her reply obviously support critics out to implicate her; Kenneth Muir glosses as follows: 'At the beginning of this quotation Death is a beadle whipping a harlot; Isabella thinks of stripping herself for punishment, but the image takes on a sexual meaning'.[15] Lever adds to this that the occurrence of the image here 'is psychologically revealing'. This is so, arguably. Nevertheless we may note two things; first that, whatever the metaphor may import, she adheres firmly to her rejection; indeed, the metaphor may be seen as a poetic strengthening of her disinclination, a way of emphasizing her denial, as much as an unconscious admission of its figurative sense. Secondly, and more importantly, we see that Isabella's implication occurs only as metaphor; if she is guilty in the metaphor, she is also innocent in it since the metaphor, in context, may always be interpreted either in her semantic or in her rhetorical register; indeed, her metaphor, on the sexual interpretation, is as much part of an impersonal rhetoric which, even if she employs it at this point, does not necessarily equate with the exposure of some hidden impulse; quite obviously, the situation is itself charged not only with a specific emotional content, but the emotion released by the pressure Angelo exercises on her is structured according to a symbolic system of rhetorical substitution which is entirely non-personal. Not properly herself in her rhetoric, Isabella exploits the metaphor to her proper purpose (as when she later agrees to have Mariana replace her); yet she is also undeniably caught unawares in the sexual connotation of her metaphor, and she is forced as much by its inherent logic as by any sexual impulse of which she might be ignorant. The metaphor, in short, is a means of saying something and speaking otherwise, a perfect vehicle for substitution.

In any case Isabella's desire is negative; in relation to Angelo she desires not to be desired; her desire for Christ may only be achieved by denial, and her desire for her brother's release is expressed in the shadow of his imminent death. Apparently Isabella disclaims desire as such. This, as I said, has led many critics (Wilson Knight, F.R. Leavis and others) to mistrust her, even dislike her; to quote Northrop Frye again: 'Isabella, in her invulnerable virtue, would not be anyone's favourite heroine'.[16] A.W. Schlegel, by contrast, invokes the traditional romantic heroine: 'the heavenly purity of her mind is not even stained with one unholy thought'.[17] Too much or too little, once again. R.M. Smith catches the ambiguity when he says that Isabella is the object either of 'excessive admiration' or 'excessive repugnance'.[18] This contradiction may be resolved if we argue that her refusal is not only not a negation of desire, but indeed the crowning formula for it, since desire, as organized in the symbol that structures it, is invariably negative.[19] What she desires is desire as such. To achieve this, her invulnerable virtue is decisive. If we question it, we fail (like Claudio and Frye) to perceive her position as coherent.

On the verge of entering the convent, and before she clashes with Angelo, Isabella is informed of her future privileges as novice. However, as we learn, she desires not privileges, but 'rather ... a more strict restraint' (I, iv, 3-4). This is answered by Francisca, a Nun, who instructs her:

> When you have vow'd, you must not speak with men
> But in the presence of the prioress;

> Then, if you speak, you must not show your face;
> Or if you show your face, you must not speak.
> (I, iv, 10-13)

The announcement of the prohibition is occasioned by the advent of Lucio who comes to ask Isabella to intercede on behalf of her brother, with the ironic result that she becomes the unwilling agent of violating the above rule. Since she has not taken the vow at this point and since, of course, she cannot know what awaits her, she does not break the rule. Indeed, she adheres to it throughout her meeting with Angelo. It is probably safe to assume that this meeting must be read in dramatic contrast not only to the injunction but also to the desire to submit to it which Isabella explicitly states. Indeed, Isabella's progress in the drama is symbolically lodged in the above rule and allowed the full emotional amplitude and ambiguous scope between desire and negation of desire implicit in it.

Isabella explicitly desires circumscription and restraint, and when Francisca spells it out to her in the convent rule she provides, in metaphoric terms, the formula for desire as such, ironically defining the path Isabella will follow. As we readily recognize, the above prohibition is phrased in terms of the body's parts; we learn, specifically, that these parts should not act in conjunction, but should stand in a complementary relation where the presence of one part of the body is parallelled by the depreciation of the other part; when the face shows (a – b), the mouth must close and *vice versa* (b – a); the emergence of one part is followed by the veiling of the collateral part.

Veiling and unveiling in the presence of a man represents the formula for desire and it structures Isabella's confrontation with Angelo: when she promotes her case this leads to an increase in his desire (a – b); when, concomitantly, he states his desire as lust, she reciprocates by rejecting him (b – a); when Angelo subsequently thinks he has won her, she is veiled in Mariana, her metaphor, while Mariana, on her part, is unveiled to Angelo as his true mistress. One part appears, the other part disappears. Angelo and Isabella are the agents of desire, yet they are not free agents, but act *via* metaphoric substitution. Angelo, as we have seen, is even shocked at finding himself in the grip of an emotion he has not sought. I agree with Eagleton that Angelo's *volte face* from 'repressive legalist to rampant lecher' is not so mysterious as one might think, since his lust, at one level, structurally equates with his abstract advocacy of formal law. However, his lust is not just the obverse face of his repressive legalism, although it is also that, but originates specifically in the symbolic structure, the formula for desire, of his confrontation with Isabella.

As for Isabella, she speaks with passion and may do so freely and without contradicting herself on the literal level. Whatever else she says is taken hand of by the anonymity of the metaphor and the alienation of her desire in the name of the other for whom she speaks. The anonymity of her rhetoric is in fact made explicit in terms of the formality of the convent rule. From this impersonal (improper) point of view, Claudio's claims on her virginity seem to her a continuation of Angelo's, and rejecting her brother's suggestion to comply with Angelo only serves to fire her passion. Critics who charge her with excessive prudery fail to take stock of what goes on here. It is neither an excess of puritanism, emotional coldness, lack of compassion nor fear for her life that motivates her rejection of Claudio — one might even guess that she would have joyfully surrendered body and life, as she in fact proclaims ('I had rather give my body than my soul', II, iv, 56). What happens is that a new object accrues to her in the process of rejecting Angelo and Claudio. Not Angelo's person, as he would have it (along with Frye), but her own virtue. This object is in itself a perfect formula for what she wants: she wants not to be wanted and she wants it fervently — she wants it, indeed, so vehemently that she is willing to give her own life and to see her brother's head cut off; she desires only it; to have it she needs someone (Angelo, Claudio — even her physical self) to reject. What Angelo (and later Claudio) offers her is an experience which releases desire in her in its perfected form — the object she wants is not a thing, but a pure sign. As for Angelo, he remains behind in the world of gross matter; suffering from lust instead of love, he is unblessed by any sign — if not the disgust in which Shakespeare envelops him as objective correlative to Isabella's excess of emotion.

The Substituted Bedmate

Isabella's confrontation with Angelo is her finest hour. From then on the play develops into a comedy, she is effectively silenced and becomes a pawn in the Duke's game. By the sheer impetus of dramatic speed, The Substituted Bedmate (and the material associated with it), which Shakespeare grafts on to the two other narratives, provides a resolution of sorts. Mariana is only cumbersomely superimposed on Isabella and the addition, as invented by the bustling Duke, invariably promotes the farcical element in the play, which is otherwise restricted to Lucio, Elbow, Abhorson, Overdone, Pompey and consorts. If the link between the two previous narratives appears fortuitous, the addition of the Substituted Bedmate seems even more surprising, as curious as Barnardine's desire for sleep or Ragozine's head. Of course, the substitution leads to the final reconciliation. But, in the process, the seriousness of Isabella's confrontation with Angelo is considerably reduced, the comic element outfaces the potentially tragic encounter betweeen death and virtue — with the result that the three narratives interact in a way so unforeseen that it surely argues Eliot's equation of the play's intractability with *Hamlet*.

Any form of replacement of something with something else (or, more importantly, somebody with somebody else) involves a redistribution of value. This is obvious in the comedies where the chain of misrepresentations, displacements and substitutions is the very machinery of the plot; but in plays like *Hamlet* and *Measure for Measure* substituting something with something else is only achieved at the price of representational paradox where otherwise inalienable value is depreciated as alienable. In *Hamlet* the loss is obvious everywhere; and if, in *Measure for Measure*, we choose to see Mariana not only as a measured substitution for Isabella but as her nominal metaphor, the plot tacks from one perspective to another and we hardly know what to think; *via* her name Isabella is admitted to an experience not her own. But (in contrast to Hamlet who gets nowhere however much he tries to adjust his perspective on things) the point of view in *Measure for Measure* by and large follows the pragmatic strategies of the Duke and the symbolic debt incurred by Isabella's alienation in Mariana is deferred by the sheer speed and craft of his inventiveness. From ruler he becomes a stagemanager; Frye calls him a trickster. Keir Elam warns us that

The creation of *fictional personae* by the very *fictional personae* is one of the major sources of trouble ... in the canon, most insistently so in *Measure for Measure*.[20]

That is no doubt true. Yet both the ambiguity of replacement and the solution to it results from the Duke's genius for rôle-playing and symbolic engineering. In particular we note that the chain of replacements is continued right through to the end, as in the comedies.

We are reminded by J.W. Lever that Shakespeare's duplication of deputies is without precedent in any of the earlier versions of the play.[21] In fact the dramatic development is based on a surplus substitution of something with something else which it both repeats and differs from. Thus the substitution of Mariana for Isabella is part of a whole series of major and minor symbolic transfers between virtue, mercy, lust and law, whose final end is the dissolution of the intractability inherent in the logic of absolute identity and absolute difference; whenever someone replaces someone else there is a readjustment in the internal balance between measure and measure. Let me list only the most important substitutions: Angelo substitutes for the Duke, (but Angelo also deputizes for Escalus, the traditional deputy); Isabella substitutes for Claudio in Angelo's proposed bargain; Mariana replaces Isabella (but she in fact also substitutes for herself); Barnardine, as represented by the promise of his dead body, is supposed to substitute for Claudio; but Barnardine counts out and is replaced by 'One Ragozine, a most notorious pirate' who is subsequently represented to Angelo by his head; Friar Peter substitutes for Friar Lodowick who, in turn, substitutes *via* his name for the Duke — in another variation of the Duke's substitution of himself; finally, at the end, the Duke, rôle-playing as Friar Lodowick, is replaced by Escalus (who also, at this point, deputizes for Angelo, whose function has changed from judge to accused). In short, the play abounds in substitutions, some of which, Barnardine and Ragozine, appear to sidetrack the development of the plot as much as they promote it.

Even if we recognize the tendency to indulge in substitution as a well-known feature in the comedies, the number of major and minor substitutions in *Measure for Measure* vastly outnumber the overt replacement of one person with another and exceeds what one might argue as dramatically motivated *strictu sensu*; everything in this play, from the substitution of law for mercy to one head for another is submitted to exchange and concomitant alienation of value. It is probably a good guess that, discounting the comic relief, this dramatic surplus is at least partially caused by Shakespeare's arbitrary conjunction of the three distinct narrative structures from his source material (the strata we may define, by implication, as Eliot's archaic left-over).

Can we account for this dramatic surplus? Or must we submit to Eliot's final verdict? One answer might be that the Duke, who is the author of the substitutions, attempts to clear a space between himself as head of state and his nominal identity with Angelo in this capacity; indulging beyond measure in substitution, he effectively dissociates himself from his deputy, creating a new state of affairs where their symbolic identity is erased and Angelo officially returned first to the status of law-breaker and hypocrite and subsequently raised to a level of ordinary citizen by the act of mercy. In the process, the deputy is de-deputized and captured under a new heading. This refashioning of Angelo further explains the Duke's otherwise callous secretiveness in keeping Isabella in the dark about her brother (another source of unease with this play); only Isabella could confer mercy on Angelo, and only in the light of her belief that Angelo's orders to execute

Claudio were carried out to the letter does Shakespeare raise her final act
of forgiveness to a level where the Duke's mercy may include Angelo without entirely endangering the basic substitution of measure for measure.

The continuous play of substitutions that runs through the play may be
seen as an ironic effect of this discrepancy between measure and measure;
everything and everybody change symbols, value and position; everything
is flux, movement, replacement, arrangement and rearrangement, all balls
hang suspended in mid-air throughout the duration of the play; this
continual deferral is the very substance of the plot and the plotting, of
course, and therefore geared to get things right in the end; but it clearly
also serves to prevent the symbolic order from either petrifying in the dead
letter of the law or succumb to the brute materialism of life as pure lust,
that is it prevents the system of representations from collapsing between
opposites impossible to reconcile.

The Duke is as busy as Friar Laurence in *Romeo and Juliet* — but has
better luck. Barnardine represents the odd exception, his refusal of the Duke
is absolute. According to Jacques Lezra, 'it is the moment of the play when
substitution is denied ...'[22] However, moments later the refusal is reversed
with the advent of Ragozine's head upon which the chain of substitutions
is continued almost as if nothing had happened. Lack of availability in one
head is substituted with surplus accessibility in another. As for Angelo, he
remains behind and in the background, like Malvolio in *Twelfth Night* he
is the evil eye,[23] and the Duke's surplus inventiveness may be seen as a
way of averting it. Conversely, we may say that Angelo remains outside
the symbolic transfer because he thereby, in contrast to Barnardine, upholds
the flow of substitutions. As for himself, Angelo is a blank space; reduced
to deputizing for someone else, he is improper, a signifier pure and simple;
as such he is nameless and there is no outlet he can fashion to enter the
game of substitutions; while everything around him is subject to transformation, he remains fixed and rigid; the only symbolic system available
to him is what may be expressed in terms of the law; however, the very
nature of the law is precisely that it leaves no escape route open to follow
but remains as it is when everything else fluctuates; what remains for
Angelo when he breaks this law is the naked lust of someone unblessed
with any symbol; if the viewpoint had been his, we might have seen him
as tragically caught up in a substitution that does not come off (like
Macbeth, *mutatis mutandis*). In short, Angelo remains ambushed, in the
name of someone else, between his desire to enforce the law and his unhappy substitution of it with his lust. If, in the end, his lust for Isabella is
replaced with marriage to Mariana this final substitution is brought about

merely to accommodate the others who have all achieved what they want at this point, closing the gap between fact and fiction. Angelo, by contrast, remains literally stuck in the metaphor.

Notes

1. I discuss John Dover Wilson's *What Happens in* Hamlet at some length in *Hvad er et navn? Shakespeare i rænæssancen,* (Copenhagen: Tiderne Skifter, 1994).
2. T.S. Eliot, 'Hamlet and his Problems', in *The Sacred Wood,* (London: Faber & Faber, 1920), the quotations are from pp. 96, 99 and 101 respectively.
3. Northrop Frye, *'Measure for Measure'* in *Northrop Frye on Shakespeare,* ed. Robert Sandler, (New Haven: Yale University Press, 1986), p. 148.
4. Mary Lascelles, *Shakespeare's 'Measure for Measure',* (London: University of London Press, 1953), p. 111.
5. A.W. Schlegel, *A Course of Lectures on Dramatic Art and Literature* tr. by John Black, (London, 1815). I quote from *The Romantics on Shakespeare,* ed. Jonathan Bate, (Harmondsworth: Penguin, 1992), p.451.
6. Terry Eagleton, *William Shakespeare,* (Cambridge, Mass.: Harvard University Press, 1986), p. 57.
7. The chiasmus is a rhetorical favourite in Elizabethan drama and poetry. It abounds in Shakespeare who exploits its full range from tautology to paradox. Notably, the chiasmus is not always explicit, but veiled in various forms (thus the title of *Measure for Measure* may be analysed as an imperfectly stated chiasmus); quite often it organizes the semantico-semiotic (frequently even the narrative) rather than the syntactic level (thus: Angelo's proper name is Duke; the Duke is not, properly speaking, Angelo; or as narrative: an increase in law destroys life; and increase in life destroys the law. Usually its two constituent parts are contradictory and their combination in a single figure points to a paradox or dilemma (hence its dramatic value); an instance may be found in what I later term the formula for desire, explicit as a chiasmus in the convent's injunction ('Then, if you speak, you must not show your face;/ Or if you show your face, you must not speak' (I, iv, 10-13)). Interestingly, and no doubt often ironically, the chiasmus nevertheless also trans-figures harmonious relationships, as in the play's antepenultimate line where the Duke informs 'dear Isabel' that 'What's mine is yours, and what is yours is mine' — the formula for marriage and the end to desire, presumably.
8. François Guizot, from 'On the Life and works of Shakespeare', repr. in Guizot, *Shakespeare et son temps* (Paris, 1852), tr. as *Shakespeare and his Times* (London, 1852). I quote from *The Romantics on Shakespeare,* op. cit., p. 203.
9. Northrop Frye, op. cit., p. 146.
10. William Empson, *The Structure of Complex Words,* (London: Chatto and Windus, 1951), p. 274.
11. For a discussion cf. Jonathan Dollimore, 'Transgression and Surveillance in *Measure for Measure'* in Dollimore and Sinfield (eds.), *Political Shakespeare,* (Manchester: Manchester University Press, 1985).
12. Eagleton, op. cit., p. 49.

13. Isabella's position has alternately been claimed as divine or discredited as lacking in humanity — or the two contrastive positions have been conflated upon which she has been charged with ambiguousness and duplicity. Jacqueline Rose defends Isabella in 'Sexuality in the Reading of Shakespeare', in *Alternative Shakespeares*, ed. John Drakakis, (London: Methuen, 1985).

14. William Hazlitt, from the Preface to *Characters of Shakespeare's Plays*, (London, 1817), I quote from *The Romantics on Shakespeare*, op. cit., p. 453.

15. Kenneth Muir, *London Magazine*, Dec. 1954, p. 106 (I quote from Lever's note to the passage in question).

16. Northrop Frye, op. cit., p. 148.

17. Schlegel, op. cit., p. 451.

18. R.M. Smith, 'Interpretations of *Measure for Measure*', *Shakespeare Quarterly*, I, (1950), p. 212.

19. If desire is what Fielding in *Tom Jones* terms 'the Desire for satisfying a voracious Appetite with a certain amount of delicate white Flesh' it is, as he adds, 'properly Hunger'. This covers Angelo, but according to Hegel (and his psychoanalytic French offspring), desire differs from need (Fielding's Hunger) — what you desire is desire itself, not its object. This is Isabella's position.

20. Keir Elam, *Shakespeare's Universe of Discourse*, (Cambridge: Cambridge University Press, 1984), p. 220.

21. J.W. Lever, Introduction to the New Arden edition, p. lxvi.

22. Jacques Lezra, 'Pirating Reading: The Appearance of History in *Measure for Measure*', *ELH*, 1989, p. 257.

23. I owe this point to Geoffrey Hartman's 'Shakespeare's Poetical Character in *Twelfth Night*' in *Shakespeare and the Question of Theory*, ed. by Patricia Parker and G. Hartman, (New York: Methuen, 1985), p. 49.

Is All Well That Ends Well? A Historical Reconstruction of *All's Well That Ends Well*

Michael Skovmand

> Our wooing doth not end like an old play:
> Jack hath not Gill. These ladies' courtesy
> Might well have made our sport a comedy.
> (*Love's Labour's Lost*, V, ii, 874-76)

> This play has suffered at the hands of critics
> whose tastes are more delicate than Shakespeare's.
> (C.J. Sisson, 1953)

From its first known performance in 1741 until the present day, *All's Well That Ends Well* has consistently been ranked among Shakespeare's most controversial plays. As W.W. Lawrence points out, 'Critical explanations have nowhere shown wider divergence than in regard to this play ...'[1] At the heart of the debates over this play are basic questions of genre, related to basic uncertainties about its date. Is this a comedy? If so, what sort of comedy? Early lyrical comedy? Tragi-comedy? Dark comedy? Problem play? Symbolic Christian early romance? The radical nature of the critical divisions over this play is unsettling to any critic with illusions about a basic consensus existing in the matter of Shakespeare's plays.

Historically, the fortunes of the play, both in terms of critical history and performance history, have varied considerably. The absolute historical silence concerning this play, from its date of composition until 1741 (apart from its presence in the First Folio) makes it quite exceptional[2] among Shakespeare's plays. There is no evidence that this play was ever performed before an Elizabethan or Jacobean audience. Accordingly, we must assume that what we have, with the Folio text, is a *virtual* text for performance, not a text tested and evolved in the crucible of acting experience and audience response. Consequently, any approach to *All's Well* which considers the audience relation as a determining factor in the makeup of the play should be mindful of this aspect of *virtuality*. Arguably, its *lack* of performance is a potentially significant lack. What made this particular play unacceptable/uninteresting to Shakespeare's audience? Obviously, this question opens up the field to any kind of conjecture, textual as well as circumstantial. Nevertheless, what remains is the fact, or at least the likelihood that *All's Well* was not deemed sufficiently attractive for performance by the London theatres in Shakespeare's time — an aspect of the play almost invariably overlooked by critics.

The fortunes of *All's Well* from 1741 to the 1960's are chronicled by Joseph Price's *The Unfortunate Comedy* (1968), along with J.L. Styan[3] and others. Without going into the details of the history of the play, what is striking are the parallel courses of performance history and critical history of the play, the salient points of which are the inordinate prominence of Parolles in the 18th century (he was frequently seen as a minor version of Falstaff), the sentimental representation of Helena in the Romantic theatre, the growing disapproval of the play in the Victorian and early Modern age, (with exceptions, such as G.B. Shaw), and finally, after World War II, a reappraisal of the play, in terms of its 'ideological' potential, either as proto-Feminist,[4] or as moral allegory, or even as a self-reflexive dark comedy of manners. Moving back into the unknown before 1741, one may ask oneself what was, or would have been the position of *All's Well* to Shakespeare and his contemporaries?

Before that question can be answered, the question of *dating* the play needs to be dealt with, because an answer to this question is a precondition to any overall assessment of the play.

The Dating Game

The problems of dating *All's Well* are at the centre of any attempt at understanding the uncertainties and ambiguities surrounding the play. With the possible exception of *King John*, *All's Well* is the most intriguing of all of Shakespeare's plays when it comes to fixing a date of composition. The first appearance of the play is in the First Folio in 1623, and there is no historical evidence of any performance before 1741. Accordingly, critics are left exclusively with so-called *internal evidence*, i.e. the thematic and stylistic properties of the Folio text, for dating the play.

In 1764, Bishop Percy suggested the identification of *All's Well* with the mysterious, missing play *Loue Labours Wonne*, mentioned in 1598 in Francis Meres' *Palladis Tamia*, and ostensibly a companion-piece to *Love's Labours Lost*. Although there is no evidence to support this theory other than the semantic appropriateness of calling *All's Well* 'Love's Labours Won', the theory has held wide currency into this century. A variant form of this theory — the most prominent supporters of which are Coleridge and John Dover Wilson — suggests that the Folio text of *All's Well* is a revised or re-written form of the earlier *Loue Labours Wonne*, the great number of in-coherencies and inconsistencies of *All's Well* being proof of this. Indeed, Dover Wilson, in the 1929 New Cambridge edition of the play sees the hand of a 'collaborator or reviser, with a passion for sententious couplets and a mind running on sexual disease',[5] thus virtually exculpating Shake-speare of what he sees as the failure of the play. However, as pointed out by G.K. Hunter and others, the textual inconsistencies of the play need not be taken as evidence of revision or re-writing.[6]

The coupling of *All's Well* with the phantom *Loue Labours Wonne*, com-bined with the theory of a Jacobean revision of an Elizabethan play, is, however, indicative of the central critical concern: Is the play early robust folk-tale comedy in the manner of *The Taming of the Shrew* (a comedic in-version of the male chasing the female — pattern)? If not, is it a late, sym-bolically oriented romance comedy in the manner of *The Winter's Tale*? The linchpins of a late dating are primarily two arguments, both tying *All's Well* to *Hamlet* (ca 1601) and *Measure for Measure* (ca 1604), neither of which is conclusive: The first argument relates to the 'echoes' of *Hamlet* in Act I: A Polonius-like send-off to Bertram by the Countess:

> Love all, trust a few
> Do wrong to none. Be able for thine enemy
> Rather in power than in use, and keep thy friend
> Under thy own life's key. Be checked for silence,
> But never taxed for speech.
>   (I, i, 52-56)

In addition, a Hamlet-like posture by Helena, followed by a Claudius-like admonition:

HELENA:	I do affect a sorrow, but I have it too.
LAFEW:	Moderate lamentation is the right of the dead; excessive grief the enemy to the living.
	(I, i, 42-44)

Finally, there are strong echoes of the Ophelia-Hamlet relationship in He-lena's description of her inferiority to Bertram:

> That I should love a bright particular star
> And think to wed it, he is so above me.

In his bright radiance and collateral light
Must I be comforted, not in his sphere.
(I, i, 74-77)

The second thematic resemblance which allegedly points to a late dating of the play is the use of the bed-trick — Helena luring Bertram into bed while pretending to be someone else. Since the bed-trick is also used in *Measure for Measure*, it is argued that the plays must have been composed about the same time — *All's Well* before *Measure*, arguably because in *All's Well* the bed-trick is integrated in the plot and taken over from the source-texts, whereas in *Measure* the bed-trick is an extraneous device, used to get Isabella out of the painful dilemma of saving her brother or her chastity. The bed-trick, accordingly, is likely to be a re-use of an earlier dramatic device, as is generally acknowledged. But what about the *Hamlet* parallels in *All's Well*? They are obviously there, and abundantly so, and only in Act I. There are two ways of accounting for them: (a) the passages are clearly not as extended, as rhetorically developed, or as psychologically integrated in plot or character as in *Hamlet*. Consequently they can be seen as early, *undeveloped* ideas in a play *earlier* than *Hamlet*, later cannibalized because the manuscript was shelved, or the play flopped, or simply because it seemed like a good idea at the time; or (b) as a rather uninspired *recycling* of ideas in a play *later* than *Hamlet*, attesting to the often-mentioned 'tired', 'lacklustre', quality of the play. So the thematic arguments point to a dating of the play as earlier than *Measure* and either earlier or later than *Hamlet*!

The other area under investigation, the stylistic evidence, is highly ambiguous, as pointed out by G.K. Hunter and others.[7] The use of couplets, letters, blank verse and metaphor in general are seen either as full of 'the lyrical sweetness and dainty artifice of the early comedies' (Coleridge) or 'contorted and gnarled ... in a way which is totally unlyrical' (Hunter). What is characteristic of this 'dating game' is the circularity of argument. Thematic parallels are used to firm up stylistic arguments; external arguments, however dubious, are used to bolster internal points, and vice versa. *All's Well* and *Measure* are not just connected by the common use of the bed-trick, no, they are 'obviously twins'.[8] The part of the Clown/Lavatch may have been designed for the actor Robert Armin, who (possibly) took over from Kempe about 1599 — begging the question: how consistently did Shakespeare design his parts with particular actors in mind? Again, the part of Lavatch may or may not be seen as more akin to the later 'fools' rather than the earlier 'clowns' in Shakespeare, or vice versa.

An even more elaborate attempt at dating by contextualization is made by David Farley-Hills, in *Shakespeare and the Rival Playwrights 1600-1606*. Farley-Hills argues that a comparison with Chapman's play *The Gentleman Usher*, roughly contemporary, is a clue to an understanding of *All's Well*. Both plays are 'romance seemingly deprived of romance', 'essentially mythic comedy and both describe spiritual journeys'.[9] He argues the likelihood of the play being played at the Globe, because of the theme of the superiority of virtue over birth, a recurrent bourgeois theme which would appeal to a popular audience. The weakness of the arguments of Farley-Hills and like-minded critics is that the allegorical underpinning of the play is more or less taken for granted — usually because a long tradition of criticism has idealized Helena and allegorized the love-plot, reading the play along parallel lines with *Measure for Measure*, as moral allegory with Christian overtones of grace and redemption. Textual and contextual issues intertwine in a circularity of arguments, mutually bolstering each other.

Dating a play is a fairly pedantic exercise, if nothing more than chronology is at stake, even if it is Shakespearean chronology. In the case of *All's Well*, however, more than a date is dependant upon the outcome of this debate. My tentative conclusion to the ongoing controversy over the dating of *All's Well* is this: the play, as most critics would agree, is stylistically and thematically 'uneven'; consequently, it is possible to find textual support for any date between the mid-1590's and 1604. I suggest that a broader approach to the play is necessary, if the dating game is to make sense.

The Mode of Representation of *All's Well That Ends Well*

At the heart of the critical controversy is a largely unresolved *generic* issue with a built-in chronology of its own: beyond asking what sort of comedy it is one might ask what is the *mode of representation* of *All's Well*? In other words: what are the characters supposed to be doing on stage in that play? To put it bluntly: are they *showing* their roles or *being* their roles? Or, to put it differently: to what extent is early modern individualized subjectivity defining the substance of the parts of the play? Or, by contrast, to what extent are the parts defined by the late medieval mode of figural representation found in the source texts?

Initially, one should be aware of the basic structure of *All's Well*. The narrative building blocks of *All's Well* are a fusion of two classic folk-tale prototypes: the Curing of the King and the Clever Wench. The two prototypes were combined in the ninth story of the third day in Boccaccio's

Decameron, and Shakespeare's immediate source was in all probability the English translation, William Painter's *The Palace of Pleasure* (1566). The first two acts tell the story of the Curing of the King, by Giletta (Shakespeare's Helena), the physician's daughter who cures the King of France of a fatal disease, and who is rewarded with Beltramo (Shakespeare's Bertram), Count of Roussillon, as a husband.

The last three acts, the Clever Wench story, are the story of Bertram's attempt to evade the responsibilities of being a husband: how he flees to Italy to join the war there, how Helena pursues him and tricks him into impregnating her, and how he is finally reconciled with his wife. Shakespeare adds a number of characters to the story: Bertram's mother, the old Countess of Roussillon who, surprisingly, sides with her new daughter-in-law; Lafeu, an old Courtier who is also on Helena's side; Lavatch, a melancholy clown in the service of the old Countess. Shakespeare's main addition, however, is *Parolles*, a follower of Bertram and, as indicated by his name (French paroles = words), a braggart and a coward in the Roman and *commedia dell'arte* tradition of the *miles gloriosus*. In addition, Shakespeare introduces a number of alterations to the characters. As well as adding psychological depth to the major characters, Shakespeare actually blackens the character of Bertram, making him one of the least likeable male protagonists of the entire *oeuvre*

Shakespeare seems deliberately to break up the smooth narrative of Boccaccio/Painter. Susan Snyder uses the formerly fashionable term 'deconstruct':

In dramatizing the tale of the clever wench, then, Shakespeare also deconstructs it. He brings to the surface its latent tensions by getting inside awkward moments rather than simply gliding over them (how would a nobleman react when handed over in marriage to a commoner woman? how would it feel to receive the love-making your husband means for another woman?[10]

Of course, this is the sort of thing that is one of the hallmarks of Shakespeare in his use of source materials for his plays, whether it be the Histories, the Tragedies or the Comedies — to use the old divisions of the First Folio.

Shakespearean plays of the early and mid-1590's are characterized by their emerging, but uneven individualization of the character of the protagonists. A schematic taxonomy (which transcends the divisions of history, tragedy and comedy) drawing on some of the more well-known examples from this period, might look like this:

Stage 1:
The character of Richard III in *Richard III* (c. 1592): a *hybrid* between the late medieval figure of the Vice[11] of the morality play and a modern individualized character complete with psychological motivation.

Stage 2:
The character of Kate in *The Taming of the Shrew* (c. 1593-4): *emergent* individualization, stereotypical character ('the shrew'), but capacity for development. The ongoing critical controversy over the ambiguity of the ending is ample testimony of the unresolved tension in the play between figure and individual. Figures don't develop, individuals do (sometimes).

Stage 3:
The character of Juliet in *Romeo and Juliet*: early individualization of characters; unevenly personalised idiom; moderate capacity for development.

Stage 4:
The end-point of this taxonomy of dramatic character development in Shakespeare in the 1590's is Brutus of *Julius Caesar* (1599), and the character of Hamlet (*Hamlet*, ca 1600), where the idiom is distinctly personalized, where consciousness and self-consciousness are dramatized, and development of character is an integral part of plot development. Beyond 1600, we see the growth in the plays of a new kind of figurality, a symbolic figurality, moving away from maximum emphasis on individualized dramatic characterization.[12]

This, of course is an excessively crude taxonomy which does not take into account the relative autonomies of genre, and which says little about the ever varying relations between plot and character, and of minor, 'flat' characters throughout the plays subordinated to the exigencies of plot or aesthetic structures of contrast and variety. However, with all these provisos in mind, I suggest that this parameter of mode of character representation is a developmental axis running the full length of Shakespeare's dramatic works, and, consequently, a useful tool in dating a play like *All's Well*.

The real discussion, accordingly, is whether *All's Well* belongs to the phase of late pre-individualist story-oriented figurality in Shakespeare before *Hamlet*, or to the early post-individualist phase of symbolist figurality after *Hamlet*; the source of confusion, in my view, is in the surface similarity between these two transitional states.

Helena's soliloquy, at the end of Act I.i is a case in point:

> Our remedies oft in ourselves do lie
> Which we ascribe to heaven; the fated sky
> Gives us free scope; only doth back ward pull
> Our slow designs when we ourselves are dull.
> What power is it which mounts my love so high,
> That makes me see, and cannot feed mine eye?
> The mightiest space in fortune nature brings
> To join like likes, and kiss like native things.
> Impossible be strange attempts to those
> That weigh their pains in sense, and do suppose
> What hath been cannot be. Who ever strove
> To show her merit that did miss her love?
> The king's disease — my project may deceive me,
> But my intents are fix'd, and will not leave me.

This is Helena's 'project' — curing the king and winning Bertram — defined from the very first scene of the play in seven formal couplets, and relentlessly pursued to the successful completion in Act V. This is our first privileged, inside view of Helena, establishing, as soliloquies do, that special *rapport* between character and audience — we are made the *confidants* of the character, and are put in a position where we know more about her than the other characters in the play do. She is thus positioned as the heroine of the play; the fulfilment of her desire is seen to be the chief project of the play, and our sympathies are engaged by her efforts to achieve her goal. But what is the exact nature of this representation of her project? We can see how, reluctantly, Helena moves from the almost chorus-like 'we' of the opening into the first person singular of 'my love', only to move back after a single couplet to the impersonal third person and passive voice of the next lines, and then finally gathering courage in the closing couplet with a resounding first person statement of 'intents'. The female subject of this soliloquy has not quite found her voice yet, but of course her project of upward mobility is indeed truly revolutionary, militating as it does against no less than three powerful forces of conservatism: rules of gender, social class, and literary convention.

How does it compare to similar 'project representations' in Shakespeare? The first point to be made is that Helena's 'project soliloquy' is an unusually *bald* and direct declaration of intent. There is, however, a development between Helena's more personalized, intimate revelation to the

audience of her intentions, and the brash commedia dell'arte-like audience
address of the medieval Vice, in Richard III's opening statement:

> Plots have I laid, inductions dangerous
> By drunken prophecies, libels and dreams,
> To set my brother Clarence and the King
> In deadly hate, the one against the other:
> (*Richard III*, I, 32-35)

or the dramatically plain opening exposition of *Love's Labour's Lost*:

> Our late edict shall strongly stand in force:
> Navarre shall be the wonder of the world;
> Our court shall be a little academe,
> Still and contemplative in living art.
> You three, Berowne, Dumaine, and Longaville,
> Have sworn for three years term to live with me.
> (I, i, 12-16)

This technique with an opening project statement we find again, but
dramatically sophisticated, in *Measure for Measure*.

> Hold therefore, Angelo:
> In our remove be thou at full ourself
> Mortality and mercy in Vienna
> Live in thy tongue and heart.
> (I, i, 42-45)

The statement, in other words, is no longer simply a performative utterance;
simultaneously, it sets in motion the multiple ambiguities and ironies of the
play, circling around the idea that Angelo's meting out of 'mortality and
mercy' will be a judgement on himself. Accordingly, (accepting that this
example is representative of the play as a whole) the mode of representation in *Measure for Measure* displays a degree of complexity in the
dramatic *intertwining* of plot, character and thematic structure which is not
in evidence in *All's Well*.

Compare Helena's project-statement with our first private moment with
Hamlet who, like Helena, has 'that within which passes show/These but
the trappings, and the suits of woe'; as soon as he has the stage to himself
for the first time, we are presented with a virtual *eruption* of pent-up agony:

> O that this too too sullied flesh would melt,
> Thaw and resolve itself into a dew,
> Or that the Everlasting had not fixed
> His canon 'gainst self-slaughter. O God! God!
> How weary, stale, flat and unprofitable
> Seem to me all the uses of this world!
>   (*Hamlet*, I, ii, 129-34)

Beyond the mid-point of *Hamlet* in this taxonomy of representation, we find Edmund making his famous statement echoing Helena, asserting the idea that everyone is the architect of his own destiny — a strongly individualist statement not normally given authorial approval in Shakespeare — Helena, in fact, being the exceptional case:

This is the excellent foppery of the world, that, when we are sick in fortune, often the surfeits of our own behaviour, we make guilty of our disasters the sun the moon, and stars; as if we were villains on necessity, fools by heavenly compulsion, knaves, thieves, and treachers by spherical predominance, drunk-ards, liars, and adulterers by an enforced obedience of planetary influence; and all that we are evil in, by a divine thrusting on. (*King Lear*, Act I, ii, 124-32)

At this point in his career, however, Shakespeare relishes the multiple ironies of having villains tell us the truth, only to demonstrate that this truth in the hands of Edmund is of no use. It is hard not to believe that we are far removed from the time of the conception of *All's Well*.

All's Well That Ends Well as a Comedy

A central question remains, however: whether Shakespeare retains the foundation of comedy, or whether *All's Well* marks a move away from comedy, a 'deconstruction' of the genre, putting it to more complex uses, questioning the generic properties of comedy itself, a move onto the terrain of the last plays, of symbolically oriented romance. I shall try to argue in favour of a *comedic* reading of *All's Well*. The play makes excellent sense as a comedy, indeed a pre-1600 comedy: a comedy which foregrounds *the outsider*, as we see it in *The Merchant of Venice*; which privileges female fortitude and intelligence, as seen in *Much Ado about Nothing*, *As You Like It*, and *The Merchant of Venice*, and which grapples with the dramatization of individual consciousness, seen at full stretch in *Hamlet*. Why has it been so difficult for literary criticism in the past 150 years to read *All's Well* as a comedy?

In accounting for what is seen as the unevenness or even the failure of the play, E.M.W. Tillyard sees *All's Well* as an early example of what Shakespeare did in his romances (*The Winter's Tale* and *The Tempest*): 'adjusting symbolism and real life'.[13] This is an alternative formulation of the issue articulated so frequently in criticism of the play: its problems in fusing folk-tale elements and three-dimensional psychological representation of characters. A.P. Rossiter calls *All's Well* an 'off-play':

... a piece in which the writer was aware of the off-notes, by which I mean those discords produced by playing off a harsh, disturbing human reality against conventional story-book or play-book sentimental expectations.[14]

The operative word in Rossiter's statement is 'off'. However, all of Shakespeare's comedies 'play off a harsh, disturbing human reality against conventional story-book or play-book sentimental expectations'. *The Taming of the Shrew*, *A Midsummer Night's Dream*, *As You Like It*, *The Merchant of Venice*, *Much Ado about Nothing*, *Twelfth Night*, all the major comedies are 'off' in this sense. Incongruity is a major component of comedy, and these 'discords' are virtually the stuff Shakespeare's comedies are made of. In other words, comedic 'propriety', like any other sense of decorum, is historically variable, and *All's Well*, for a number of reasons, has been seen not to be containable within consensual definitions of the genre of comedy. What are those reasons? It is frequently pointed out how this play *inverts* or *subverts* genre expectations: the most obvious example is the motif of woman chasing man (at the heart of a long comedic tradition of the clever wench).

A second feature, pointed out by Snyder and others, is the inversion of the pattern of the older generation as blocking the happiness of the young lovers — in *All's Well* the old characters, the King, The Duchess and Lafew, actively support Helena's project. Thirdly, and perhaps crucially, is the view of Bertram as incompatible with the role of the lover-in-chief of comedy. Psychologically, he is seen to be devoid of redeeming human qualities, to such an extent that a marriage between him and Helena is unacceptable, even within the bounds of comedy.

At the bottom of this question lurks a major issue: what are the properties of Shakespearean comedy? I find myself in agreement with W.W. Lawrence when he argues that the play is far more 'unsavoury' to a modern audience than to Shakespeare's audience, and 'that the effect which it was intended to create has been generally misunderstood'.[15] This echoes the statement quoted earlier on by C.J. Sisson: 'This play has suffered at the hands of critics whose tastes are more delicate than Shakespeare's'.[16] Most modern approaches to *All's Well* are more or less thinly disguised 'defences' or 'apologies', that is, new ways of reading the play and in the process, redeeming the play from its disastrous critical reputation. My point of departure has been an examination of what one might term the *audience contract*, that is, the terms of understanding established between the audience at any given time and the 'play' — the latter term understood in its most extended sense: the playwright's script combined with the words as performed under specific historical circumstances.

This is meant as an *archaeological* investigation into the intrinsic meaning of the term: an investigation into the *old sense* of the problem plays, and in the process, an investigation into how making sense of Shakespeare has changed over the centuries — not simply because different actors or directors have imposed different interpretations upon the plays over the years, but equally because our sense of the theatre has changed since the time of Shakespeare. If one is willing to accept an early dating of this play, these issues of genre are far more easily resolved: this is a comedy whose major comedic device is the story of the clever wench getting her man. As with Helena and Egeus in *A Midsummer Night's Dream,* or Kate and Petrucchio in *The Taming of the Shrew*, we are probably well advised not to speculate too intensely on whether they will actually live happily ever after. And we are not likely to, except academically. Northrop Frye's comments on the 'nature' of comedy are a welcome reminder:

We should be aware that comedy is a context word and not an essence word. If a play in a theatre is subtitled 'a comedy', information is being conveyed to a potential audience about what kind of thing to expect, and this type of information has been intelligible since the days of Aristophanes. But to answer the question of whether it really 'is' a comedy or not would involve us in a limiting definition of the essence of comedy, as something not found in other things, whereas comedy is a term indicating a certain group of literary phenomena which may be found to a greater or lesser extent anywhere in literature. There has never been such a 'thing' as comedy, though most people are familiar with the range and ambience of what the word indicates.[17]

Notes

1. Lawrence, W.W., *Shakespeare's Problem Comedies*, (New York, 1931), p. 43.
2. *Two Gentlemen of Verona* can 'boast' a longer stretch of non-recorded performance — its first known performance was in 1762. But it received historical mention in Meres' *Palladis Tamia* in 1598.

3. Price, Joseph, *The Unfortunate Comedy*, (Liverpool: Liverpool University Press, 1968), and Styan, J.L., *All's Well That Ends Well*, (Shakespeare in Performance series, Manchester: Manchester University Press, 1984).

4. See e. g. Asp, Carolyn, 'Subjectivity, Desire, and Female Friendship in *All's Well That Ends Well*', in *Shakespeares Comedies*, ed. by Gary Waller (London: Longman, 1991). According to Asp, the play is unique in the Shakespeare canon, in that it is 'written out of the history of the female subject and this history is the history of her desire. The inadequacy of the male as subject is not only *not* repressed; it is emphasized' (p. 176).

5. Sir Arthur Quiller-Couch and John Dover Wilson, eds, *All's Well That Ends Well*, (Cambridge: Cambridge University Press, 1929), p. 110 et passim.

6. G.K. Hunter, Introduction to the Arden edition of *All's Well That Ends Well*, (London: Methuen, 1959), pp. xx et passim.

7. Ibid., pp. xx-xxi.

8. Ibid., p. xxiii.

9. Farley-Hills, David, *Shakespeare and the Rival Playwrights 1600-1606*, (London: Routledge, 1990), p. 89.

10. Snyder, Susan, Introduction to the World's Classics edn of *All's Well That Ends Well*, (Oxford: Oxford University Press, 1994), p. 6.

11. Spivack, Bernard, *Shakespeare and the Allegory of Evil* (New York: Columbia University Press, 1958), and more recently: Doctor, Jens Aage, *Shakespeares Karneval*, (Aarhus: Aarhus Universitetsforlag, 1994), Ch. 1 et passim.

12. Russel Fraser, in his Introduction to the New Cambridge edition of *All's Well That Ends Well* (Cambridge: Cambridge University Press, 1985), uses the term 'diminishing of character': 'the great wheel of his *oeuvre* is coming full circle. The diminishing of character under Shakespeare's eye and hand enforces this suggestion' (p. 11).

13. Tillyard, E.M.W., *Shakespeare's Problem Plays*, (Toronto, 1949), p. 109.

14. Rossiter, A.P., *Angel with Horns*, ed. Graham Storey (London, 1961), p. 93.

15. Lawrence, op. cit., p. 48.

16. Sisson, C.J., *William Shakespeare*, (London: Odhams Press, 1953).

17. Frye, Northrop, *The Myth of Deliverance, Reflections on Shakespeare's Problem Comedies*, (Toronto: University of Toronto Press, 1983), p. 15.

Dr. Johnson and the Martial Spirit

Lee Morgan

Twentieth-century scholarship has shown convincingly that the long-held popular image of Dr. Johnson as something of a jingo was erroneous, that, instead, he was apparently opposed to war as a means of settling international disputes and that he was an outspoken opponent of aggression, imperialism, and colonialism. These facets of his character, along with his well-known charities toward the poor and unfortunate menagerie that made up his London household, caused Richard Harries, Bishop of Oxford, to propose Johnson for special commemoration in the Anglican calendar, which recognizes outstanding Christians since the Church no longer canonizes.[1] It would, however, be a mistake to think that the martial spirit was extinct in him; indeed, it was rarely dormant, and there are accounts about him wherein he expresses admiration for the military calling, demonstrates unmistakably martial responses to insults and injustice, and generally evidences appreciation of a healthy martial outlook.

Perhaps it should be pointed out that the connotations of 'martial' are almost uniformly favourable. We speak of martial music, a martial bearing or carriage, a martial air; and we mean stirring, manly, brave. These are precisely the aspects of the word that Dr. Johnson illustrates in so many opinions and episodes in his life. In a sense, 'martial spirit', as it is being here applied to him, is something of a redundancy: 'martial' implies 'spirit' or 'spiritedness'. There is implicit in the word 'martial' a vigorous, male competitiveness, the kind to be found on British playing fields from Johnson's day to our own. Moreover, so imbued with this spirit was he that he carried it over into non-athletic, even non-physical endeavours such as scholarship and drawing-room conversation, often impressing both adversaries and spectators with an aggressive, 'win-at-all-costs' attitude. This is well illustrated in his panegyric to taverns, where all the good service and congenial atmosphere, he claimed, 'exhilarates my spirits, and prompts me to free conversation ... I dogmatise and am contradicted, and in this conflict of opinions and sentiments I find delight'.[2] *Any* kind of discourse, even the most relaxed, aroused 'delight of battle with [his] peers' in Johnson. He viewed it as a martial exercise. Nor is the physicality without a feeling of good-naturedness. Confrontation, physical or mental, is fun, has zest; and,

if defeated, one 'takes his lumps'. Remember Johnson's 'surrender' and confession of 'pure ignorance' when his erroneous definition of *pastern* as the
knee of a horse is brought to his attention by a lexically querulous lady.[3]

Whence derives, though, the popular image of Johnson as jingoistic and
tetchy to the point of pugnaciousness? It comes often from the misinter-
pretations of others about his speech and actions, usually in social contexts
where he is either expressing, in exaggerated form, his righteous indig-
nation at some immorality, hypocrisy, or other reprehensible conduct or
demonstrating his English bulldog relish of a good scrap. In such encounters, once the battle is joined, Johnson's blood is up; he wants to make
his point, to convince others, to win. Pacific reflections he is more likely to
write elsewhere; and this is in large measure the key to interpreting his
seeming aggressive nationalism or personal bellicosity: with a few glaring
exceptions of admittedly political propaganda, his writings seem more truly
indicative of his real feelings and opinions. This is why, in the main, modern scholarship in focusing on Johnson's writings constitutes a more reliable guide to his essential, studied thoughts about a subject. This is by no
means to say that his conversations are regularly to be discounted as primarily exhibitions of polemical and rhetorical skill without reference to his
honest opinions; but it is to suggest that they should not always be adduced as his last word on a topic.

The popular image of Johnson as John Bull incarnate, a Tory super-
patriot, is traceable almost exclusively to a few notorious anti-American
outbursts. 'I am willing to love all mankind, *except an American*', he
maintained at a dinner party at Mr. Dilly's on April 15, 1778, where, Boswell tells us, he 'breathed out threatenings and slaughter', referring to
Americans as 'Rascals-Robbers-Pirates', adding that he would 'burn and
destroy them'.[4] His *Taxation no Tyranny* three years earlier was as intem-
perate. In commenting on its vehemence, Boswell says, '... the extreme violence which it breathed, appeared to me ... unsuitable to the mildness of a
Christian *philosopher* ...'[5] In the same passage, Boswell notes that this was
at variance with 'the principles of peace which he had so beautifully recommended in his pamphlet respecting Falkland's Islands ...' Some years
earlier, Johnson had said to Dr. John Campbell regarding Americans, 'Sir,
they are a race of convicts, and ought to be thankful for anything we allow
them short of hanging'.[6]

What was it about Americans that could produce this degree of de-
testation in Johnson? It was primarily their sanction of Negro slavery
coupled with canting, humbugging, hypocritical professions of liberty and
freedom. He had asked in *Taxation no Tyranny* '... how is it that we hear the

loudest *yelps* for liberty among the drivers of negroes?'.[7] Johnson seems always to have been strongly opposed to slavery and to the exploitation of native populations by colonial powers, and he saw Americans guilty on both counts. To Johnson, Americans were not victims of rapacious, imperialistic government. Rather, they were transplanted Britons in whom the capitalistic impulse had run wild. Some of his statements reflecting national bias are intended solely as pleasantry, for example, his reckoning the superiority of one Englishman to forty Frenchmen in compiling the dictionaries of their respective languages.[8] The anti-American outbursts and the political pamphlets remain then the principal reasons why so many have persisted in seeing Johnson as chauvinistic and hawkish.

However, like most people, Johnson was not consistent; and when one examines his writings closely, it appears that throughout his life, he criticized things military, both actions and actors. As a young man of thirty, he wrote *Marmor Norfolciense*, a satirical essay on an alleged inscription found in Norfolk near Lynne. The piece is antagonistic to the Hanoverian succession and government and to Walpole. In it, Johnson describes a soldier as

a red animal, that ranges uncontrouled over the country and devours the labours of the trader, and the husbandman; that carries with it corruption, rapine, pollution and devastation; that threatens without courage, robs without fear, and is pamper'd without labour.[9]

He repeats some of these sentiments in an undated letter to 'an eminent friend':

My god-son called on me lately. He is weary, and rationally weary, of a military life. If you can place him in some other state, I think you may increase his happiness, and secure his virtue. A soldier's time is passed in distress and danger, idleness and corruption.[10]

Similar opinions are voiced in *Idler* No. 21, which speaks of 'the most contemptible of all human stations, that of a soldier in time of peace'[11] and in his life of Gilbert West, who spent some time in the army, 'though it is reasonable to suppose that he never sunk into a mere soldier'.[12]

As general editor of the *Literary Magazine* for a time in the mid-1750's, during the Seven Years' War, Johnson wrote several articles where his anti-war sentiments were forcefully presented, so forcefully in fact that the proprietors had to remove him. He was decidedly not reflecting their views on expanding trade, extending the empire, and conducting the war. Put simply, Johnson was out of step with most of his countrymen on war, imperialism, and commercialism — on moral grounds. He was unsuccessful in persuading others to his point of view, holding, in James Clifford's description, 'resolutely to his moral view of international affairs'.[13] Johnson also demonstrated his humanity toward victims of war. In the summer of 1760, a charity was undertaken in England for the raising of money to clothe French prisoners of war. Johnson furnished the introductory essay to *Proceedings of the Committee on French Prisoners*, an exceptionally powerful appeal.[14]

Among Johnson's finest anti-war arguments is his *Thoughts on the Late Transactions Respecting Falkland's Islands* (1771), in which he delineates the disputed claim of Britain and Spain over the sovereignty of those islands. His eloquence and humaneness in describing the miseries of war and his harsh criticism of those in government who advocated a military solution to settle the controversy were crucial in averting war at that time.[15]

The main point of this paper, however, is to show that Johnson's hatred of war and its causes by no means eradicated his essentially martial spirit, evidenced in a proclivity to decide matters of right and honor by combat, physical or mental, as the case required.

A number of episodes in Johnson's life indicate that he possessed combativeness and physical courage, two martial characteristics, in high degree. Garrick described one such episode to Boswell. As a young man, Johnson was attending a performance at the playhouse in Lichfield. He left his seat during intermission and returned to find that a man had taken it. Johnson courteously asked him for his seat; the man rudely refused. Where-upon, Johnson picked up the man and the seat and threw both into the pit.[16] Johnson himself told Boswell of being attacked one night by four men in the street and holding them off until the watch came and took the whole group to the round-house.[17] He also told Mrs. Thrale of beating Osborne the bookseller in his [Johnson's] chambers for being impertinent to him. He seemed surprised that Osborne would go around telling people. 'I have beat many a fellow', said Johnson, 'but the rest had the wit to hold their tongues'.[18] When James Macpherson, putative author of the spurious *Ossian* poems, threatened Johnson with bodily harm for having detected and publicly exposed his fraud, Johnson wrote him a letter of defiance and bought a six-foot oak cudgel, with a head the size of a large orange, to defend himself against the much younger man.[19]

Not all Johnson's combativeness and courage were exhibited in conflict with other men. Once at Topham Beauclerk's country home, two large dogs were fighting, and Johnson, not knowing whether they might attack him, interposed himself, and beat them till they separated. On another occasion, when told that a gun might explode if overloaded, he crammed six or seven balls into it and discharged it into a wall. Bennet Langton tells of warning Johnson against the treacherous current of a stream outside Oxford where the two were once swimming. Johnson immediately headed directly into it.[20] When he was on his deathbed, his surgeon superficially lanced his legs to relieve the pressure of the accumulated dropsical fluid. Unsatisfied with these timid measures, Johnson plunged scissors deep into the calves of each leg.[21]

Such headstrong intrepidity and instant recourse to daring measures to decide dangerous matters seems almost to be an inborn part of Johnson's character, something he might have inherited. Indeed, his father's brother Andrew once reigned for a year as champion wrestler and boxer at Smith-field, taking on all comers. Johnson told this 'good-humouredly' to Mrs. Thrale, who noted that he was 'very conversant' about boxing, having learned it from this uncle and that he discoursed upon it, thereby surprising people who would not have expected the subject to have interested him.[22] It did, however. He once said during his trip through Scotland with Boswell that he was sorry prize-fighting had 'gone out'. He justified the opinion on the grounds that 'every art should be preserved', especially the art of self-defence. He went on to explain that boxing taught people not to panic at the sight of their own blood or upon feeling a little pain.[23] Thus, an activity involving physical vigor and prowess serves two functions in Johnson's mind: it is worthwhile in itself as manly sport, and it preserves people from panic in time of violence or trauma. Johnson was knowledge-able not only about boxing but about knife-fighting. He criticized the heavy, two-handed claymore sword which fatigued a soldier to handle and with which he could strike only once. Were he himself in such a fight, Johnson said he would run in under the claymore and stab his antagonist with a dagger 'as if he were a calf'. In this particular discussion, he further showed his martial predilections by elaborating on the necessity of English soldiers to take advantage of their superior physical strength against the French in hand-to-hand combat.[24]

It is interesting how often Johnson makes use of martial illustrations in proposing immediate and necessary solutions to a problem. In discussing the right of the state to regulate the open teaching of singular religious points of view as it relates to freedom of speech, he said, 'Every man has a right to utter what he thinks truth, and every other man has a right to knock him down for it. Martyrdom is the test'.[25] Similarly, when talking about the toleration, even pity, of obviously wrong opinions, he asserted,

If a madman were to come into this room with a stick in his hand ... our primary consideration would be to take care of ourselves. We should knock him down first, and pity him afterwards.[26]

Two variations of this instant recourse to martial measures involve humorous episodes in Johnson's life. Both occurred when he was in his forties. His two young friends, Beauclerk and Langton, had been drinking in a tavern till 3:00 a.m., when they decided to awaken Johnson and invite him to accompany them on a romp. They knocked loudly at the door of his lodgings in the Temple. He appeared in his nightshirt brandishing an iron poker with which he had armed himself, 'imagining probably', Boswell speculates, 'that some ruffians were coming to attack him'. On learning the identity of his callers, he was more than ready, despite the late hour, to join them in whatever high-jinks they were up to: 'What, is it you, you dogs! I'll have a frisk with you'.[27] The martial spirit appears here not only in the poker but in the embracing with almost kinesthetic joy the prospect of a 'frisk' that could have easily resulted in violent encounters with other inebriated young bucks full of animal spirits.

The second incident involving a humorous martial response took place in 1756. Johnson was considering the publication of an international periodical. William Adams recommended that he might well study or consult Matthew Maty, author of *Bibliotheque Britannique*. Johnson, probably still smarting from Maty's criticism of the *Dictionary* in his publication, said angrily, 'Damn Maty — little dirty-faced dog — I'll throw him into the *Thames*'.[28]

Though a hater of most wars, Johnson was not a hater of them all. He assumed that everyone would think it right to fight for justice and morality. This was his rationale for defending duelling. Since we acknowledge that 'public war' may be consistent with morality, he reasoned, so may private, individual conflicts like duelling.[29] This conviction that people may resort to combat for reasons of honour, justice, and self-defence is surely one of Johnson's most strongly held views. Time and again, he articulates it for various contexts. He condoned slaves' seeking their freedom by violence as evidenced in his famous toast at Oxford: '... Here's to the next insurrection of the negroes in the West Indies'.[30] He opposed all governmental oppression, royal or republican.

... no government power can be abused long. Mankind will not bear it. If a sovereign oppresses his people, they will rise and cut off his head. There is a remedy in human nature against tyranny ...[31]

In short, Johnson believed in martial measures to deal with oppressive governors.

In direct contrast to the aforementioned slurs on the military profession in *Marmor Norfolciense*, the *Idler*, and a letter, may be offered a number of high compliments to military men and their profession wherein Johnson evinces a pronounced martial spirit. He does this in one episode by showing how highly regarded soldiers are as a whole. Dining on April 10, 1778, in the Temple with a Mr. Scott and Boswell, he asserted,

'Every man thinks meanly of himself for not having been a soldier or not having been at sea'. BOSWELL: 'Lord Mansfield does not'. JOHNSON: 'Sir, if Lord Mansfield were in a company of General Officers and Admirals who have been in service, he would shrink; he'd wish to creep under the table ... No, Sir, were Socrates and Charles XII of Sweden both present in any company, and Socrates to say "follow me and hear a lecture in philosophy"; and Charles, laying his hand on his sword, to say, "Follow me and dethrone the Czar"; a man would be ashamed to follow Socrates. Sir, the impression is universal ... the profession of soldiers and sailors has the dignity of danger. Mankind reverence those who have got over fear, which is so general a weakness'.[32]

This echoes a conversation at the Mitre some two years earlier when he expressed a similar opinion: 'The character of a soldier is high. They who stand forth foremost in danger, for the community, have the respect of mankind'. He went on to comment on the respect that officers command from society generally though they have relatively little money. Even gross common soldiers if they are civil, receive respect merely for being soldiers.[33]

Indeed, Johnson had a real fondness for common soldiers as well as respect for their dangerous occupation. When he and Boswell were on the road in Scotland on August 31, 1773, they encountered a group of soldiers on a work detail repairing the road under the command of a sergeant. Johnson and Boswell gave them two shillings to drink. Later that evening, they ran into the soldiers again at their inn, where the latter were celebrating in the barn. The travellers went to them, and Johnson said, 'Come, let's go and give 'em another shilling a piece'. All the soldiers called Johnson 'MY LORD'; he loved it and told Boswell, 'I am quite feudal, Sir'.[34] Next day, he demonstrated it again by distributing pennies to the children of a wild-looking crowd of M'Craas, 'Lord Seaforth's people', none of whom could speak English. Boswell told Johnson he would make a good clan chief, an opinion that pleased him greatly and to which he responded, 'Were I a chief, I would dress my servants better than myself, and knock a fellow down if he looked saucy to a Macdonald in rags ...'[35]

Johnson's contemporaries thought the martial spirit among his most distinguishing characteristics. Sir Joshua Reynolds described his conversational *modus operandi* as invariably military, remarking his rejection of feints and sallies in favour of a frontal attack, one might even say a storming of the ramparts. '"He fought with all sorts of weapons"; Sir Joshua says, "with ludicrous comparisons and similies [*sic*]; and if all failed, with rudeness and overbearing"'.[36] Johnson's aggressiveness may be inferred from an exchange between Reynolds and Boswell. Sir Joshua commented on the 'extraordinary promptitude' with which Johnson charged into an argument. Boswell agreed: 'Yes ... he has no formal preparation, no flourishing with his sword; he is through your body in an instant'.[37] The best known expression of this trait of Johnson's is Goldsmith's famous remark, 'There is no arguing with Johnson; for when his pistol misses fire, he knocks you down with the butt end of it'.[38]

The martial spirit in Johnson was not dampened by age. Fanny Burney gives an account of a dinner party at Streatham, two months after Henry Thrale's death, and in Johnson's seventy-second year, where he attacked Sir William Weller Pepys for having expressed a critical opinion of his *Life of Lord Lyttleton*. '"What is it you have to say against it?" he stormed. "Come forth, man! Here am I, ready to answer any charge you can bring"'. The quarrel carried from the dinner table to the drawing-room, where Mrs. Thrale feelingly requested that they let it drop. Johnson, by no means completely mollified, answered, 'Well, Madam, you *shall* hear no more of it; yet I will defend myself in every part and in every atom'.[39]

The evidence seems clear. The martial spirit virtually permeates Johnson's being. He consistently approved martial responses on the part of a nation or an individual for purposes of self-defence or the avenging of an insult to honour. His metaphors on the most disparate subjects are war-like or pugilistic. His knowledge of martial technicalities is impressive. Though deploring war as a solution in human affairs, he nevertheless had great respect for the courage of military men and thought 'the military spirit of a people' essential to national health. Indeed, this is how he was perceived by those who knew him best. Of all the teachings of Christianity, Dr. Johnson would have had the most trouble with the one which enjoins us to 'turn the other cheek'.

Notes

1. Harries, Richard, 'Should Dr. Johnson be made a Church of England Saint?', *The Independent*, Thursday 22 September, 1988.
2. Boswell, James, *The Life of Samuel Johnson*, ed. George Birkbeck Hill and L.F. Powell, (Oxford: Clarendon, 1934-50), vol. 2, p. 452, n. 1.
3. Ibid., vol. 1, p. 293.
4. Ibid., vol. 3, p. 290.
5. Ibid., vol. 2, p. 312.
6. Ibid.
7. Greene, Donald J., ed., *The Works of Samuel Johnson*, (New Haven: Yale University Press, 1977), vol. 10, *Political Writings*, p. 454.
8. Boswell, vol. 1, p. 186.
9. Greene, ibid., p. 36.
10. Boswell, ibid., vol. 3, pp. 266-67.
11. Bate, W.J., John M. Bullitt, and L.F. Powell, eds., *The Works of Samuel Johnson*, (New Haven: Yale University Press, 1963), vol. 2, *Idler and Adventurer*, p. 66.
12. Hill, George Birkbeck, ed., *Samuel Johnson, Lives of the English Poets*, (Oxford: Clarendon), 1905, vol. 3, p. 328.
13. Clifford, James L., *Dictionary Johnson*, (New York: McGraw, 1979), p. 187.
14. Ibid., pp. 233-35.
15. Boswell, vol. 2, p. 134.
16. Ibid., p. 299.
17. Ibid.
18. Ibid., vol. 1, p. 154, n. 2.
19. Ibid., vol. 2, p. 300.
20. Ibid., p. 299.
21. Bate, W. Jackson, *Samuel Johnson*, (New York: Harcourt, 1975), pp. 598-99.
22. Hill, George Birkbeck, ed., *Johnsonian Miscellanies*, (New York: Harper, 1897), vol. 1, p. 149.
23. Boswell, vol. 5, p. 229.
24. Ibid.
25. Ibid., vol. 4, p. 12.
26. Ibid., vol. 3, p. 11.
27. Ibid., vol. 1, p. 250.
28. Quoted in Clifford, op. cit., pp. 165-66.
29. Boswell, vol. 2, p. 226.
30. Ibid., vol. 3, p. 200.
31. Ibid., vol. 2, p. 170.
32. Ibid., vol. 3, pp. 265-66.
33. Ibid., p. 9.
34. Ibid., vol. 5, p. 136.
35. Ibid., p. 143.
36. Ibid., vol. 2, p. 100, n. 1.
37. Ibid., p. 365.
38. Ibid., p. 100.
39. Ibid., vol. 4, p. 65, n. 1.

Fanny Burney's 'Styles'

Knud Sørensen

Some 45 years ago I first read Macaulay's essay on Fanny Burney in which, while characterizing *Evelina* (1778) as 'the best work of fiction that had appeared since the death of Smollett', he described Madame D'Arblay's later style as 'the worst style that has ever been known among men',[1] referring to her later novels as utter failures. At the time I had read *Evelina* and shared Macaulay's view of it, while his strictures on *Cecilia* (1782), *Camilla* (1796), and *The Wanderer* (1814) had acted as a disincentive to embarking on these works. However, considering Macaulay's well-known propensity for overstating his case, I have sometimes wondered over the years whether his harsh assessment of the later novels was entirely well-founded. I decided, then, to re-read *Evelina* and to read the last three novels for the first time, and in the pages that follow I shall record my impressions.[2]

Fanny Burney's first novel was a success — and no wonder. In it the reader was presented with a lively account of a 17-year-old inexperienced heroine's entrance into the world, a world peopled by an upper stratum of well-off gentry and noblemen and by a lower stratum of lower-middle-class tradesmen. The novel strikes a modern reader as a halfway house between Smollett and Jane Austen. What reminds one of the former is the element of social comedy and practical joking, and there are obvious Austenian similarities in the many reports of elegant and somewhat formal conversation among the upper classes, the TON. It is true that there is also a moralizing strain in the book, but it does not assume undue proportions. If proper allowance is made for the social and intellectual scene of the late 18th century, *Evelina* can be read with pleasure today, not least owing to its author's skilful use of English.

The main concern of this essay is with the development of Fanny Burney's style. Let us begin by considering *Evelina*. It is obvious that Fanny Burney has a very fine ear for dialogue, which she renders convincingly at more than one level. Her unpleasant or ridiculous characters are generally made to use substandard English with its double or triple negations, its breaches of concord, and its superfluous repetitions. The first two phenomena are too familiar to call for illustration. As for needless repetition, the best examples can be culled from the members of the vulgar Branghton family. Here, for instance, is young Branghton:

So I says to the porter, says I, tell his Lordship, says I, one wants to speak to him as comes from Miss Anville, says I (*Evelina* p. 282).

This is a feature that is very much alive in the colloquial speech of today.

What further contributes to vivifying the style is the use of colloquialisms; these are sometimes employed by characters whose unwelcome attentions are resented by the heroine:

I was accosted by another, who begged the favour of hopping a dance with me (*Evelina* p. 252).

Some of the colloquialisms turn out to be at the same time neologisms. According to the *OED*, it was Fanny Burney who first used the words that are italicized in the following passages:

She lamented that I had been brought up in the country, which, she observed, had given me a very *bumpkinish* air (*Evelina* p. 68).

it's as arrant a *take-in* as ever I met with (*Evelina* p. 97).

Miss is so *uppish* ['ready to take offence'] this morning, that I think I had better not speak to her again (*Evelina* p. 287).

Such expressions — and there are a few additional ones — must have struck 18th-century readers even more forcefully than they do a modern reader.

By way of contrast let us briefly consider the speakers of standard English, first and foremost Mr. Villars and the narrator-heroine. Mr. Villars's style is formal and dignified, and he tends to drive his points home through the use of triplets:

to bestow her upon some worthy man, with whom she might spend her days in tranquillity, cheerfulness, and good humour, untainted by vice, folly, or ambition (*Evelina* p. 139f).

On the whole Evelina herself sticks to a plain style, although she makes occasional use of a triplet:

The benevolence of his countenance reanimates, the harmony of his temper composes, the purity of his character edifies me! (*Evelina* p. 297f).

There is a stylistic subtlety that is quite frequent in Jane Austen and which also appears sporadically in Fanny Burney, namely the use of free indirect speech. This is a mode of speech-rendering that is not — as in normal indirect speech — preceded by an explicit 'he said', etc.; instead it is suggested by pointers in the context that speech is being reported. Consider the following passage:

The young ladies, in some confusion, expressed their surprise that their papa should not know the opera prices, which, for their parts, they had read in the papers a thousand times (*Evelina* p. 95).

This account of what the Branghton girls said is a mixture of a fairly colourless statement ('expressed their surprise') and a vivid suggestion of their actual words conveyed through the hyperbolic 'a thousand times'.

The favourable reception of *Evelina* encouraged Fanny Burney to try her hand again at novel-writing. In the three later novels the theme is basically the same as in her first novel: a young heroine's trials and tribulations. From a modern point of view it may at times be hard to stomach her impossibly virtuous heroines; there is too much melodrama, and an excessive number of tears are shed in these novels. As for their style, it may be noted that all the features found in her first novel reappear in the later ones, which are about twice the length of *Evelina*. It is partly this fact and partly the fact that as she grows older, Fanny Burney tends to use some stylistic devices to excess, that produce in the reader the impression of a mannered and monotonous style which in some passages reads like a parody of Johnson's *Rambler*.[3] As we shall see, some aspects of the style tend towards the abstract and the impersonal, and this is a style that goes hand in hand with a generalizing and moralizing strain which is patent in the later works. But why should she have turned moralist to such an extent? In that age the novel was in low repute. Mr. Delvile in *Cecilia* makes the statement that

a lady ... should never degrade herself by being put on a level with writers, and such sort of people (p. 179).

and Fanny Burney may have endeavoured to strengthen her own position by becoming a moral teacher. Judging from a passage in the dedication to *The Wanderer* she held that there was no genre that offered 'fairer opportunities for conveying useful precepts' (p. 7) than the novel.

The abstract and impersonal character of the style is manifested for instance in the frequent use of psychological nouns as subjects. Psychological nouns are intellectual, moral, or emotional terms that describe the characteristics of people. While a concrete formulation would promote a person to the subject slot, in Fanny Burney it is often a psychological noun that takes over:

his pride might readily object to her birth (*Cecilia* p. 467).

in her faded cheeks and weakened frame, his agonizing terror read the quick impending destruction of all his earthly happiness! (*Cecilia* p. 885).

The total want of delicacy shewn in this transaction, made the wishes of Ellis send back the instrument (*The Wanderer* p. 224).

In the last example, what is meant in plain English is that Ellis 'wished to send back the instrument'.

Besides this use of psychological nouns there are many instances of the traditional substitution of abstract for concrete terms referring to people; for instance, *timidity* is employed in the sense of 'timid people', and *pride* is made to stand for 'proud people':

Timidity solicits that mercy which pride is most gratified to grant; the blushes of juvenile shame atone for the deficiencies which cause them; and aukwardness itself ... is perhaps more interesting than grace (*Camilla* p. 62).

... where distress sighs for succour, where helplessness solicits support (*The Wanderer* p. 515f).

What further contributes to lending an abstract and generalizing flavour to the style is the fact that the narrator, whose account is in the past tense, frequently moves into the present tense to add a general comment:

The observations of Camilla had broken that spell with which a first declaration of regard is apt to entangle unreflecting inexperience (*Camilla* p. 121).

The lateness of this resolution, made her application for its accomplishment so completely fill up her time, that not a moment remained for those fears of self-deficiency, with which diffidence and timidity enervate the faculties, and often, in sensitive minds, rob them of the powers of exertion (*The Wanderer* p. 92).

This makes for prolixity, and so does the novelist's occasional lapse into periphrasis:

that finely scrutinizing monitor to which Heaven, in pity to those evil propensities that law cannot touch, nor society reclaim, has devolved its earthly jurisdiction in the human breast (*Camilla* p. 680).

What a mouthful! — considering that a single word might have been used: *conscience*. And elsewhere *Stonehenge* is referred to as

a stupendous assemblage of enormous stones, of which the magnitude demanded ocular demonstration to be entitled to credibility (*The Wanderer* p. 765).

Over and above this one may add the novelist's predilection for bookish and stilted words: 'This anxiously awaited *æra* at length arrived' (*Camilla* p. 29); 'the short *epoch* she reserved for sleep' (*Camilla* p. 686). Words like *conference* 'talk', *ejaculate* 'exclaim', *felicity, interrogatory* 'question', *palliation, tranquillity,* and *velocity* crop up continually in preference to their plainer synonyms. In many passages of the later novels this produces a ponderous style, and the ponderousness is reinforced by heavy syntax, for instance the construction in which a concessive clause is inserted into a relative clause:

The first circumstance among these was the evident ill will of Lady Margaret, which, though she had constantly imputed to the general irascibility for which her character was notorious, she had often wondered to find impenetrable to all endeavours to please or soften her (*Camilla* p. 818)

Syntactic involution may further be exemplified in a passage like

Mr. Tedman conceived, immediately, a warm partiality for Ellis, whose elegant manners, which, had he met with her in high life, would have distanced him by their superiority, now attracted him irresistibly (*The Wanderer* p. 239).

Here we have the beginning of a main clause, interrupted by the beginning of a relative clause which is followed by a second subordinate relative clause that is in its turn modified by a conditional clause.

The demotion of the personal element is further evidenced in a sometimes peculiar use of a passive construction where an active formulation with a person as subject would have been more natural:

Where her counsel and opinion were demanded, they were certain to reflect honour on her capacity and discernment; but where her assistance or her pity were supplicated, her purse and her tears were immediately bestowed (*Camilla* p. 518f).

scenes of disappointment and despair on the part of Sir Sedley, were anticipated by her alarmed imagination (*Camilla* p. 558).

There are other syntactic peculiarities that appear so regularly that they are felt to be mannerisms. Thus, when a transitive verb is introduced, one normally expects its object to follow immediately, but in Fanny Burney it is often placed at the end of the sentence after a second transitive verb because a parallel or an alternative has been added:

the appearance of beauty alarmed, and of cheerfulness disgusted her (*Cecilia* p. 6).

but, while his softness had soothed, his approbation had invigorated her (*Camilla* p. 345).

... the assiduity with which he visited, or the wealth with which he purchased, works of art (*The Wanderer* p. 231).

The construction just referred to may conveniently lead on to a discussion of Fanny Burney's use of doublets and triplets. These appear with such frequency that they produce the impression of having been mechanically applied. A doublet may serve to convey an idea of the happy mean:

Her equipage, therefore, was without glare, though not without elegance; her table was plain, though hospitably plentiful (*Cecilia* p. 776).

A particularly frequent type of doublet is the negatively introduced com parison or contrast which tends to acquire a decidedly artificial ring:

Cecilia, not more tired of the beginning of the evening than entertained with its conclusion, was handed to the carriage by Mr. Arnott (*Cecilia* p. 42).

a world of formalities, not more customary than fatiguing (*Camilla* p. 246).

He had left Tunbridge in a manner not more abrupt than comfortless (*Camilla* p. 536).

Another rhetorical favourite is the triplet, whose third member is sometimes expanded so as to ensure a resounding climax:

she resolved to select such [friends] only as by their piety could elevate her mind, by their knowledge improve her understanding, or by their accomplishments and manners delight her affections (*Cecilia* p. 51).

She determined, therefore, to see him, to pronounce a farewell, and then to bend all her thoughts to the partner destined her by her friends (*Camilla* p. 334).

She now apologized for having stayed away, professed a design to be frequent in her future visits, and presented, with generous importunity, the trifles which she blushed to have offered so abruptly (*The Wanderer* p. 76).

Above, a number of features have been reviewed that tend to grow stylistically forbidding owing to their overuse. Some of them make for prolixity and monotony, and if Fanny Burney herself suspected this,[4] she may have believed that monotony might be counteracted by the use of unconventional word-order. Be that as it may, one notes a number of passages in which she resorts to an arrangement of words that conveys unwarranted foregrounding; note the position of objects and predicatives in examples like

even truth from imagination she scarcely could separate (*Cecilia* p. 563).

That to hear the name of this lady, said the young man, should not be necessary to inspire me with respect for her, who can wonder? (*Camilla* p. 649).

Strange, however, she thought such behaviour (*Cecilia* p. 449).

hard, therefore, she found it to endure such a change (*The Wanderer* p. 131).

In some passages one may note another mannerism: chiastic word-order:

That he loved her with tenderness, with fondness loved her, seemed no longer to admit of any doubt (*Cecilia* p. 466).

The consternation was general, and general was the silence (*Cecilia* p. 611).

There also occurs a somewhat unconventional placement of adjectives after nouns as in 'an indecorum unpardonable' (*Cecilia* p. 366), 'a doubt inexplicable' (*Cecilia* p. 746), and 'a choler indescribable' (*The Wanderer* p. 112).

Up till now we have been concerned with stylistic features that are used to excess and thus tend to become disfiguring mannerisms. Fanny Burney's later style has, however, its redeeming features as well. First of all, in her apt handling of social comedy she displays a knack of characterizing individuals through their language. In a general way she is critical of the manner in which some of her contemporaries used the English language. This is brought out indirectly in a remark that she has one of her characters make in *Camilla*:

You descant too much upon words, sir; we have left off, now, using them with such prodigious precision. It's quite over, sir (p. 601).

A number of characteristic idiolects are convincingly illustrated. In *Cecilia*, for instance, we are introduced to the emptyheaded Miss Larolles, whose inflated and sometimes doubtfully acceptable language stamps her as a frivolous person:

where have you hid yourself these twenty ages? (p. 127).

Only think how monstrous ... only conceive how horrid! (p. 128).

It's horrid shocking, I assure you (p. 579).

Perhaps it was this character which inspired Jane Austen to create the vulgar Isabella in *Northanger Abbey*.[5] From *Camilla* one remembers Sir Hugh Tyrold, most of whose rambling and inconsequential speeches take up three quarters of a printed page, and from *The Wanderer* absentminded and naive Mr. Giles Arbe, the bore Mr. Scope, and Mrs. Ireton and her interminable harangues come to mind. Fanny Burney undoubtedly had an acute ear for vulgarisms and colloquialisms. It is noteworthy that when she renders the direct speech of her characters, she repeatedly makes them use a construction with an indefinite pronoun that is treated as a singular while the object, and a later personal or possessive pronoun that refers back to the indefinite pronoun, are in the plural:

and then the next news I heard, was that he was shut up in this poor bit of a place, with nobody troubling their heads about him! (*Cecilia* p. 308).

and if any one plays their tricks upon me, they shall pay for their fun (*Camilla* p. 433).

Probably this construction, which has become fully acceptable today, would have been frowned on by 18th and 19th-century grammarians as being illogical, and it is interesting to note that when the narrator intervenes in her own voice, she prefers something else: either a construction with the later personal or possessive pronoun in the singular or the stilted 'he or she' construction:

every one seemed rooted to the spot on which he stood (*Cecilia* p. 611).

every one broke off abruptly from what he or she was saying (*The Wanderer* p. 125).

From the above examples it is obvious that the novelist makes a clear distinction between on the one hand the relaxed spoken idiom of her day and on the other hand the standard that she adheres to herself as the narrator. She is sometimes language-conscious to the extent of lapsing into the pitfall of hypercorrection:

I have not the smallest knowledge whence this young lady comes, nor whom she may be ... (*The Wanderer* p. 613).

where the presence of *whom* may be compared with the *I* of 'between you and I'. And language-conscious though she is, her grammar does not always pass muster. Thus she falls into the trap of using the so-called un-attached participle as in

for though burning to assert the integrity of his conduct, the fear of uttering a word that might be offensive to Indiana, embarrassed and checked him (*Camilla* p. 214).

where there is an unacceptable link between *burning* and *fear*. When an adverb is made to convey agency rather than manner, as in

in the despondence of believing herself parentally rejected, she was indifferent to appearances (*Camilla* p. 860).

one is reminded of a similar unconventional formulation in Dickens: 'the family retired; she [i.e. Mrs. Wilfer] cherubically escorted', i.e. she was escorted by her husband, nicknamed the cherub. (*Our Mutual Friend* 1.4.42).

Another device that points forward is Fanny Burney's use of free indirect speech, a mode that in suitable contexts allows 'private' verbs like *hope* and *suppose* to acquire a pregnant sense: 'say that one hopes/supposes':

Startled, and astonished, she hoped that Miss Ellis was not again indisposed? (*The Wanderer* p. 101).

They could give no account of her, but supposed she was broke loose from Bedlam. (*Cecilia* p. 876).

A further device for suggesting the wording of direct speech is the use of italics:

the necessity of *bringing the young ladies out*, and the duty of *thinking of their establishment*, were the sentences with which he was so regularly assailed, that ... (*Camilla* p. 54).

The later novels, too, contain a number of neologisms[6] whose novelty must have counteracted the heavy style; for instance:

she *rouged* well (*Cecilia* p. 19).

the insignificant *click-clack* of modish conversation (*Cecilia* p. 23).

a young Ensign ... *stroamed* into the ballroom (*Camilla* p. 76; = 'to walk with long strides').

This true *John Bullism*, Lynmere had neither sense to despise, nor humour to laugh at (*Camilla* p. 588).

give her as much of your *tudeling* as will come to this (*The Wanderer* p. 239; a depreciative or humorous expression for playing on a musical instrument).

I might just as well have talked to the post; which *huffed* me a little, I own (*The Wanderer* p. 460; put me into a huff).

To return now to the question that was asked at the beginning of this essay: was Macaulay too harsh in his assessment of Fanny Burney's later novels? I believe he was. He appears to have become thoroughly fed up with Fanny Burney the ponderous and verbose moralist, disregarding the lively and humorous aspects of her novels, and that is hardly fair. As I have tried to show, the same elements recur in all four novels, and so it makes doubtful sense to speak of Fanny Burney's *styles*. However, the last three novels are very long and therefore contain a great quantity of the less attractive stylistic features.

By way of conclusion it may be noted that in recent years all Fanny Burney's work has been very favourably assessed by feminist readers who have concentrated on her message rather than on her style. To one of her modern critics she is 'the first novelist seriously to express sympathy for the working women in their normal conditions of work'.[7]

Notes

1. Thomas Babington Macaulay, 'Madame D'Arblay' in *Critical and Historical Essays*, (London: Everyman, 1946), vol. II, pp. 577 and 564.
2. Quotations are from: *Evelina; or, The History of a Young Lady's Entrance into the World*, (London: 1854). *Cecilia or Memoirs of an Heiress*, (Virago Press: London, 1986). *Camilla or a Picture of Youth*, edited with an introduction by Edward A. Bloom and Lillian D. Bloom, (Oxford: Oxford University Press 1983). *The Wanderer; or, Female Difficulties*, edited by Margaret Anne Doody, Robert L. Mack, and Peter Sabor, with an introduction by Margaret Anne Doody, (Oxford: Oxford University Press, 1991).

3. It can hardly be doubted that Fanny Burney took her cue from Dr. Johnson to an increasing extent, though one must query Macaulay's assertion that Johnson 'revised *Cecilia* and that he retouched the style of many passages' (op. cit. p. 607).

4. The revised second edition of *Camilla* (1802) is over 500 pages shorter than the first edition.

5. While we are on the subject of such influence, it may be added that in all likelihood Jane Austen borrowed the title *Pride and Prejudice* from *Cecilia*: '"The whole of this unfortunate business", said Dr. Lyster, "has been the result of PRIDE AND PREJUDICE."' (p. 908; cf. Frank W. Bradbrook, *Jane Austen and her Predecessors*, Cambridge: Cambridge University Press, 1966, p. 97).

6. Cf. J.N. Waddell: 'Fanny Burney's Contribution to English Vocabulary', *Neuphilologische Mitteilungen*, 81 (1980), 260-63.

7. Margaret Anne Doody in *The Wanderer*, (Oxford: Oxford University Press, 1991), p. xxxi.

Domesticating Science: The Liberal Politics of Mary Shelley's *Frankenstein*

Inger Hunnerup Dalsgaard

> Why should my reflections perpetually centre upon myself? — self, an overweening regard to which has been the source of my errors! ... Thy intellectual powers were truly sublime, and thy bosom burned with a godlike ambition. But of what use are talents and sentiments in the corrupt wilderness of human society?
> (William Godwin, *Caleb Williams* (1794))

When she wrote her first novel, Mary Shelley was very much the child of her parents, Mary Wollstonecraft and William Godwin. Not only does *Frankenstein* incorporate a good deal of autobiography, as does Mary Wollstonecraft's *Mary, a Fiction*; it is also a novel with a purpose, demonstrating high philosophical objectives, much like Godwin's *Caleb Williams*. Shelley was also a child of her parents' time: an age of transition in which many were concerned with justice for the individual and responsible behaviour on the part of those in power. Debates over such issues as the rights of man and the status of the individual are particularly important contexts within which the didactic tendencies of *Frankenstein* should be seen. What makes Mary Shelley's views about the era's prevalent power structures distinctive, however, is what I call her *liberal* stand-point and the fact that her philosophy is personal rather than explicitly political.

Unlike the radicals surrounding her, Shelley does not seem to advocate an egalitarian *redistribution* of power so much as a responsible and considerate *use* of it by those in positions of authority. She conceives of imbalances of power as aggravating only when those subjected to them are forced to challenge their masters in order to survive. *Frankenstein* suggests that if the former are respected and cared for, the master/subject relation may instead become dynamic, engendering creative interaction rather than destructive conflict. Shelley's call for greater responsibility within an enlightened, secularized society appears as a modest proposal compared to the more radical, revolutionary plans for overturning society embraced by those around her.

If Mary Shelley's views are not as radical as those of her father or spouse, neither are they reactionary, politically or philosophically. What can be read out of *Frankenstein*'s call for scientific and parental responsibility is, rather, the belief that the privileges of personal liberty should necessarily be constrained by duties towards others. More specifically, Shelley's idea of liberalism is differentiated by its solid anchoring in family and affection. According to Shelley, who believed affection to be central not only to man's character but also to his happiness, the moderation duty imposes on freedom ought to be cherished.[1] In *Frankenstein* one can read her tentative subscription to an original Lockean definition of liberalism, the belief in a coincidence between public and private interests, alloyed by a faith in man's natural social virtue that is more modified than the one her father entertained in his *Enquiry Concerning Political Justice* (1793). In fact, by focusing on nuclear families — the Frankensteins and the De Laceys — in her first novel, Shelley de-emphasizes the social or public element (with which individual interests should be fused). The interests of the family are placed above those of the individual and the larger society in a position of 'benevolent dicatorship'.

Correspondingly, her critique of Victor Frankenstein and the modern science he represents is much less condemnatory than is often assumed. It is not his act of creation that is sinful, but his refusal to subordinate his desire for solitude by remaining within his own family structure, and his failure to live up to the new family responsibilities parenthood demands of him. In addition, however, though Victor's failure as a family man — rather than his failure as a scientist — is an obvious warning to *Franken-stein*'s readers, it is significant that Shelley allows *none* of her characters a happy ending; nor are her ideal models for family behaviour as faultless as they seem at first. This may well be the radical strength, or perhaps Romantic quandary, of Mary Shelley's cultural critique: her attack on fanaticism and blind idealism of *any* kind.

As Mary Shelley was growing up around the turn of the eighteenth century, attitudes in English society were rapidly changing. On the British side of the Channel the repercussions of the French revolution had already led to the burgeoning of a new political awareness. Though Conservative-backed 'Gagging Acts' and anti-Jacobin watchdog publications (secretly subsidized by the government) soon quashed extra-Parliamentary political activity and overt challenges to the establishment, radical political philosophy left a mark on intellectual debates — as did its opponents. The predominant view of those who had inherited public power was that the need for social order justified political manipulation of individuals while the brutish nature of man required it. In both private and public spheres there was a widespread conviction that authority — in the shape of a father or politician — was necessary to regulate (and at times determine) the needs and wants of his dependents. Such regulation was considered essential if a balance was to be struck between the mutually exclusive interests of the individual and society. At the same time, however, other groups asked whether all men were not, after all, individuals to be reckoned with, and as such had natural privileges and political rights. In the early 1790s, the main concerns expressed in the radical political writings of Thomas Paine, Wollstonecraft, Godwin and others involved the rights of man; in the course of their debates, light was also shed on the *nature* of man and his role in society. All would leave their mark on the social message of *Frankenstein*.

Many critics have attempted to identify the philosophical ideas of prominent thinkers in *Frankenstein*. But while Shelley was obviously influenced by many people, it is important to acknowledge that she was capable of remodelling their ideas to her own design, and to respect the message of *Frankenstein* as essentially her own. One particularly interesting example involves Shelley's father, William Godwin. Godwin did not believe that individual and social interests opposed one another. In his *Enquiry Concerning Political Justice* he challenges the pessimistic Hobbesian view that human beings are fundamentally 'self-interested' and in need of government. In its place he offers his belief in human perfectibility and intellectually character-building education (based on an optimistic reading of Condorcet and Helvétius) and the proposition that all individuals have a natural *need* to share social responsibility. He emphasizes that neither moral virtue nor happiness spring from solitude, enforced or chosen: justice, he insists, *has* to be a product of mutual social responsibility. Though Mary Shelley would agree in principle with her father's social theory, *Frankenstein* questions with more than filial scepticism not only its general applicability but also its realistic viability. Having seen the Romantic movement pursue individualism to the point of self-centredness, it must have seemed unlikely to Shelley that either 'sociability over self-seeking' or the concept of perfectibility and the moral value of education (significant in early Godwinian idealism) would ever prevail, even in an enlightened society.

The differences between father and daughter concerning virtue and justice are illustrated in *Frankenstein*. Through her depiction of the trial of Justine in the republic of Geneva, for example, Mary Shelley clearly demonstrates a conservative understanding of personal injustice. As a result of Victor's silence concerning his monstrous creation, the innocent servant Justine is wrongly condemned to death by both public opinion and the court. Having failed to save a member of the extended Frankenstein-family, Elizabeth may voice a Godwinian condemnation (present in both *Political Justice* and *Caleb Williams*) of the pointlessness of institutions such as law courts: 'When one creature is murdered, another is immediately deprived of life in a slow and torturing manner'.[2] But the implications of her statement — that, in enacting Old Testament norms, current judicial practices simply reproduce what they seek to eliminate — are immediately modified. Alluding less to the injustice of a legal system *per se* than to the individual unjustly subjected to it, she continues: 'then the executioners, their hands still reeking with the blood of *innocence*, believe that they have done a great deed' (p. 67, my emphasis). It is immediately obvious to the reader that Justine's execution is judicial murder, yet the blame is diverted from the law court to a flawed individual. Thanks to Victor no mutual social responsibility is available to save Justine.

A second, and crucial, example of Mary Shelley's distinctive views concerns her use of parent-child metaphors to express ideas about social responsibility in ways distinct from other, explicitly political, thinkers. In his *Reflections on the French Revolution* (1790), for example, Edmund Burke uses familial metaphors as alibis for authoritarianism, comparing radicals (who, like Paine, considered government a necessary evil at best) to rash and horrible children who, rather than 'approach the faults of the state as the wounds of a father, with pious awe and trembling solicitude[,] ... hack that aged parent in pieces'.[3] One can identify here a latent perception of the monstrous within the social order: on the one hand, the mob, child of democracy; on the other, the aristocracy, all-powerful parent. In Shelley, by contrast, it is up to the reader to decide who is the greater monster, father or son. Moreover, the conclusion is not obviously political. For though both radicals and conservatives drew on the parent-child metaphor to explain the *natural* distribution of power in society, and though Shelley's liberal philosophy could be — and has long been — applied to politics, in *Frankenstein* parent-child relations are metaphorical only insofar as they parallel other social hierarchies. They express Shelley's conscious effort to expose social dilemmas and real conflicts in the area of child-rearing and family life. Her careful description of Victor Frankenstein's upbringing, as well as the treatment the Monster receives in its formative years, bear witness to this.

Mary Shelley belongs firmly within what Anne Mellor has called the intense cult of domesticity generated from the increasing number of non-arranged love-marriages in the seventeenth and eighteenth centuries [which] idealized the nuclear family as the primary source of psychological and spiritual comfort.[4]

Yet caught between the ideas and practices of domestic intimacy associated with those diverse groups (radical, romantic, middle class) to which she might have felt affiliated, Shelley in her first novel expresses duly ambiguous views. This was, perhaps, to be expected as her personal position on the subject of the affectionate nuclear family was ambivalent. Her life with Percy Shelley — by no means a family man — made her long for the closeness such a structure could give, yet she was also acutely aware that such a closed community had the potential to bar as well as bond. Few of her contemporaries considered the problems confronting motherless or step-children in that idealized model with as much personal involvement as did Mary Shelley.

Parents in this new intellectual, middle class, affectionate family structure had been encouraged by the spread of Enlightenment beliefs and a new interest in the individual, identity or consciousness to start thinking beyond the basic needs of food and clothing to the importance of education and even the merits of entertainment. In many enlightened families the Godwinian notion that a child had a perfectible consciousness (rather than a defective character) encouraged parents to respect the individual integrity of their children and teach them by setting examples rather than punishing them to break their will.[5] As the bourgeoisie grew in size and importance through the seventeenth and eighteenth centuries, their 'accumulation of wealth from commerce' allowed them to let other middle-class professions take care of the education of children they could now afford to regard more as valuable than as expensive.[6]

The late eighteenth and early nineteenth centuries saw a corresponding growth in the publication of advice books about child-rearing and education inspired by these new, humane and 'secular' theories, such as Mary Wollstonecraft's *Thoughts on the Education of Daughters*. They also witnessed the appearance of regular children's books, intended to stimulate the imagination rather than improve religious rigour, as previous publications had sought to do. Co-publishing a good many of these works (with his second wife) between 1805 and 1824, Godwin articulated the new atmosphere of affection and intimacy clearly:

The way to make children good is to make them happy, and how better to do that than to sit with a laughing child on your lap turning over pages of a jolly book?[7]

Through the Frankensteins and the De Laceys, the apparently ideal affectionate nuclear families of her best-known novel, Mary Shelley herself describes the merits of enlightened education. At the same time, however, she also seems to demonstrate that the inborn character of a child (good or bad) might ultimately override or undermine its healthy upbringing. Though the inevitable corruption of nature by society in *Frankenstein* seems unmistakably Rousseauist, Shelley also recognized (from a much more rationalist, Lockean standpoint) the limitations of a complete rejection of nurture and culture. The values of education and civilization's other benefits made it impossible for her to endorse the anti-rational, anti-social element in Rousseau's Romantic thought. In *Frankenstein* she cannot make her Monster feel happy outside human society because, equipped with a human capacity for intelligence, it is impossible for him not to use his potential instead of remaining in a state of nature.

However, encoded in the development of both Victor and the Monster is Shelley's criticism of the apparently progressive society in which she lived, a society such education was meant to sustain. Because the Monster's birth categorizes him as a lower sort of being, even enlightened people with high moral standards refuse to practice what they preach by recognizing his human values. As the Monster tries to obtain the social benefits he has learnt he is entitled to, all those who believe themselves above him by birth — be they strangers, villagers, the De Lacey family, the father of the girl he saves from drowning or Victor Frankenstein himself — deny him his human rights of company, hospitality, gratitude, Christian forgiveness, fatherly affection and even the love of a like-bodied, if not like-minded, spouse. The Monster strives to prove that he too has all the qualities that make up a human being. But his birth as mere matter deprives him of human rights: nobody sees beneath the surface to recognize that he has acquired — if not by birth then by education — what makes matter into man, namely *mind*. Unsuspected by all, the hideous monster to which Victor has given birth possesses both a beautiful soul and a potentially benign, enlightened nature. One senses that Shelley, like her father, was concerned with human rights, but unlike him she treated the matter in ways more philosophical and personal than political. She does not simply express the abstract corruption of human nature by society in her fictional description of the rise, decline and fall of Victor Frankenstein and his Monster; she also exposes the real faults of people as she experienced them, even when they think they have, or should have had, faultless human natures.

Disenchanted, perhaps for personal reasons, with theories like Godwin's which equated self-interest with social interest, Mary Shelley in *Frankenstein* hints at a central Romantic problem: the danger of *selfishness within* Romantic introspection. The authority of the self, which had led radicals of the early Romantic movement towards the concept of social action, was always liable to be theorized and personalized in ways which effectively marginalized such concerns. Growing introspection and interest in the individual in practice revealed a tension between personal and social interests when the need for social cohesion was perceived as a culturally created obstacle to the free exercise of one's will. Ideally, man's natural tendencies to independence had to be tempered by duty to his neighbour. In literature especially, however, Godwinian social virtue lost out to the Romantic idealization of solitude, as even the idea of a moral duty towards society (paradoxically, because it was perceived as a *personal* choice) edged the subject towards a more central position. Certainly, what Bertrand Russell calls the 'revolt of solitary instincts against social bonds' — which he claims anchors the 'Romantic outlook' in human nature — is evident in the philosophical concern with self-interest which in Victor Frankenstein becomes an all-exclusive instinct for self-preservation at the expense of society.[8]

It is no coincidence, then, that Shelley has Victor Frankenstein contemplate and execute his plans for creation in a social vacuum: 'I thought of returning to my friends and my native town', he writes, but was 'forced to spend days and nights in vaults and charnel houses'. Victor actually sacrifices his *social* bonds to further a completely *personal* ambition — to discover 'whence ... the principle of life proceed[s]' (p. 35) — thinly disguised, after the fact, as a social benefit. Dangling from a chain of conditionals — 'I thought ... I might in the process of time (although I now found it impossible) renew life' — the real objective is 'a new species [who] would owe their being to me' (p. 37). Later, shying away from the responsibility his creature and its actions impose on him, he responds to the tension-fraught situation with what is for others a fatal passivity. In Victor's case morality cannot function in a personal capacity, because it is in his self-interest to make what, from a social stand-point, seems a morally wrong choice. Thus Justine and most of Victor's family fall victim to his silence about the existence, as much as to the revenge, of the Monster.

As noted, not even Shelley's idealized families escape punishment in a book which contains both cultural critique and Gothic thrills. Reviled at the time for its crudeness, Shelley's strategy of 'domestic horror' is not only an ingenious improvement on the delapidated abbey atmosphere of earlier novels in the genre to which *Frankenstein* is often seen to belong. Paradoxically it also elevates Gothicism to a higher critical plane by applying shock-treatment to the bourgeois smugness and safety of 'affectionate nuclear families' in order to reproach them for their loss of humanity in refusing to extend benevolence beyond their own water-tight units. At the heart of Shelley's criticism is the individual's willful neglect of what she feels must be a natural human need for inclusion in the family. To Shelley, being human is in all respects a social skill: even within a micro-society, self-centredness is disruptive. While Caroline and Elizabeth Frankenstein both sacrifice their individuality in order to keep their family together, Victor avoids society and destroys his family by seeking solitude. Shelley criticizes such egotism when it is turned against affection *inside* the family. In an act of supreme self-indulgence, Victor loses his humanity to secure for mankind a breakthrough it neither wants nor needs. Indeed Shelley also criticizes pretenses at doing what seems best for *society* at the expense of family. Victor claims (only once) that his Monster is endowed with human nature (rationality) and human rights (to happiness and well-being) but adds with utilitarian logic that such 'familial' bonds are negligible as 'My duties towards my fellow creatures had greater claims to my attention, because they included a greater proportion of happiness and misery' (p. 186). Victor refuses to realize that it is by failing to create happiness on the micro-level that he has engendered more general misery.

For better or worse, however, the autonomy of the individual gained legitimacy. As the literary movement progressed, so individuality, increasingly a solitary, introspective ideal, seemed to supersede the need for social cohesion. The 'interior journey' in search of one's true identity became separated from the politicial consequences of recognizing the human rights and human nature of others. Tipping the scales towards subjectivism in the eighteenth century, the thinking of Locke, Berkeley and Hume led progressively towards the breakdown of reason and a departure from (to the point of abolition of) the material, prompting the importance of ideas and the mind to approach the absolute. As the spiritual or ideal gained supremacy over matter, one logical consequence of placing in the mind of the beholder full authority over a (subjective) reality (as philosophy had done) was for the Romantic poet to see the mind as creator of what it perceived.

In literature, such creative imagination was limited to the sensitive qualities of the artist. He could convey to others the idea or real nature of things by evoking in them an emotion sympathetic to his own; the original emotional experience of the artist remained, however, the focal point. As the advance of subjectivity shed doubt on the reliability of the laws of Newton (and even God), moreover, an existential crisis was avoided by replacing divinity with pantheism and natural laws with Nature idealized. As a result, nature as an object of the artist's experience lost its material qualities too; and in many respects poetry changed from being mimetic, a 'mirror held up to nature' and the material universe, into a mirror the individual poet held up in front of himself in order to explore the truth of his inner psyche and his self-formation. This lifting of the 'inner veil from his own perceptions and soul' furthered the creative imagination, allowing the poet to lift 'the veil from the face of the eternal and beautiful ... [and] to create the world anew' for his readership.[9] Imagination had become a unifying link between mind and matter. However, the uneasy union between mind and matter, reason and nature, was evident throughout, causing conflicts to arise within Romantic (self-)consciousness.

It is important to clarify Mary Shelley's frequently simplified and misunderstood attitude to science. Her knowledge of scientific progress and processes was greater than most critics would have us believe: the material basis for *Frankenstein* was more than a flimsy reproduction of one single scientific discussion overheard by her in the Villa Diodati in 1816. One look at Mary Shelley's reading lists alone confirms her interest in the philosophy of science. Moreover, she was not anti-science *per se*. Recognizing that science was appropriating, in a negative sense, the sole right to locate and define (measurable) truth to the exclusion of all other approaches, in *Frankenstein* she offers instead a schematic critical history of the development of science which articulates the dangers she feared such processes might entail. As young Victor abandons his alchemic obsessions, briefly, in favour of Krempe's empiric studies, before turning towards Waldman, whose visionary rhetoric promises to reap the fruits of the former through the labours of the latter, we are presented with not only a struggle between mind and matter-oriented attitudes but also a symbolic meeting of 'pre-' and 'post-Enlightenment'. In Victor's volatile mixture of pre-scientific ambition and modern technique, Shelley demonstrates how in Romanticism the intersection of the two areas calls forth and helps realize grandiose and dangerous dreams.

The danger, it should be emphasized, lies not in science itself, but in its instrumental function within processes of increasing polarization and single-mindedness which ultimately lead to anti-social carelessness and shedding of responsibilities. In her fiction, Shelley advocates neither a radical redistribution of power nor even an egalitarian one, proposing instead domesticity as a unifying factor and affection between the sexes as the glue capable of holding communities together. Victor's mind is, however, 'filled with one thought, one conception, one purpose', while in his narrative women become cardboard figures, no longer part of the reproductive process. Fostered by science, a dominant (male) party within a hierarchical power structure fails to take care of a subordinate (male/ female). Such neglect or rejection of 'the other half' (whether cultural, social, psychological, philosophical — or sexual) completely unbalances the hierarchy. As if to salvage the social, most of the men who surrounded Mary Shelley, as well as her fictional characters, indulged in 'homosocial desires'. Having substituted individuality for public conscience, they replace marriage with male bonding. Victor Frankenstein is in this regard representative. At one level, he thinks he needs no one but himself. To the extent that he, and Romantic men, acknowledge that 'no man is an island' he does so in the belief that together *two* men create perfect harmony. In *Frankenstein*, 'masculine' men befriend men who have 'feminine' Romantic qualities — either impressionable and sensitive (in Victor's case, like Clerval) or submissive and willing to be instructed (like Walton) — in pursuit of a gendered balance. Within such a philosophy, male perfectibility renders women superfluous, while potential female mates — the Monster's and Victor's — are destroyed. Such conditions are not unique to Shelley's novel. The uniqueness lies in the fact that they leave her males so obviously unfulfilled.

If balance can derive from a certain kind of male-bonding, then it is science itself that in Victor's eyes enables the creation of 'a human being in perfection'. Such a belief not only challenges the Godwinian notion that man could be 'perfected' through education (perhaps partly illustrated in the early life of the Monster). Victor's blind faith in technology is also in keeping with his historical context, exemplified for our purposes in the thought of his contemporary, English scientist Sir Humphry Davy. Davy, whose works are echoed in the enthusiastic tone of Victor's and Waldman's scientific philosophies, claimed that science and knowledge *could* satisfy all those human needs — beauty, tranquillity, happiness, order, consolation — which Victor had briefly admitted might stem only from domesticity.[10] Indeed, in Davy's work scientism becomes an all-inclusive technocratic world-view. Frankenstein's more enduring conviction — that scientific improvements can also lead to the perfection of man in one stroke — resembles Davy's claim that science may fulfill even social needs (something it singularly fails to do in Shelley's novel). In his *Discourse*, Davy writes:

The unequal division of property and labour, the difference of rank and condition amongst mankind, are sources of power in civilized life, its moving causes, and even its very soul: and considering and hoping that the human species is capable of becoming more enlightened and more happy, we can only expect that the different parts of the great whole of society should be intimately united together by means of knowledge and the useful arts; that they should act as the children of one great parent, with one determinate end, so that no power may be rendered useless, no exertions thrown away. In this view we do not look to distant ages, or amuse ourselves with brilliant, though delusive dreams, concerning the infinite improvability of man.[11]

This perfectibility, not of man's actual conditions but of his *thoughts* about them, rests on the assumption that individuals, when enlightened, will recognize and accept their place in the social hierarchy and, having realized that such a hierarchy is necessary for civilized life, no longer be discontented or rebellious. The social and political assumptions which may be inferred from Davy's words include an endorsement of inequality as industrialism's motor and a dream of reining in and controlling the power embodied by the growing but uncultivated working class. Science, in Davy's Burkean model, becomes the strong 'parent' which its 'children' (once sufficiently enlightened) will obey.

While Davy posits an alternative to philosophical solutions, he like Victor is more concerned with means than ends. He shies away from defining specific realistic goals, concentrating instead on the immediate benefits of science. While embracing the concept of improvement, he is reluctant to relate it specifically to *human* perfectibility, as did Godwin, so much as to abstract mechanistic ideas for improving the system.[12] Though they might seem deceptively similar, this distinction between the humane and the mechanical is the key to the difference between the views of Davy and Mary Shelley. The liberal Shelley also seeks to justify a reasonable use of power within a necessary hierarchy. Yet the *basis* upon which her views rest makes them incompatible with Davy's. For if a mechanistic, technocratically-inspired model like Davy's were successful in appropriating space otherwise occupied by humanistic philosophies, as it threatens to be, neither conscious social responsibility nor free moral choice — both crucial to Mary Shelley's liberal ideals — would be possible. If *Frankenstein* had ever been intended as proof that such a model might work, then the scientific irresponsibility of its sole practitioner effectively disproves it.[13]

While the idea of science as the basis of a socially desirable world-view (as well as a source of personal satisfaction) is clearly not one Shelley agrees with, her handling of the broader theme of personal responsibility extends the scope of her critique. For justifying the shedding of ethical constraints by reference to the Romantic concept of 'genius' — 'understood not as a peculiar capacity possessed by a creative artist, but as the power which possessed him' — was not unique to natural philosophy.[14] On the contrary, such a definition of inspiration in the New Science was similar to a stream of thought within the arts. Just as scientists guided by inspiration from an *outside power* were relieved of personal responsibility for their own dis-coveries and inventions, so similar beliefs in interference from outside (in the form of inspiration) brought relief to the existential despair underlying the Romantic sentiment described earlier. In spite of the existence of radical poetry and populist sciences, both were rendered liable to accusations of irresponsibility, either social or political.

To this extent, Victor appears to be at least as much a Romantic as a modern, rational scientist. Indeed, his own statements about his approach to science show that the creative imagination of Romantic sensibility did not *necessarily* stand in strict opposition to the *minutiæ* of science: this occurred only where the latter signified the 'idea of pedantry ... tinged by dogmatism' (p. 34). 'In other studies', Victor says, 'you go as far as others have gone before you, and there is nothing more to know; but in scientific pursuit there is continual food for discovery and wonder' (p. 35). He im-plies that non-scientific studies merely allow their student to achieve profi-ciency, whereas science promises the glory of originality, creativity and invention. Enraptured by the potentials of the latter, Victor falls short of the ideal of objectivity and cool aloofness we have now come to identify with the scientific project. He rises above the potential tedium of the 'minutiæ of science' — things that anyone can learn — to *create*. The implication is that Victor has a talent or an unusual mental capacity for intuition which allows him to delve deeper and go further than others before him, very much in accordance with the poetic ideal described earlier.

Significantly, Victor Frankenstein ignores the quest — so important to the Romantic psyche — for a higher philosophical meaning within a personal framework.[15] Instead, he uses his genius to pursue the outward, Newtonian quest for the *physical* boundaries of the cosmic framework. There is, however, no fundamental opposition between the spontaneous creativity of the Romantic poet and Victor's scientific creativity (which might just indicate that Shelley aims to criticize *both*). The cross-overs exemplified by Victor, Krempe and Waldman were, it is important to note, not merely fictional. Davy, Bacon, Newton, Erasmus Darwin and other 'modern scientists' all cultivated alchemical interests. Paracelsus had searched for medicine rather than gold, praised 'reason and experiment' as the sources of knowledge, and had even acted as a medical doctor. But between science (or natural philosophy) and poetry there were no airtight boundaries either. Davy and Darwin wrote poetry, and the views of Romantic poets such as Wordsworth, Coleridge, Goethe and Percy Shelley ranged from ambivalence or curiosity to enthusiasm about science. The mythical figures of modern science, Newton especially, were so fascinating that they were 'cleared' of pure empiricism and their works raised to the level of 'act[s] of genius'. Science was poeticized, and metaphors in the Romantic natural sciences shifted from the mechanical to the organic — even becoming gendered: science ceased to be a Renaissance clock-work — 'the philosophy of mechanism, which ... strikes *Death*' in Coleridge's words — and became a personal interaction with a mysterious female, Mother Nature.[16] Moreover, structural homologies only strengthen these associations between the romantic and the scientific. For all his spontaneity and radical innovation, the poet still forces his words into metres and stanzas and remains dependent on the same basic systems, grammatical and syntactical, as those predecessors he reacts against. Similarly, Victor's revolutionary ideas rest on and within the framework of laborious scientific research furnished by Krempe's enlightened rationalism.

Yet such homologies contain functional tensions, for in Victor's — and the Romantic — mind a hierarchy exists between dogmatic proficiency (reproduction of a given knowledge) and the freedom of genius or imagination (original creation).[17] It follows that if, in order to go further than any other scientist before him, Victor builds on the basis of the work of his predecessors, he does so reluctantly, as if fearing that his creative imagination will be hemmed in by established natural laws. Their unidealistic labours are beneath him, so to speak, while he reaches for the sky. Incorporating other elements only of necessity, he remains single-mindedly set on his course. Rather than observing and understanding with respect for his object (being a *student* in the original sense, in other words), Victor seeks to master and perfect Nature.

The suggestion that Victor's ambition was to become not a sensitive Romantic student of organic science but a glorified master scientist, 'penetrat[ing]' like Humphry Davy 'into the recessess of nature, and show[ing] how she works in her hiding places' (p. 32), carries within it allusions to the attitudes of great Enlightenment scientists who acted on the aggressively potent Baconian metaphor: Nature as passive female, scientists as men who seek the secrets in her womb. The patriarch of experimental philosophy, Francis Bacon, derided the organic view of nature as science for 'boys'. In its manhood, he argued, science would turn 'with united forces against the Nature of things, to storm and occupy her'. Not satisfied with observing miracles due to the 'many secrets ... still laid up in the womb of nature', Bacon promised that 'time will show ... what she may do when her folds have been shaken out'.[18]

Such metaphors are significant, for they call into question the conventional belief that Romantic science was a *reaction* to the scientists whose views, following those of Bacon, had 'conceptually transform[ed mother nature] into a lifeless, machine-like entity of mere matter in motion'.[19] Personifying Nature and 'minding' her matter, Romantic poetics may have attempted to relieve her of the constraints of matter and mechanistic explanatory models. Yet their trains of thought were in some ways deceptively similar. When Davy says 'the skirt only of the veil which conceals these mysterious and sublime processes has been lifted up, and the grand view is as yet unknown', for example, his language echoes the description of how the creative imagination of the poet may help him lift 'the veil from the face of the eternal and beautiful ... to create the world anew'.[20] Though the veil the materially-oriented scientists sought to lift up may have been a little further down Mother Nature's body, there is not only a coincidence of metaphor but a pattern of thought.[21] Both poet and scientist seek interactive creativity with the object, Nature, one with her mind the other her matter. Such is the nature of the relationship that exists between the idea of 'genius' and that of 'creative imagination'.

Frankenstein, who represents a particular brand of Romantic natural science which challenged the primarily 'objective, dogmatic' view later to become dominant, literally gives a body to the idea of an immaculate male conception:

My imagination was vivid, yet my powers of analysis and application were intense; by the union of these qualities I conceived the idea, and executed the creation of a man (p. 181).

Victor's insistence on the supremacy of mind (eternal life) over matter (mortality) reinforces the suspicion that the Monster may be the product of a warped mind, or even that it exists not as ugly matter but as a hideous thought alone. He is, according to Victor's own description, very elusive — almost a shadow. Like the few people Victor reveals his story to, even the creator himself doubts the existence of Frankenstein's monster but concludes that 'the mere presence of the idea was an irresistible proof of the fact' (p. 57). Whatever its ultimate status, Frankenstein insists upon a permanent imbalance and hierarchy. Allowing 'the charms of nature' at its most fertile to pass him by, his 'human nature' is filled with disgust as he gathers the material which is to give life to his idea. Keeping his mind on the glory, Victor proceeds with his 'filthy creation'. In a passage resonant with the warning tone of Wordsworth's 'The Tables Turned' (*Lyrical Ballads*, 1798), where scientists and scholars — approaching nature as material only — 'murder [her] to dissect', he 'pursue[s] nature to her hiding places ... tortur[ing] the living animal to animate the lifeless clay' (p. 38).

Not only does Victor's dead mother warn him (in his dream) of the ugly truth of death; the Monster's shape — 'more hideous than belongs to humanity' (p. 57) — reveals a misconception (at once literal and metaphoric) not unique to Victor alone. Teratology (the study of the creation of actual monsters) shows that prior to the Romantic era monsters were considered the 'intellectual' property of their *mothers*. (Mere vessels carrying the 'material' provided by the father, women could conveniently be blamed for imprinting with their fanciful imagination any flaws on the child, thus producing monsters as '"demonstrations" of the mother's unfulfilled desires'). But the Romantics reclaimed the *vis imaginativa* 'as a masculine attribute'. They no longer reproduced images mimetically, the way women had, but created new ones.[22] Viewed in this light, only Victor's creative imagination could be responsible for the deformity of his Monster.

Victor conceives of his behaviour not as a terrible crime but simply as the act of giving life to matter. He does not realize that what condemns his procreative act is its exclusion of a female partner. What to Shelley is a crime takes place on a number of levels. Excluding all emotions and postponing his wedding night indefinitely, Victor literally makes his Monster by himself. Separating mind and body, making his creative imagination the sole source (and perhaps the sole *locus*) of the Monster, he also denies (because it disgusts him) the significance of matter, which in the creative process is traditionally (and semiotically) thought of as feminine. In addition, Victor refuses to acknowledge that his Monster can and, after all, does grow up spiritually to become a sentient, intelligent human being. Instead, he thinks of him if not as a reanimated corpse then certainly as death personified. Both mentally and through his actions (or inaction), Victor denies his creation any right to belong, as an equal member, within human society, even if such membership amounts only to the 'right' to be tried at a court of law for the murder of William. The Monster feels driven to seek extra-legal justice in terms of *personal* revenge as he finds himself excluded from the support of a community.

Last but not least, Victor's final significant rejection of matter, mother-hood and the feminine in general, occurs with his destruction of his second monster, whose creation would (in human terms) have made the existence of the first more justified. Though it might seem that, having had the ex-perience of the first, Victor is able to anticipate more realistically the out-come of a second creative act, what really mortifies him is the prospect of their natural procreation. It is the female monster who is the ultimate threat because, like Eve, she can create a race, which as a community will live for ever. Victor, the solitary egoistic male, seeks to triumph over the individual mortality of the one person he animates (the Monster) or wants to re-animate (his mother); he tries to conquer individual death, too, by seeking the glory that would immortalize his own name. To Mary Shelley, humble procreation offers a better, more *democratic* way of conquering death than the quest for personal immortality. It also offers the only proper way of achieving eternal life, for whereas a masculine nurturing model merely creates the embryo, leaving it to grow up a monster, a feminine model creates bonds and harmony. Having a mother thus seems to ensure access to a social network. Nurturing, or 'mothering', facilitates social cohesion and responsibility; and the balance provided by the understanding and affection of nuclear families upon which this model rests is, in Shelley's liberal, humanistic opinion, not only sensible and natural but *best* for most people. The single-minded denial of responsibility to and for society, which leads Victor to father a child or an idea without mothering it, is what creates monsters, both of the mind and of matter.

Notes

1. James O'Rourke, '"Nothing More Unnatural": Mary Shelley's Revision of Rousseau', *ELH*, 56, 3 (Fall, 1989), p. 548.
2. Mary Shelley, *Frankenstein* (1818 edn), ed. by Paddy Lyons, (London: Everyman's Library, 1992), p. 67. All references in the text are to this edition.
3. Edmund Burke, 'Reflections on the Revolution in France' in Robert B. Dishman, *Burke and Paine on Revolution and the Rights of Man*, (New York: Scribner, 1971), p. 142.
4. Anne K. Mellor, *Mary Shelley: Her Life, Her Fiction, Her Monsters*, (New York: Rout-ledge, 1989), p. 214.
5. Linda A. Pollock, *Forgotten Children: Parent-Child Relations from 1500 to 1900*, (Cam-bridge: Cambridge University Press, 1983), pp. 18-28; Lawrence Stone, *The Family, Sex and Marriage in England 1500-1800*, (London: Weidenfeld and Nicolson, 1977), pp. 10, 433.
6. Jonathan Cook, 'Romantic Literature and Childhood', in *Romanticism and Ideology: Studies in English Writing 1765-1830*, eds. David Aers, Jonathan Cook and David

Punter, (London: Routledge, 1981), p. 44. Cook's argument relies on the interpretation in E.P. Thompson's *The Making of the English Working Class* of the role
of the bourgeoisie in industrialization, which with the intensification of child-
labour, ironically, made the children of the lower clases valuable too.

7. Godwin quoted in William St. Clair, *The Godwins and the Shelleys*, (London: Faber
& Faber, 1989), p. 282.

8. Bertrand Russell, *A History of Western Philosophy*, 2nd edn, (London: Unwin, 1984),
p. 657.

9. James Engell, *The Creative Imagination: Enlightenment to Romanticism*, (Cambridge,
Mass.: Harvard University Press, 1981), pp. 239-40.

10. Laura E. Crouch, 'Davy's *A Discourse, Introductory to A Course of Lectures on
Chemistry*: A Possible Scientific Source of *Frankenstein*', *The Keats-Shelley Journal*,
27 (1978), p. 41. Some disagreement exists as to which of Davy's works Mary
Shelley was reading while writing *Frankenstein*, but the general source of her
inspiration is clear.

11. Sir Humphry Davy, *A Discourse, Introductory to A Course of Lectures on Chemistry*,
in *The Collected Works of Sir Humphry Davy*, ed. John Davy, (New York: Johnson
Reprint Corporation, 1972), vol. 2, p. 323.

12. Both Laura Crouch ('Davy's *A Discourse*', p. 40) and certain scholars writing in
her wake appear to have gravely misread Davy's social philosophy. The previous
quotation does *not* bear out their claim that Davy foresaw 'social changes that will
erase class distinction, leading to near-perfect society'. To Davy, social inequality
was clearly the very soul and motivator of a well-functioning system.

13. As an excuse for not thinking through the practical consequences of his experiment, Victor uses one of Davy's apologies for scientific imperfection: 'my
work [might] be imperfect: yet, when I considered the improvement which every
day takes place in science and mechanics, I was encouraged to hope my present
attempts would at least lay the foundations of future success' (p. 37). This
ideology of trial-and-error is taught by Waldman who affirms that: 'the labours
of men of genius, however erroneously directed, scarcely ever fail in ultimately
turning to the solid advantage of mankind' (p. 32). A scientific ideology con-
doning the use of power freed from the constraints of ethics is an expression of
Baconian optimism. Davy himself invests in early natural philosophical 'scientists'
a benevolent objective: 'to ameliorate the condition of humanity, and to support
the interests of Religion'. He also excuses their mistakes as 'errors natural to an
infant science'. See Patrick J. Callahan, '*Frankenstein*, Bacon, and the "Two
Truths"', *Extrapolation*, 14, 1 (December, 1972), p. 41; Davy, *Works*, vol. 1, p. 146.

14. Simon Schaffer, 'Genius in Romantic Natural Philosophy', in *Romanticism and the
Sciences*, ed. Andrew Cunningham and Nicholas Jardine, (Cambridge: Cambridge
University Press, 1990), p. 83.

15. Engell, *Creative Imagination*, p. 263.

16. Henry M. Pachter, *Paracelsus: Magic into Science*, (New York: Henry Schuman,
1951), p. 25; Kant's *Critique of Judgement* quoted by Schaffer, 'Genius', p. 89;
Samuel Taylor Coleridge, *Letters*, ed. E. H. Coleridge, (Cambridge, Mass.: Harvard
University Press, 1895), II, p. 649, quoted in Andrew Cunningham and Nicholas
Jardine, 'The Age of Reflexion', in *Romanticism and the Sciences*, p. 4.

17. This distinction applies within both arts and sciences. The difference between

learning an oriental language and the experience of reading or writing one is comparable to the difference between the study of natural philosophy and the 'creative' experimental science Victor finally pursues.

18. Francis Bacon, quoted in Brian Easlea, *Fathering the Unthinkable*, (London: Pluto Press, 1983), pp. 20-21.
19. Easlea, *Fathering*, p. 22.
20. Engell, *Creative Imagination*, pp. 239-40.
21. Davy, *Works*, vol. 8, pp. 175-76.
22. Marie-Hélène Huet, *Monstrous Imagination*, (Cambridge, Mass.: Harvard University Press, 1993), pp. 6-8. The latin roots of 'monster' (*monstrare* or *monere* meaning to show/demonstrate or warn) suggest its function is to warn Victor and others against that which causes deformity.

Modern Voices

An Allotropic Triangle
in D.H. Lawrence's *Women in Love*:
The Philosophical and Psychological Genesis of
the Gerald-Gudrun-Loerke Relationship

Per Serritslev Petersen

> You mustn't look in my novel for the old stable ego of the character. There is another ego, according to whose action the ego is unrecognisable, and passes through, as it were, allotropic states which it needs a deeper sense than any we've been used to exercise, to discover are states of the same single radically unchanged element.
>
> (Lawrence's announcement of his modernist psychology of the allotropic [that is, radically unstable, dynamic] ego in a letter to Edward Garnett, dated 5 June 1914[1])

> Criticism which does not get beyond the words on the page sterilizes and emasculates literature. Each published work is only the latest bulletin of the writer's battle to achieve and articulate a vision of life adequate to his experience.
>
> (Keith Sagar, *D.H. Lawrence: Life into Art* (1985))

At the end of the final, published version of *Women in Love* (1920) — the result of seven long years of gestation, false starts, and radical revisions — Gudrun ironically refers to her past relationship with Gerald and Loerke as a 'pretty little sample of the eternal triangle'.[2] With 'the cold devil of irony' (*WL* 577) freezing her soul after Gerald's suicide in the Tyrolese alps, she knows that a romantic triangle never really existed between the three of them, that it had always been a fight between Gerald and herself, and that 'the presence of the third party [that is, Loerke] was a mere contingency' (*WL* 578).

However, if you visit the Harry Ransom Humanities Research Center at the University of Texas, Austin, you may actually find, amongst the library's extensive Lawrence holdings, a pretty little textual sample of a genuinely romantic Gerald-Gudrun-Loerke triangle, that is, a triangle un-touched by the cold devil of modernist irony. In a fourteen-page holograph manuscript comprising two fragments of a very early version of the story,[3] Lawrence has Gudrun invite the German sculptor to England: 'You sent for me, Miss Brangwen', Loerke reminds Gudrun when the trio is having its first, and last, conversation/negotiation. The romantic scenario of this early version is, as far as one can reconstruct it from the surviving fragment, as follows. After their Tyrolese skiing holiday, Gerald and Gudrun have come back to England *together*, so, unlike the final version of *Women in Love*, they have not split up in the Tyrol (and Gerald, consequently, has not committed suicide). Still, their relationship appears to be on the rocks because Gerald cannot make up his mind whether he really loves Gudrun, and whether he is going to marry the woman, who is now pregnant with his child. In this version Gudrun plays the victimized, that is, conventionally stereotyped, female part in the sex war, and, as a romantic damsel in distress, she must have decided to send for Loerke, her German lover and Gerald's rival, who promptly comes to her rescue, complete with *romantische Liebe* and, if neces-sary (and culturally feasible!), *Liebestod* by duel:

'I think', he [that is, Loerke] said, we place Miss Brangwen in a rather awkward position. Gerald turned and looked at her. She was still and impassive, regarding neither man. The sculptor fretted on his chair.
    'Yes', said Gerald Crich mildly, constrained also to wait.
    'If we were in Germany', said the sculptor, with an agitated smile, 'we might settle it with pistols'.
    'We are not in Germany, are we?' said Gerald Crich.
    'No', said the sculptor, his head bowed. Then he looked up at Gerald Crich, an anger blazing in his eyes. 'That is the pity', he said.
    The other man went pale, and looked aside. Gudrun sat aloof.

Probably as a result of Loerke's dramatic appearance on his English turf, Gerald has, at long last, made up his mind to marry Gudrun. Naturally, Gudrun cannot help feeling humiliated and exasperated by his overbearing manner, and suddenly, during the two rivals' argument, she 'burst[s] into life' and turns against Gerald: 'You pretend *now* you want to marry me — [...] You pretend it now,' she said, 'but why? — Why now rather than at any other time these last six weeks?'
    This pathetic feminine outburst then triggers off the final masculine show-down between the passionate German lover and the somewhat self-

complacent English aristocrat, who has 'still retained the queer unseeing look in his eyes, as of a creature that follows its instinct blindly, thoughtlessly as a leopard running in the sunshine, for the sake of running':

'If you say any more,' said Gerald Crich, turning at bay, 'I'll break your neck.' He sat leaning forward, staring at the other man. His fists were clenched and he breathed hard.

'One of your noble English threats, because you know you are a little bigger, physically,' said the sculptor, his face twisted with pain. He looked back into the other's eye. He was too much moved to be afraid. 'You trust to your position to play with *her*, you trust to your muscles to threaten me, just as you would threaten an unarmed man with your loaded gun — and shoot him righteously — that is what you would do.' The sculptor was showing all his teeth, like an animal, with suffering and passion.

Loerke leaves when he realizes that Gudrun has made her choice: she wants to marry the father of her child. Gudrun still claims to have loved Loerke, but she could not marry him. Why, Gerald asks: 'Because of the child? — Without that, would you have preferred him to me?' Well, Gudrun of course is entitled to her quota of feminine nagging and teasing after what she has been through, but basically she is a good woman in the Lawrentian-patriarchal sense of 'a good woman', so she ends up offering Gerald what Lawrence in *Fantasia of the Unconscious* (1922) singled out as a woman's 'true female self', 'that beautiful and glamorous submission which is truly the wife-submission'.[4] Gerald's instant response is that of a true Lawrentian *homo religiosus et allotropicus*, for he is miraculously converted from arrogant machismo to true love and marriage, 'the right way to be happy — a nucleus of love between a man and a woman, and let the world look after itself', as Lawrence summed up this romantic love-and-marriage philosophy in a letter:[5]

She buried her face in his shoulder. And the love went through him like a hard flame, love for her movement, like a wild thing hiding itself from fear and misery against him. [...] He did not want to speak. It was enough to hold her close, like this, whilst she pressed her face against him for shelter. And he felt himself giving her shelter, relief, and ease, and his heart grew hot with a trembling joy. He was something he feared he never could be: he had got something he had pretended to disbelieve in. And, breathing hard, he knew this was his life's fulfilment, and a wave of faith, warm, strong, religious faith went over him.

However, Gerald's new sense of existential fulfilment and religious faith of course also reflects Lawrence's own feelings about his relationship with

Frieda Weekley, whom he had met and eloped with in 1912. 'I know in my heart "Here's my marriage"', [he assures Frieda in a letter while they are still living apart]. 'It feels rather terrible — because it is a great thing in my life — it is *my life* — I am a bit awe-inspired';[6] and after they have moved and lived together for about a year in Germany and Italy, Lawrence can still report eulogistically on his marital condition: 'You'd be surprised, how I am married — or how married I am. And this is the best I have known, or ever shall know'.[7]

Gerald is glad that they are going to have a child, but he is also worried that Gudrun might think more of the child than him, and 'it's you I want most', he tells her. It is as if Lawrence himself does not really believe in the happy ending of his love story because once again he feels obliged to spell out the psychological details of Gerald's romantic conversion: 'In his new conversion, he had almost a passion for submission: it was so new a thing to him'. Perhaps Lawrence found his happy ending too good, too romantic, to be true. Perhaps he realized that he had somehow confused life with fiction, the story of his own marriage with that of his fictional characters, Gerald and Gudrun? So perhaps the author's allotropic ego had already, subconsciously, started rewriting the story. Whatever, this denouement of the triangle was written off as another false start in 1916.

If we compare this early version of the Gerald-Gudrun-Loerke relationship with the final version, we can at least start by observing that the original triangle has suffered a sea-change into something much richer and stranger. What principally caused this dramatic transformation of the triangle, was the traumatic impact of World War I on Lawrence, who was also, thanks to his possession of a Hunnish wife and a suspiciously Hunnish *Weltanschauung* (witness, for instance, the notorious 'obscenities' of *The Rainbow*), treated as a potential traitor by the English authorities and refused permission to leave the country. To quote James T. Boulton and Andrew Robertson's succinct summary of this critical period:

In 1915 *The Rainbow* was suppressed for immorality — and the sense of detachment from the bourgeois world, the world which controls press, publication and all became almost complete [during the period of the war].[8]

In a 'Foreword' written for the American edition of *Women in Love* (it was only printed in an advertising leaflet distributed by Seltzer, the American publisher), Lawrence himself starts by pointing out that '[the] novel was written in its first form in the Tyrol, in 1913', and that it was 'altogether rewritten and finished in Cornwall in 1917':

So that it is a novel which took its final shape in the midst of a period of war, though it does not concern the war itself. I should wish the time to remain un-fixed, so that the bitterness of the war may be taken for granted in the characters.[9]

As Lawrence reveals in a letter, 'Mrs Lawrence' wanted the misanthropic and apocalyptic 'bitterness of the war' to be reflected in the actual title of the new 1916 version of the novel: instead of *Women in Love* it should, she suggested, 'be called "Dies Irae" [that is, "Day of Wrath"]'.[10] Lawrence decided to keep the title *Women in Love* though, but, as he confessed in another letter: 'The book frightens me: it is so end-of-the-world',[11] And one more quotation from the letters written during the last months of 1916, viz. a passage from a note to E.M. Forster that illustrates not only Lawrence's anger and despair at the time, but also the kind of animal imagery he was to deploy in the final version of *Women in Love* to articulate his sense of 'Apocalypse Now':

I am in a black fury with the world as usual. One writes, one works, one gives one's hand to people. And the swine are rats, they bite one's hand. They are rats, sewer-rats, with all the foul courage of death and corruption, darkness and sewers. But of openness and singleness — ah well — I am weary to death of my fellow men. I think it would be good to die, because death would be a clean land with no people in it: not even the people of myself. Where to go, where to go away from them![12]

However, before we reach the definitive configuration of the Gerald-Gudrun-Loerke relationship in *Women in Love* (1920), there is one more false start (or rather 'ending') to record in the textual genesis of the novel, viz. the 'epilogue', which Lawrence began writing in 1916, but crossed out in his exercise book and never rewrote or completed:

A year afterwards, Ursula in Italy received a letter from Gudrun in Frankfurt am Main. Since the death of Gerald in the Tyrol, when Gudrun had gone away, ostensibly to England, Ursula had had no news of her sister.
 'I met a German artist who knew you,' Gudrun said, 'and he gave me your address. I was silent for so long because there was nothing I could say. I have got a son — he is six months old now. His hair is like the sun shining on the sea, and he has his father's limbs and body. I am still Frau Crich — what actually happened is so much better, to account for one's position, than a lie would be. The boy is called Ferdinand Gerald Crich. As for the past — I lived for some months with Loerke as a friend. Now I'm staying [sentence incomplete][13]

In this version, then, Gudrun is still made pregnant with Gerald's child, but

Gerald has now — as in the final version — chosen to commit suicide as a result of the show-down with Gudrun and Loerke in the Tyrolese alps.[14] But how did Gudrun become Frau Crich? Seeing that the manuscript, which contains the whole of the 'Exeunt' chapter, does not mention any marriage, 'Frau Crich' is probably just the name Gudrun has adopted, for reasons of convenience and decorum, during her pregnancy abroad; and her 'friend' Loerke, in this version of the triangular story, is no longer the passionate German lover. A fascinating fellow-artist and demonic Nietzschean nihilist, the new Loerke allotrope instead becomes Gudrun's mentor and soul-mate:

A certain violent sympathy [...] came up in her for this street arab. He seemed to be on the bed-rock of life, planted. There was no going beyond him. He was a real *ne plus ultra*.[15]

In the final version of the novel Gudrun is, at long last, relieved of her pregnancy and her conventionally, that is, romantically stereotyped sexual persona so that she can now — as an allotropically reborn Lawrentian character, along with the two male characters of the triangle — 'fall into the form of some other rhythmic form', to quote again from the famous letter to Edward Garnett.[16] Within this new rhythmic or dynamic form of the triangle, Gudrun has become the New Woman, the emancipated modern artist-feminist, and as such she can now challenge, humiliate and finally break up with Gerald instead of being obliged to follow him back to England and eventually marry him. 'Gudrun went to Dresden' (*WL* 583), the author laconically reports at the end of the novel, presumably to work in Loerke's studio. So this time Loerke is the winner, but, of course, in an entirely different ball game. What has happened to the original romantic triangle in the process of this textual metamorphosis; and how, precisely, has the new rhythmic/dynamic form of the triangle impinged upon the individual characters that 'fall into the form'?

My answer to the first question is simply that the conventionally *romantic* triangle of the first versions has been converted into an essentially *philosophical* triangle in the final version. At the beginning of 1916 Lawrence had sent Lady Ottoline Morrell 'the first, the destructive half of [his] philosophy',[17] viz. the unpublished essay 'Goats and Compasses', and in a letter written at the beginning of 1917 Lawrence notes that, at this juncture of his life, 'the pure abstract thought interests me [...] more than art':

I am tired of emotions and squirmings of sensation. Let us have a little pure thought, a little perfect and detached understanding. [...] I am sick to death of struggling in a cauldron of foul feelings, with no mind, no thought, no under-standing; no clarity of being anywhere, only a stinking welter of sensations.[18]

The triangular dialectics of the final version can be read, I suggest, as part of Lawrence's philosophical diagnosis, in *Women in Love*, of that cultural pathology which had brought about the bitterness of the war and the con-comitant 'draught of blasphemous living'.[19] As far as the philosophical dia-lectics is concerned, the crucial character of the triangle is now Loerke, who had already, in the previous manuscript version, been promoted to a philo-sophical *ne plus ultra*. The German sculptor has become the exponent of not only a sophisticated *l'art-pour-l'art* aestheticism, but also a Nietzschean 'radical nihilism', that is, to quote one of Nietzsche's definitions in *The Will to Power*, 'the conviction of an absolute untenability of existence when it comes to the highest values one recognizes'.[20]

In this game of triangular dialectics there are, predictably, two con-flicting types of response to Loerke and his philosophical position. Gud-run's response is one of deep fascination and admiration. In a way her close relationship with Loerke (a platonic or spiritual relationship at this stage, because the Loerke of the final version has also metamorphosed into a homosexual) represents the existential-philosophical consummation of her initial response to the alpine whiteness of the Tyrol, 'the sleeping, timeless, frozen centre of All' (*WL* 502); in other words, Melville's symbolic 'land-scape of snows — a colorless, all-color of atheism'.[21] For Gudrun cannot help feeling Nietzschean in this sublime environment: '*übermenschlich* — more than human' (*WL* 486). And when she encounters Loerke, she must needs welcome him as another Zarathustra descending from the mountains to tell the old saint in his forest that '*God is dead!*' and the rest of mankind that '[t]he superman is the meaning of the earth'.[22] As a Nietzschean soul-mate, Gudrun pays homage to Loerke, celebrating his nihilism and stoicism, 'devoid of illusions and hopes':

To Gudrun, there was in Loerke the rock-bottom of all life. Everybody else had their illusion, must have their illusion, their before and after. But he, with a perfect stoicism, did without any before and after, dispensed with all illusion. He did not deceive himself in the last issue. In the last issue he cared about nothing, he was troubled about nothing, he made not the slightest attempt to be at one with anything. He existed a pure, unconnected will, stoical and momentaneous. There was only his work (*WL* 521).

Indeed, there was his work, his work as an artist, and in Gudrun's and Loerke's joint nihilism-*cum*-aestheticism gospel, the Nietzschean superman becomes identified with the modern artist beyond human or humanistic good and evil. As Loerke, in his broken English, explains to the indignant Ursula, his statuette of a naked girl sitting on a great naked horse is a *Kunstwerk*, an autonomous work of art, and as such it is 'a picture of nothing, of absolutely nothing':

It has nothing to do with anything but itself, it has no relation with the everyday world of this and other, there is no connection between them, absolutely none, they are two different and distinct planes of existence, and to translate one into the other is worse than foolish, it is a darkening of all counsel, a making confusion everywhere. Do you see, you *must not* confuse the relative work of action, with the absolute world of art (*WL* 525-26).

Gudrun and Loerke agree that Life and Art represent 'the Reality and the Unreality' respectively, so life, Gudrun argues, 'doesn't *really* matter — it is one's art that is central' (*WL* 546). Thus Gerald becomes a mere 'bagatelle', and love 'one of the temporal things in her life, except in so far as she was an artist' (*WL* 546). As eroticist-artist Gudrun enlists in the company of 'exoteric exponents of [female] love' — Cleopatra, Mary Stuart and Eleonora Duse: 'After all, what was a lover but fuel for the transport of this subtle knowledge, for a female art, the art of pure, perfect knowledge in sensuous understanding' (*WL* 546-47).

Gudrun can still admire and appreciate the masculine charisma of Gerald, her Don Juan, but after meeting Loerke, her awareness of Gerald's existential limitations increases drastically: 'He was limited, *borné*, subject to his necessity, in the last issue, for goodness, for righteousness, for oneness with the ultimate purpose' (*WL* 551), the ultimate purpose being, in Gerald's case, the construction, in society as well as in his mining industry, of 'a great and perfect machine, a system, an activity of pure order, pure mechanical repetition, repetition ad infinitum' (*WL* 301). Gerald as a 'Deus ex Machina' (*WL* 301), with 'such a lot of little wheels to his make-up' (*WL* 566) becomes Gudrun's recurrent nightmare: 'Oh God, the wheels within wheels of people, it makes one's head tick like a clock, with a very madness of dead mechanical monotony and meaninglessness' (*WL* 564).

In the existential-philosophical rivalry between Gerald and Loerke (as distinct from the romantic rivalry of the original version), the values of masculinity and virility in the form of Gerald's glamorous Don Juan eroticism, are questioned and depreciated: 'His maleness', Gudrun reflects, 'bores me. Nothing is so boring as the phallus, so inherently stupid and stupidly conceited' (*WL* 563). Gerald might have penetrated the 'outer places' of Gudrun's body and soul, but it took 'little, ultimate *creatures* like Loerke' to reach 'the inner, individual darkness, sensation within the ego, the obscene religious mystery of ultimate reduction' (*WL* 550). Gerald was not capable of touching the quick of her: 'where his ruder [phallic as well as mental] blows could not penetrate, the fine, insinuating blade of Loerke's insect-like comprehension could' (*WL* 550). As a *l'art-pour-l'art* artist and Nietzschean nihilist, Loerke has the advantage of Gerald in this existential-philosophical game because he is 'detached from everything', 'admits no allegiance', is 'single and, by abstraction from the rest, absolute in himself' (*WL* 551).

Gerald, on the other hand, is handicapped by his attachment to his *borné* human constructions. In the modern industrial and technological world, Gerald was undoubtedly, Gudrun reflects in one of her moods of 'terrible cynicism', a perfect instrument, who should 'go into Parliament in the Conservative interest' and 'clear up the great muddle of labour and industry' (*WL* 511), but immediately Gudrun is faced with 'the ironical question "What for?"' (*WL* 511). With 'the perfect cynicism of cruel youth' she has reached the Loerkean-Nietzschean position of radical nihilism. 'The whole coinage of valuation was spurious' (*WL* 512), she tells herself, thus echoing Nietzsche's answer to the question, 'What does nihilism mean', viz. '*That the highest values devaluate themselves*. The aim is lacking; "Why?" finds no answer'.[23]

Throughout the novel, however, Gerald himself appears to have a kind of subliminal modernist awareness of his own existential 'aimlessness'; witness, for instance, the scene in Chapter 17 ('The Industrial Magnate') where Gerald looks closely at his own face in the mirror, fearing that it is not real, but only a mask, and that behind the progressive social mask of the 'Industrial Magnate' there is nothing, only a vacuum: 'He was afraid that one day he would break down and be a purely meaningless bubble lapping around a darkness' (*WL* 306). After his father's death Gerald is once more 'faced with the ultimate experience of his own nothingness', feeling 'suspended on the edge of a void, writhing' (*WL* 422), and if he fell into this void, he knew he would never rise again. It is Gudrun who, with 'the wonderful creative heat' of her sexuality, saves and restores him in this existential crisis. As *Magna Mater*, Gudrun is his 'great bath of life', and, through the sex act, Gerald becomes 'perfect as if he were bathed in the womb again' (*WL* 430).

However, the price Gerald has to pay for his existential salvation and restoration is his fatal dependence on Gudrun and her body (or, to put it more precisely and bluntly, her 'pussy power'). He constantly needs her, and, at the apocalyptic climax of this modern love story, Gerald is 'dominated by the constant passion, that was like a doom for him' (*WL* 492). Gudrun, in one of her moods of perfect cynicism, despises this Don Juan crying in the night like an infant:

Perhaps this was what he was always dogging her for, like a child that is famished, crying for the breast. Perhaps this was the secret of his passion, his forever unquenched desire for her — that he needed her to put him to sleep, to give him repose (*WL* 566).

In the final triangular show-down, Gerald realizes that he must be as 'self-sufficient' as Gudrun (and Loerke), and that 'it only needed one convulsion of his will for him to be able to turn upon himself also, to close upon himself as a stone fixes upon itself, and is impervious, self-completed, a thing isolated' (*WL* 543). But that one convulsion of the will is beyond the philososophically *borné* Gerald because that would have been tantamount to a leap into Nietzschean nihilism. His brain 'turned to nought at the idea. It was a state of nothingness' (*WL* 543). Gerald's nature is 'too serious, not gay enough [also in the sense of Nietzsche's *The Gay Science*) or subtle enough for mocking licentiousness' (*WL* 543). Instead Gerald opts for a kind of Dionysian martyrdom and *Liebestod*: 'like a victim that is torn open and given to the heavens, so he had been torn apart and given to Gudrun'. He insists on 'keep[ing] the unfinished bliss of his own yearning even through the torture she inflicted upon him' (*WL* 543):

A strange, deathly yearning carried him along with her. She was the determinating influence of his very being, though she treated him with contempt, repeated rebuffs, and denials, still he would never be gone, since in being near her, even, he felt the quickening, the going forth in him, the release, the knowledge of his own limitation and the magic of the promise, as well as the mystery of his own destruction and annihilation (*WL* 543-44).

Also in the previous manuscript version of *Women in Love* Gerald had insisted, in a conversation with his friend Birkin, that he would not have missed this erotic experience *in extremis*, 'to die when you are with a woman [...] so beautiful, so perfect, so good to you, her flesh like a silk, and every slope and bit perfect'. Yet Gudrun, this 'magnificent woman', would be his life's 'final experience', he tells Birkin: 'God — I think she is deathly, I do really'.[24] So Gerald's suicidal exit from the triangle — leaving Loerke the winner of the existential-philosophical contest — was already a foregone conclusion.

Outside the triangle, however, Loerke's victory is seen as a human tragedy. Loerke, after all, is only Gudrun's hero: the other characters — Birkin, in particular — never tire of denouncing and traducing the 'little' German artist-nihilist. As a fictional articulation of Lawrence's psychology of the allotropic ego, *Women in Love* represents one of the more extreme cases of what Mikhail Bakhtin termed the dialogic or polyphonic novel; but as far as the on-going existential-philosophical dialogue about Loerke is concerned, critics of Lawrence's dialogic novel *par excellence*, invariably and unquestioningly, side with Birkin's position in the argument.[25] The same critics, it should be noted, may blithely admit that Birkin is also the most allotropic, volatile, and self-contradictory character in the novel. In other words, the truth-value of any existential-philosophical position taken up by Birkin in the course of the novel is inherently questionable (the position is bound to be questioned at least by Birkin himself in the next paragraph or the next chapter). Even the woman that loves Birkin, viz. Ursula, readily confesses that '[Birkin] says one thing one day, and another the next — and he always contradicts himself' (*WL* 374). Well, the name of Lawrence's allotropic-dialogic game — and the contested character of Loerke is a perfect case in point — is, I suggest, *ambivalence*, the acute existential-philosophical ambivalence evinced by the author himself as well as his fictional *alter ego* Birkin.

Why does Birkin hate Loerke with such intensity? He calls him 'a little obscene monster of the darkness' (*WL* 522), 'a rat [living] in the river of corruption, just where it falls over into the bottomless pit' (*WL* 522-23). Yet, throughout the novel, Birkin himself has been deeply fascinated and attracted by what he calls the black river of darkness as distinct from 'the silver river of life':

'It is your reality, nevertheless,' he said [to Ursula], 'the dark river of dissolution. — You see it rolls in us just as the other rolls — the black river of corruption. And our flowers are of this — our sea-born Aphrodite, all our white phosphorescent flowers of sensuous perfection, all our reality, nowadays' (*WL* 238).

There is also Birkin's notorious letter about the Flux of Corruption, which Halliday quotes from in Chapter 28 ('Gudrun in the Pompadour'), and which advocates extreme regression as part of what R. D. Laing would have called 'a project of [psychological] deconstruction-reconstruction' or '[r]eculer pour mieux sauter':[26]

It is a desire for the reduction-process in oneself, a reducing back to the origin, a return along the Flux of Corruption, to the original rudimentary conditions of being [...] And in this retrogression, the reducing back of the created body of life, we get knowledge, and beyond knowledge, the phosphorescent ecstasy of acute sensation (*WL* 474-75).

So Birkin and Loerke could actually be said to be philosophical allotropes, the Loerke allotrope being the more demonic form. For, compared with Birkin, Loerke is also a decadent artist, a Nietzschean nihilist, a 'Jew — or part Jewish' (*WL* 523), a German, and a homosexual: Loerke and his male companion, Leitner, have 'travelled and lived together in the last degree of intimacy' (*WL* 516). But why does the less demonic allotrope hate the more demonic so intensely? My answer to that question brings us back to what I called Lawrence's acute existential-philosophical ambivalence and, I should add at this stage, his sexual ambivalence as well. As late as in December 1913 (that is, shortly before the bitterness of the war with its draught of blasphemous living began traumatizing his soul), Lawrence made no bones about his personal interest in homosexuality when, in a letter to Henry Savage, he starts philosophizing, in a type of discourse closely resembling Loerke's aestheticism, about the question of the great artist and his sexual identities/priorities:

I should like to know why nearly every man that approaches greatness tends to homosexuality, whether he admits it or not: so that he loves the *body* of a man better than the body of a woman — as I believe that the Greeks did, sculptors and all, by far. I believe a man projects his own image on another man, like on a mirror. But from a woman he wants himself re-born, re-constructed. So he can always get satisfaction from a man, but it is the hardest thing in life to get one[']s soul and body satisfied from a woman, so that one is free from oneself.[27]

For what gives Lawrence's fictional game of ambivalence away, at least seen in the perspective of the novel's textual and philosophical genesis, is Loerke's homosexuality in the final version. In an opening chapter to *Women in Love* entitled 'Prologue', which Lawrence must have written in 1916 and later rejected, we are first introduced to an all-male trio, comprising Birkin, Gerald, and the otherwise unknown William Hoskins, and this trio is spending a week (*mirabile dictu!*) in the Tyrol, mountain-climbing. Now in this version of the story Birkin is a full-fledged homosexual character (not just a wishy-washy bisexual as in parts of the final version of *Women in Love*), who is tortured by his fascination for the 'male physique':

Why [Birkin asks himself] was a man's beauty, the beauté mâle, so vivid and intoxicating a thing to him, whilst female beauty was something quite unsubstantial, consisting all of look and gesture and revelation of intuitive intelligence?[28]

Gerald, incidentally, is in possession of the *beauté mâle* with which Birkin is most in love; but Birkin keeps his love and his homosexuality secret, this being the only secret he has ever kept to himself, 'this secret of his passionate and sudden, spasmodic affinity for men'.[29] He even keeps the secret from *himself* or, at least, tries to keep the knowledge 'at bay':

His a priori were [*sic*]: 'I *should not* feel like this,' and 'It is the ultimate mark of my deficiency, that I feel like this.' Therefore, though he admitted everything, he never really faced the question. He never accepted the desire, and received it as part of himself. He always tried to keep it expelled from him.[30]

He always tried to keep it expelled from him[self]. Here, I think, we may find the beginning of a psychoanalytic answer to the question about Loerke and his highly ambivalent functioning as a character in *Women in Love*. On the one hand, within what I have called the final existential-philosophical triangle, Loerke is permitted to humiliate and oust Gerald as the exponent of a sexually and philosophically *borné* Englishness. So, inside the triangle (serving as a kind of Trojan Horse), Loerke may be said to function as an *alter ego* or secret agent for the culturally and sexually emancipated, Continental Lawrence who, for instance, in the unpublished 'Foreword' to *Women in Love*, could argue that '[n]othing that comes from the deep, passional soul is bad, or can be bad'.[31] Hence, homosexuality — as well as other 'passional' or philosophical manifestations of un-Englishness — cannot, in principle, be bad and should not be expelled, but be accepted as part of our rich human potential. On the other hand, we have, outside the triangle, the antagonism between Loerke (plus Gudrun, his protégée) and the rest of the cast, Birkin in particular. Here Birkin, or rather the final politically correct allotrope of Birkin as anti-Loerke, tends to become the Puritan-English Lawrence's *alter ego* or superego, while Loerke (replacing, in the final version of *Women in Love*, the Birkin of the 'Prologue' as the homosexual character) turns into a sexual and philosophical scapegoat or scarecrow, a German/Jewish/Nietzschean/homosexual demon with a perverse vampirish interest in English women, who, alas, are only too willing to be corrupted, as Birkin points out to Gerald (*WL* 522).

In psychoanalytic terms, Birkin's inadequately motivated antipathy towards Loerke — plus the emotional intensity of that antipathy — may be accounted for as a psychodynamic combination of, (1) *projection*, that is, Birkin's unconscious act (triggered off by his sense of guilt or shame) of attributing to Loerke his own *ultimate marks of deficiency*; (2) *reaction formation* against the 'Loerkean' deficiencies in Birkin himself, which he still needs to repress or *expel from himself*, notably his decadent fascination for the regressive Flux of Corruption and his latent homosexual interest in Gerald ('palimpsestuously' echoing, in the diachronic-genetic perspective of the character, Birkin's manifest homosexuality in the 'Prologue'); (3) *over-compensation*, that is, an emotional reaction in excess of what is necessary (the reaction being excessive because it is a function of the reaction forma-tion). In Lawrence's non-fictional psychobiography, there are, incidentally, some interesting parallel cases of overcompensation, viz. his hysterical comments on the evil homosexual 'rats' he had met in Cambridge, John Maynard Keynes in particular.[32]

In my reading of the final form and context of the Gerald-Gudrun-Loerke triangle in the last chapters of *Women in Love*, I see Lawrence's various allotropic-dialogic games and gambits as not so much a 'struggle', in the words of the 'Foreword', to articulate his acute ambivalence into 'ver-bal consciousness', but rather as a fictionalizing, 'pulsing, frictional to-and-fro'[33] exercise in covering up and glossing over the most glaring fissures of that ambivalence — in brief, the all-too-human trick of both eating your cake and having it. But then Lawrence himself never had any romantic illu-sions about art: 'Truly art is a sort of subterfuge', he notes at the beginning of *Studies in Classic American Literature*. 'But thank god for it, we can see through the subterfuge if we choose'.[34]

Notes

1. *The Letters of D.H. Lawrence*, Vol. II, ed. George J. Zytaruk and James T. Boulton, (Cambridge: Cambridge University Press, 1981), p. 183. Henceforth cited as *Letters II*. The inspiration of Lawrence's concept of the *allotropic* ego is, of course, the so-called interconversion of allotropic forms: an element may exist in more than one molecular or structural form, and each of these forms is called an allotrope. Carbon, for instance, has graphite and diamond as allotropes, which Lawrence, in the same letter, cites by way of illustration: 'Like as diamond and coal are the same pure single element of carbon. The ordinary novel would trace the history of the diamond — but I say 'diamond, what! This is carbon'. And my diamond might be coal or soot, and my theme is carbon'.

    In terms of what I have called Lawrence's psychology of the allotropic ego, a fictional *character* may pass through several allotropes, diachronically (that is, through various textual versions) as well as synchronically (that is, within the same version). The 'generating' allotropic ego of the *author* may be seen as one of the more extreme types of what Mikhail Bakhtin termed the dialogic or polyphonic imagination.

2. Lawrence, *Women in Love*, ed. Charles Ross, (Harmondsworth: Penguin, 1989), p. 578. This Penguin edition, based on Thomas Seltzer's American 1920 edition, is

the least corrupt trade edition of the novel. Henceforth cited in my text, with page references, as *WL*.

3. Manuscript E441*a*, according to Lindeth Vasey's checklist of the manuscripts of Lawrence in Keith Sagar, *D.H. Lawrence: A calendar of his works* (Manchester: Manchester University Press, 1979), p. 265.

4. Lawrence, *Fantasia of the Unconscious and Psychoanalysis and the Unconscious*, (Harmondsworth: Penguin, 1976), pp. 126-27. Please note that *Fantasia of the Unconscious* was written six or seven years after Lawrence conceived this early version of the Gerald-Gudrun-Loerke triangle, and by then, after almost a decade of marital experience with Frieda, he appears to have resigned himself to the fact that no woman would give her 'wife-submission' to a stranger or a husband [*sic*], but only to her son, her father or her brother: 'To a stranger, a husband, a woman insists on being queen, goddess, mistress, the positive, the adored, the first and foremost and the one and only' (p. 127).

5. Letter to John Middleton Murry and Katherine Mansfield, 17 January 1916, *Letters II*, p. 507.

6. Letter dated 15 May 1912, *The Letters of D.H. Lawrence*, Vol. I, ed. James T. Boulton (Cambridge: Cambridge University Press, 1979), p. 403. Henceforth cited as *Letters I*.

7. Letter to Helen Corke, 29 May 1913, *Letters I*, p. 553.

8. 'Introduction', *The Letters of D.H. Lawrence*, Vol. III, ed. James T. Boulton and Andrew Robertson (Cambridge: Cambridge University Press, 1984), p. 1. Henceforth cited as *Letters III*.

9. Lawrence, *Women in Love*, ed. David Farmer, Lindeth Vasey and John Worthen, (Cambridge: Cambridge University Press, 1987), p. 485. Henceforth cited as *Women in Love*, CUP.

10. Letter to J.B. Pinker, 31 October 1916, *Letters II*, p. 669.

11. Letter to Catherine Carswell, 7 November 1916, *Letters III*, p. 25.

12. Letter dated 6 November 1916, *Letters III*, p. 21.

13. Manuscript E441*c* (also in the library of the Harry Ransom Humanities Research Center in Austin). Quoted in Keith Sagar, *D.H. Lawrence: A calendar of his works*, p. 74.

14. See manuscript E441*c*, pp. 472-74.

15. Manuscript E441*c*, p. 298.

16. *Letters II*, p. 184.

17. Letter dated 25 February 1916, *Letters II*, p. 556.

18. Letter to Mark Gertler, 1 April 1917, *Letters III*, p. 110.

19. Letter to Mark Gertler, 27 September 1916, *Letters II*, p. 657.

20. Friedrich Nietzsche, *The Will to Power*, ed. Walter Kaufmann, (New York: Vintage Books, 1968), p. 9. Lawrence knew Nietzsche's work, and there are quite a few allusions to Nietzsche both in his fiction and in his letters. In a note to Lady Ottoline Morrell, for instance, he comments on the 'perfect intimate relations between the men and the women' in the Ajanta frescoes, contrasting their 'very perfection of passion' with modern Nietzschean passion: 'That which we call a passion is a very one-sided thing, based chiefly on hatred and Wille zur Macht. There is no Will to Power here — it is so lovely — these frescoes' (*Letters II*, p. 489).

21. Herman Melville, *Moby-Dick*, (Harmondsworth: Penguin, 1983), p. 296. Lawrence loved *Moby Dick*, which he read at the beginning of 1916 while writing the final version(s) of *Women in Love*; see, for instance, his letters to Lady Ottoline Morrell, 7 February 1916 (*Letters II*, p. 528), and to Barbara Low, 30 May 1916 (*Letters II*, p. 614).

22. Friedrich Nietzsche, *Thus Spoke Zarathustra*, (Harmondsworth: Penguin, 1969), pp. 41-42.

23. *The Will to Power*, p. 9.

24. Manuscript E441c, pp. 326-27.

25. The founding father of the 'non-dialogic' or 'normative' school of Lawrentian criticism is, of course, F.R. Leavis, the author of, for instance, the following incredible observation: 'A strong normative preoccupation, entailing positives that are concretely present in many ways [...] informs the life of *Women in Love* — the life that manifests itself in the definition and "placing" of these opposite human disasters [notably 'the human disaster enacted by Gerald Crich]', (F.R. Leavis, *D.H. Lawrence: Novelist*, (Harmondsworth: Penguin, 1964), p. 175).

26. R.D. Laing, *The Voice of Experience*, (London: Allen Lane, 1982), p. 159.

27. Letter dated 2 December 1913, *Letters II*, p. 415.

28. 'Prologue to *Women in Love*', *Phoenix II: Uncollected, Unpublished and Other Prose Works by D.H. Lawrence*, (London: Heinemann, 1968), p. 104. Henceforth cited as *Phoenix II*.

29. *Phoenix II*, p. 107.

30. *Phoenix II*, p. 107.

31. 'Foreword to *Women in Love*', *Women in Love*, CUP, p. 485.

32. See, for instance, Lawrence's letters to Lady Ottoline Morrell, 24 March 1915 (*Letters II*, pp. 314-15), and to David Garnett, 19 April 1915 (*Letters II*, pp. 320-21).

33. 'Foreword to *Women in Love*', *Women in Love*, CUP, p. 486.

34. Lawrence, *Studies in Classic American Literature*, (Harmondsworth: Penguin, 1983), p. 8.

A World of His Own:
Dreams in Graham Greene's Novels

Niels Bugge Hansen

In 1992, the year after Graham Greene had died, appeared a slim post-humous volume from his hand, entitled *A World of My Own*. As the additional title makes clear, it is a *dream diary* — that is, a selection of items from a dream diary of more than eight hundred pages which Graham Greene had kept in the period from 1965 to 1989. The selection, which runs to just over a hundred pages, is thematically divided into nineteen short chapters, called for instance 'Famous Writers', 'In the Secret Service', 'A Touch of Religion', and 'The Job of Writing'. These chapter headings clearly suggest not only that it is a *writer's* dream diary, but also that it is an invitation into a dream world with parallels to the world Graham Greene inhabited as well as the one he created in his books. So the little book might be expected to throw some interesting light on the novelist's inner and private life and the way it has inspired and coloured his writing. But the reticence and the discretion that characterize his autobiographical volumes have also filtered the material chosen for this little book, and readers hoping to get information about the secret life of Graham Greene are much better served by the various biographical volumes that have appeared recently. However, as a supplement to the personality that emerges from the world of his books, the diary is of some interest to students of Graham Greene.

It is well known that Graham Greene was always very interested in dreams. He mentioned it himself in *A Sort of Life*, his autobiographical description of the first thirty years of his life (1971). When he was 16 he spent about six months in the home of a psychoanalyst in London after he had suffered a nervous breakdown. The treatment involved his telling his dreams to the analyst in morning sessions, and consequently — as Greene writes in *A Sort of Life*:

I kept perforce a dream diary (I have begun to do so again in old age), and fragments of the dreams I can remember still, though the diary has been destroyed for nearly half a century.[1]

He goes on to recount a few of these dreams and nightmares, and their importance in his later life is apparent from references to them in books that he wrote 15 to 20 years later. In *Journey without Maps* from 1936, a travel book of a hike through the interior of Liberia, but very much a book of a quest in search of roots and origins, there is a short section called 'Mythology', in which he explores his own dream territory:

It is the earliest dream that I can remember, earlier than the witch at the corner of the nursery passage, this dream of something outside that has got to come in. The witch, like the masked dancers, has form, but this is simply power, a force exerted on a door, an influence that drifted after me upstairs and pressed against windows. Later the presence took many odd forms: a troop of blackskinned girls who carried poison flowers which it was death to touch; an old Arab; a half caste; armed men with shaven heads and narrow eyes and the appearance of Thibetans out of a travel book; a Chinese detective.[2]

'The finest entertainment known and given rag cheap'. This is how Greene refers to dreams in the very first chapter of *A Sort of Life,* stressing the importance they have always had for him. Fine entertainment is perhaps an odd description of these more gruesome and gory dreams. Be that as it may, the significant thing is not that he dreamt, nor the nature of his dreams, but the fact that he paid so much attention to them, recorded them, returned to them and used them in his fiction. In *Ways of Escape* he mentions that in a journal he kept during a stressful period in the early thirties he noted down dreams, and in his biography of Greene Norman Sherry quotes from this unpublished journal:

... a worse dream was that I had murdered someone and deposited his body in a suitcase at a railway cloakroom. I wanted to get it away before it began to smell.[3]

A slight variation on this dream is recorded in his travel book from Mexico, *The Lawless Roads* (1939):

I dreamed that a woman and I had committed a murder and buried the body, but the smell seeped up to us through the ground until the whole world seemed to carry the scent of decay.[4]

The recurrence of these messages from the unconscious and the insistence on their importance suggest very clearly that besides the Common World (as Greene calls it in the introduction to his dream diary) this 'World of My

Own' is highly relevant for his fiction as well. This is not altogether un-
explored territory. Greene himself laid a strong scent when he wrote in the
introduction to his *Collected Stories* in 1972 that a couple of stories come
straight out of 'the free world of dreams'. And he goes on to say:

Dreams, perhaps because I was psycho-analysed as a boy, have always had an
importance when I write. The genesis of my novel *It's a Battlefield* was a dream,
and a novel which I am working on now [i. e. *The Honorary Consul*] began too with
a dream. Sometimes identification with a character goes so far that one may dream
his dream and not one's own. That happened to me when I was writing *A Burnt-
Out Case*. The symbols, the memories, the associations of that dream belonged so
clearly to my character Querry that next morning I could put the dream without
change into the novel, where it bridged a gap in the narrative which for days I had
been unable to cross. I imagine all authors have found the same aid from the
unconscious. The unconscious collaborates in all our work: it is a *nègre* we keep
in the cellar to aid us. When an obstacle seems unsurmountable, I read the day's
work before sleep and leave the *nègre* to labour in my place. When I wake the
obstacle has nearly always been removed: the solution is there and obvious —
perhaps it came in a dream which I have forgotten.[5]

It is not very clear to what extent a dream of Greene's gave him ideas or
material for the novel *It's a Battlefield*. I have found no evidence that the
main plot is based on a dream, but the dream of the body in the suitcase
left at a railway station has entered the novel as a minor topic included to
suggest the variety of crimes the Assistent Commissioner has to deal with,
and indeed to build up the picture of the city as a battlefield.

As regards the genesis of *The Honorary Consul* the information which
Greene has offered concerning an inspirational dream is brief and not very
informative. The link between the author's dream world and his fictional
world with regard to *A Burnt-Out Case* is more illuminating. *In Search of a
Character*, the journal Greene kept while he was travelling up the Congo
river to find both his setting, his plot and his protagonist, confirms that one
of Querry's dreams was an exact reproduction of one of Greene's own
dreams which occurred while he was writing the novel at the precise
moment when he needed it. And elsewhere in the journal he poses the
question: Is there a way in which I can use the dreams of X?[6]

It is worth noting that the question here is not: is there a way I can use
my own dreams? Accordingly, the focus of interest in the following brief
inquiry into the dreams of some of Graham Greene's fictional characters is
not on where they come from and how they may contribute to the author's

psycho-biography, but on how they are used in the fictional universe, how they contribute to the presentation of character and to the overall patterns of the novel in question.

The use of dreams in fiction is, of course, an age-old device, which, however, in our post-Freudian age has taken a new turn. Modern fictional characters are regularly dreamers, and especially Greene's. In fact, there is probably no main character in a Greene novel who does not have at least one dream. The first one is found on the second page of *The Man Within*, Greene's first published novel from 1929. This is a very brief dream, but at the opening af chapter II young Andrews, the protagonist in Greene's story, has a second dream, which is described at some length, and which in its surrealistic mingling of details offers a short cut through the subconscious to the sense of guilt that troubles the mind of this disturbed young man. In *Stamboul Train*, Greene's next extant novel, he has switched to a quite different narrative style, realistic, cinematic, and kaleidoscopic, but again we find him including dreams to add complexity to his characterization, especially of Myatt, the Jewish merchant.

Why do the dreams of fictional characters deserve special attention from the reader? In dream psychology the dream is a story that lends itself to interpretation and throws light on the individual in an analytical process that bears resemblance to a reader's attempt to interpret the significance of the book he is reading, looking out for symbols and their meaning, for example. In that sense a whole work of fiction is like a dream. It might also be argued that as fiction is distinguished from real life in that in stories the private, inner life of a character is or can be made accessible to the reader in a way that we seldom or never share the inner lives of 'real' people we meet, so the dream is but a variation on the thoughts and feelings of fictional characters that we are so used to, in traditional fiction as well as in the interior monologues and streams of consciousness of more recent date. As a matter of fact, one of Greene's few experiments with extended interior monologue, Anthony Farrant's night thoughts in *England Made Me*, as he is lying in his cabin on his way to Sweden, creates the state between being awake and dreaming that Joyce made so famous in *Ulysses*. So why use dreams proper to open up the private world of your characters? To try and give some kind of answer to this question I shall discuss a few dreams in Graham Greene's novels.

To interpret the dreams of fictional characters you need to see them in the context of the whole book; without this context it makes limited sense to discuss to what extent they are in character. With this reservation I turn to the specific dream in *A Burnt-Out Case* which Greene refers to in *In*

Search of a Character, a dream he himself dreamed at the precise moment when he needed it, a dream which, in his own words, 'bridged a gap in the narrative which for days I had been unable to cross'. One can hardly help wondering: Did Greene dream Querry's dream, or did he give his own dream to Querry? Or are the two too close to tell them apart? 'I suppose the points where an author is in agreement with his character lend what force or warmth there is to the expression', says Greene (in a correspondence with Evelyn Waugh) as a comment on his possible identification with Querry.[7]

The dream does indeed mark a turning point, not only in the writing of the story, but also in Querry's situation. Having left everything in his past life behind him, women, profession, religion, and escaped as far up the Congo as possible, Querry, the internationally famous architect, has just explained to the doctor at the leproserie in the jungle that he is numb, devoid of any kind of commitment.

He had a dream that night from which he woke in terror. He was walking down a long railway-track, in the dark, in a cold country. He was hurrying because he had to reach a priest and explain to him that, in spite of the clothes he was wearing, he was a priest also and he must make his confession and obtain wine with which to celebrate Mass. He was under orders of some kind from a superior. He had to say his Mass now that night. Tomorrow would be too late. He would lose his chance forever.

He finds the priest's house, is admitted and is on the point of achieving what he has come for, but at that moment, 'when he was about to lose the burden of his fear and responsibility', a second priest enters and picks up the decanter.

Then Querry broke down. It was as though he had had an appointment with hope at this turn of the road and had arrived just too late. He let out a cry like that of an animal in pain and woke.[8]

The next morning he goes back to the doctor and declares that he is willing to work, designing a new building for the hospital. We understand that the dream made him change his mind. Other means could of course have done the same, but this message from his subconscious makes the sudden change of heart plausible. The point of the whole novel is that he in some sense recovers his commitment, but though some of the other characters want to make him into an Albert Schweitzer-like, saintlike Christian hero, there is nothing in his subsequent development which shows that he recovers his religion. Hints maybe, in the doctor's comment: 'You are too troubled by your lack of faith Querry. You keep on fingering it like a sore you want to get rid of'.[9] Or in the conclusion to the fable he tells of the famous jeweller whose unbelief is seen as the conclusive proof of 'the King's' existence. But the dream, in which Querry experiences himself as a priest, in spite of the clothes he is wearing, becomes an oblique comment on the religious aspect in Querry's predicament in the novel's overall concern with giving dramatic expression to various types of belief, half-belief, and non-belief. The dream allows the author to open a deeper layer in his character's psyche than is accessible in his conversation or his conscious thoughts, and thus to create a fuller and more subtle picture of his predicament. In the surrealistic world of dreams the author transcends the limits of consciousness in the presentation of character.

Querry has three dreams in the course of the novel. This one occurs fairly early in the novel. Before this he has had one that shows his emotional numbness through his inability to share the suffering of a girl grieving for the loss of a broken vase.[10] And much later, about two thirds into the novel, after Querry has regained some sense of happiness, he dreams of being onboard a boat going further up the river with a corpse that is to be buried there:

... in his dream the boat took the contrary direction to that of Luc. It went on down the narrowing river into the denser forest, and it was now the Bishop's boat. A corpse lay in the Bishop's cabin and the two of them were taking it to Pendélé for burial. It surprised him to think that he had been so misled as to believe that the boat had reached the farthest point of its journey into the interior when it reached the leproserie. Now he was in motion again, going deeper.
The scrape of a chair woke him.[11]

The significance of this dream depends more on the context established in the course of the novel. Pendélé is an imaginary place, a dream world somewhere in the heart of the jungle, which he has heard of from his native servant. At the same time the dream content raises the question of the amount of extra-textual association it carries. Is Greene alluding to traditional mythology about ferrying a corpse, or is he with his past experiences of psychoanalysis drawing on interpretative conclusions concerning sailing with a corpse in one or another school of dream psychology? Questions of this nature are too far-reaching to be answered here. It is, however, within the scope of this paper to note that this dream has obvious parallels with one that Scobie, in *The Heart of the Matter*, dreamed some 12 years earlier:

That night he dreamed that he was in a boat drifting down just such an underground river as his boyhood hero Allan Quatermain had taken towards the lost
city of Milosis. But Quatermain had companions while he was alone, for you
couldn't count the dead body on the stretcher as a companion. He felt a sense of
urgency, for he told himself that bodies in this climate kept for a very short time
and the smell of decay was already in his nostrils. Then, sitting there guiding the
boat down the mid-stream, he realized that it was not the dead body that smelt
but his own living one. He felt as though his blood had ceased to run: when he
tried to lift his arm it dangled uselessly from his shoulder. He woke and it was
Louise who had lifted his arm. She said, 'darling, it's time to be off.'[12]

In its focus on the decaying body Scobie's dream calls to mind dreams
mentioned above, dreams Greene had recorded many years before as his
own. At the same time both these dreams, Querry's and Scobie's, anticipate
one that Maurice Castle has in *The Human Factor*, from 1978:

It was hours before he slept. He lay awake and thought of Carson and Cornelius
Muller, of Uncle Remus and Prague. He didn't want to sleep until he was sure
from her breathing that Sarah was asleep first. Then he allowed himself to strike,
like his childhood hero Allan Quatermain, off on that long slow underground
stream which bore him on towards the interior of the dark continent where he
hoped that he might find a permanent home, in a city where he could be accepted
as a citizen, as a citizen without any pledge of faith, not the City of God or Marx,
but the city called Peace of Mind.[13]

Like Scobie, Castle is reminded in his dream journey of Allan Quatermain,
the hero in Rider Haggard's *King Solomon's Mines*, who was not only
Scobie's and Maurice's childhood hero, but also Graham Greene's. Any
attempt to subject the dreams in a given novel to a purely intrinsic interpretation is likely to go astray the moment you move from one novel to the
next, and again and again the track leads you back to that dimly perceived
private universe of Graham Greene's, out of which emerge a multitude of
individualized characters who yet share many features, including features
in their dreams.

Like Pendélé in Querry's dream, Maurice Castle's golden city called
Peace of Mind is an imaginary place, a dream world somewhere in the
heart of Africa. Both these men are being hounded in one way or another,
and it is certainly both 'in character' and significant that their dreams centre
on escape and peace. Scobie's dreams, this one as well as others he has,
focus on responsibility and guilt, a guilt-feeling connected with the forbidden but tempting escape through suicide. For Scobie, too, dreams of
peace; more so, perhaps than any other Greene character:

For he dreamed of peace by day and night. Once in sleep it had appeared to him as the great glowing shoulder of the moon heaving across his window like an iceberg, Arctic and destructive in the moment before the world was struck.[14]

It is quite clear that these three men, Scobie, Querry, and Castle, are related to their author, but also that their dreams are tailored to fit their particular character and situation. It is also clear that the dream in each case occurs at a critical moment, and serves as a signal to character and reader alike. Castle, for example, has just been confronted with an ominous person from his past in South Africa, Cornelius Muller. A scheme involving the two intelligence services they work for will force him to co-operate with his old enemy, and Castle, who feels trapped all the time, finds himself in a particularly tight spot, which releases the dream of escape in his mind. In Querry's case the dream rather anticipates the situation where he realizes the need to escape, and quite possibly it anticipates more than that. Pendélé, the blissful refuge in the depth of the jungle, is an image of the ultimate peace in death, and the corpse in the cabin may be taken to be Querry's own. Dreams that carry premonitions were a familiar phenomenon to Greene, as appears from *A Sort of Life* where he records several pre-cognitive dreams of shipwrecks and similar disasters. And in *Ways of Escape* as well as in the dream diary, he refers to J.W. Dunne's book *Experiment with Time,* in which the latter writes of dreams that draw their symbols from the future as well as the past. And Greene adds an interesting com-ment: Is it possible that a novelist may do the same, *since so much of his work comes from the same source as dreams?*[15]

Scobie, Querry, and Castle are all projections of recognizable aspects of their creator's life and mentality; they are characters that the author, to borrow Greene's own term, 'is in agreement with'. So not surprisingly their most private world, the world of their dreams, is also recognizably familiar territory to the novelist. With Pinkie, the young gangleader who is the main character in *Brighton Rock,* Greene set himself a more challenging task when he moved beyond the conventions of the thriller to create a psychological and moral study of a hardened criminal. In a sense Pinkie is the embodi-ment of evil, but he is also a human being shaped by his past. Pinkie's only dream is partly precognitive, a premonition of his own violent death, partly retrospective. In his dream he is back in his childhood, experiencing the violence and cruelty of the playground:

The boy lay on his back — in his shirt-sleeves — and dreamed. He was in an asphalt playground: one plane tree withered: a cracked bell clanged and the children came out to him. He was new: he knew no one: he was sick with fear —

they came towards him with a purpose. Then he felt a cautious hand on his sleeve and in a mirror hanging on the tree he saw the reflection of himself and Kite behind — middle-aged, cheery, bleeding from the mouth. 'Such tits', Kite said and put a razor in his hand. He knew then what to do: they only needed to be taught once that he would stop at nothing, that there were no rules.[16]

As in so much psycho-analytical theory the clues to Pinkie's adult behaviour can be traced back to early childhood experiences of violence and sex, and his dream provides the clues.

The dream that opens the door to crucial childhood experiences is a recurrent motif in Greene's writings. 'If I had only known it, the whole future must have lain all the time along those Berkhamstead streets' is the opening sentence of *A Sort of Life*, and childhood dreams as well as dreams of childhood feature prominently in the first chapter of this autobiographical volume. Actually, recollecting *is* like dreaming:

Memory is like a long broken night. As I write, it is as though I am waking from sleep continually to grasp at an image which I hope may drag in its wake a whole intact dream, but the fragments remain fragments, the complete story always escapes.[17]

Nowhere are the intricate links between memory, imagination, and dream set forth more intriguingly than in 'Under the Garden', a story Greene wrote in the early 1960s about an ageing man who revisits the country house of his childhood summers and writes down the strange underground adventures he imagined, or dreamed there, when he was a young boy. The interest in dreams and the nature of dreams that is documented so frequently in his various non-fictional writings finds, however, its most detailed and striking expression within his fictional universe in an entire chapter in *The Ministry of Fear*. This wartime entertainment of a man who inadvertently becomes involved with a sinister spy ring operating in London builds on Greene's own experiences as an air-raid warden in 1940-41 in the nightmare world of the blitz. Its hero, Arthur Rowe, carries his own interior hell around with him through the bomb-ravaged streets of London. He is guilty of the mercy-killing of his wife, and though society *has* imposed its punishment on him, he is still tormented by his sense of guilt. The novel explores quite explicitly the contrasts between past and present, peace and war, childhood and adult world, innocence and guilt. Chapter 5, 'Between Sleeping and Waking', is largely a dream that runs to five pages. It opens with a general comment on dreams:

There are dreams which belong only partly to the unconscious; these are the dreams we remember on waking so vividly that we deliberately continue them, and so fall asleep again and wake and sleep and the dream goes on without interruption, with a thread of logic the pure dream doesn't possess.[18]

Rowe goes underground to find rest and goes to sleep in the lurid surroundings of the shelter. In the beginning his state is much like Anthony Farrant's in the interior-monologue passage in *England Made Me,* which I mentioned earlier, though the syntax is more straightforward, the narrative more coherent. In his dream he argues with his mother, who is firmly ensconced in the innocent past, and who refuses to believe that her little boy is a murderer. Later, as it says, 'he had worked the dream to suit himself, but now the dream began to regain control'. In this section he kills a rat which had had its back broken by a dog, an incident that in fact once took place — Rowe's first mercy killing. Next he is in a street, waiting for a girl to come out and meet him:

And then without warning the dream twisted towards nightmare; somebody was crying in the dark with terror — not the young woman he was waiting there to meet, whom he hadn't yet dared to kiss and probably never would, but someone whom he knew better even than his parents, who belonged to a different world altogether, to the sad world of shared love. A policeman stood at his elbow and said in a woman's voice, 'You had better join our little group', and urged him remorselessly towards a urinal where a rat bled to death in the slate trough. The music had stopped, the lights had gone, and he couldn't remember why he had come to this dark vile corner, where even the ground whined when he pressed it, as if it had learnt the trick of suffering. He said, 'Please let me go away from here', and the policeman said, 'Where do you want to go to, dear?' He said, 'Home', and the policeman said, 'This is home. There isn't anywhere else at all', and whenever he tried to move his feet the earth whined back at him; he couldn't move an inch without causing pain.[19]

Rowe, who cannot move an inch without causing pain, shares the predicament of Scobie, who is also a guilt-ridden man, both when he is awake ('I can't bear to see suffering, and I cause it all the time. I want to get out, get out'),[20] and in his dreams. In the distorting mirror of the dream our obsessions stand out with the force of exaggeration. Half-concealed truths, repressed or forgotten, come to the surface to complete the picture of the person.

The burden of fear and responsibility leads back to the dream of Querry's that I started with. The missed opportunity in connection with the celebration of Mass is another recurrent dream motif in Greene's fiction. It is not at all surprising to find that the whisky priest in *The Power and the Glory* has it. He has three dreams. One is a semi-conscious memory dream of his complacent past occasioned by the picture of him which has been circulated. The second is very much a guilt dream of his neglected father role. The third is the dream he has during his last night in prison, awaiting execution in the morning. In his waking thoughts that night he is very much concerned with failure. When he falls asleep, his failure as a priest and his dependence on wine fuse in his dream. The celebration of the Mass is also here a picture of missed opportunity:

A priest passed to and fro before the altar saying Mass, but he took no notice: the service no longer seemed to concern him. At last the six plates were empty; someone out of sight rang the sanctus bell, and the serving priest knelt before he raised the Host. But *he* sat on, just waiting, paying no attention to the God over the altar, as though that were a God for other people and not for him.[21]

Another variation on this motif is found in *The Comedians*. Brown, the only dreamer in the present discussion who tells his own story and thus also recounts his own dreams, started life at a Jesuit school in Monaco, but escaped as an adolescent, and would certainly not describe himself as a believer. 'Perhaps you are a *prêtre manqué*' suggests his mistress in one of their intimate scenes. His reply is: 'Me? You are laughing at me. Put your hand here. This has no theology. I mocked myself while I made love'. And yet, in his dreams he is twice cast in the role of a choir-boy. In the second of these the sense of failure and frustration is embodied in missed opportunity in a Holy Communion scene:

I fell asleep and dreamt I was a boy kneeling at the communion-rail in the college-chapel in Monte Carlo. The priest came down the row and placed in each mouth a bourbon biscuit, but when he came to me he passed me by. The communicants on either side came and went away, but I knelt obstinately on. Again the priest distributed the biscuits and left me out. I stood up and walked sullenly away down the aisle which had become an immense aviary where parrots stood in ranks chained to their crosses. Someone called out sharply behind me, 'Brown, Brown', but I was not certain whether that was my name or not, for I didn't turn.[22]

It appears that the narrator is more of a *prêtre manqué* than he is prepared to admit to himself or others. The dream (assuming it is reliably told!) becomes a means of exposing the unreliable narrator.

This paper has touched on a number of general aspects of dreams in fiction. It has raised more questions about the nature of the creative as well as the interpretative process than it could hope to answer. How consciously are these dreams composed with reference to psycho-analytical theory and practice? Or did Greene regularly give dreams he himself had dreamed to his fictional characters? The recurrence of motifs certainly suggests their common roots in their creator's private world, and makes it legitimate for the critic 'to try to track the instinctive, the poetic writer back to the source of his fantasies', as Graham Greene puts it in his fine essay 'Henry James: The Private Universe' (1936).

At least this little anthology of dreams dreamed by various main characters in Greene's fiction has shown that in the hands of an accomplished story-teller, who is at the same time a habitual dreamer and an experienced recorder of dreams, the dreams of his fictional characters become an important part of their lives and thus of our appreciation of them. As Shakespeare might have put it — and if he had, Greene would no doubt have agreed with him — *Dreams are such stuff as books are made on!*

Notes

1. Greene, Graham, *A Sort of Life* (1971), (Harmondsworth: Penguin, 1972), p. 73.
2. Greene, Graham, *Journey Without Maps* (1936), (Harmondsworth: Penguin, 1971), pp. 180-81.
3. Sherry, Norman, *The Life of Graham Greene, Volume One 1904-1939*, (London: Jonathan Cape, 1989), p. 458.
4. Greene, Graham, *The Lawless Roads* (1939), (Harmondsworth: Penguin, 1971), p. 78.
5. Greene, Graham, *Collected Stories* (1972), (London: Bodley Head, 1972).
6. Greene, Graham, *In Search of a Character* (1961), (Harmondsworth: Penguin, 1968), p. 30; see also p. 64.
7. Greene, Graham, *Ways of Escape* (1980), (London: Bodley Head, 1980), p. 255.
8. Greene, Graham, *A Burnt-Out Case* (1960), (Harmondsworth: Penguin, 1971), pp. 53-54.
9. Ibid., p. 201.
10. Ibid., p. 32.
11. Ibid., p. 137.
12. Greene, Graham, *The Heart of the Matter* (1948), (Harmondsworth: Penguin, 1971), p. 222.
13. Greene, Graham, *The Human Factor* (1978), (Harmondsworth: Penguin, 1978), p. 107.
14. *The Heart of the Matter*, p. 60.
15. *Ways of Escape*, p. 92.
16. Greene, Graham, *Brighton Rock* (1938), (Harmondsworth: Penguin, 1975), p. 186.
17. *A Sort of Life*, p. 25.
18. Greene, Graham, *The Ministry of Fear* (1943), (Harmondsworth: Penguin, 1975), p. 63.

19. *The Ministry of Fear*, p. 68.
20. *The Heart of the Matter*, p. 233.
21. Greene, Graham, *The Power and the Glory* (1940), (Harmondsworth: Penguin, 1971), p. 209.
22. Greene, Graham, *The Comedians* (1966), (Harmondsworth: Penguin, 1967), p. 207.

Making Sense of the Past for the Present: Colm Toibin and Post-Nationalist Ireland

Michael Böss

'Remember everything and keep your head'. This is the advice of the poet William Carleton in Seamus Heaney's 'Station Island'. It may seem precisely what Colm Toibin was doing when he went on his own kind of pilgrimage to the legendary islet in Lough Derg in 1986. It is the spirit of this advice that hovers over his journalism, his criticism, and his first novel, *The South*: an altogether appropriate piece of advice in a country burdened with a past that some have wanted to wake up from and others are trying to come to terms with while keeping 'at a tangent' in regard to both nationalist and cultural revivalist atavisms.[1]

Like Heaney himself, for example, whose poetry bears out his often rephrased view that 'sensitivity to the past contributes to our lives in a necessary and salutary way'.[2] The sense of the past, like the sense of place, for him being an urge to dig the bogs of the unconscious; or a way in which to rediscover both oneself and one's attachment to 'a country of the mind' by letting shafts down through layer upon layer of lost and forgotten areas of personal and collective memory.[3] This is no cult of authenticity: There is no 'last definition'. Although each layer stripped 'seems camped on before', the point is that Ireland's wet centre is 'bottomless', even 'Atlantic seepage'.[4] Hence, the poet may feel just as 'lost, unhappy and at home' in Ireland as 'Out there in Jutland'.[5] Truly, however Yeatsian in his fondness for seeking transcendence, Heaney is basically a spiritual heir of Joyce, 'The great and true liberator ... who, like Tiresias, foresuffered all'.[6] An independent, individual mind seeking adherence with past histories but who has also abolished the myths of cultural continuity.

Colm Toibin, of an even younger generation (b. 1955), is post-Joyce, but no less convinced of the necessity of striking a tangent when Ireland gets too stuffy. His is Barcelona and a small village in the Pyrenees, where he set his first novel. When I visited him in Dublin in 1994, he admitted that there was a time in the mid-1980s — the time of the referendum on the abortion amendment — when literally following Joyce's example and going into exile in his 'bolt hole', Catalunya, the 'great post-Christian society', seemed to be the only sensible thing to do.[7]

But, again, the national climate, which in the 1980s was marked by a conservative backlash, had turned considerably more clement in recent years. Anyway, Ireland of the 1990s was definitely much different from what it was in Joyce's time, he conceded with an irony that left no trace in his melancholy eyes:

I must admit that Ireland is becoming more tolerant and tolerable, unfortunately. As a writer, I'm not sure that this is all to the good. In a way, it would have been wonderful to have priests banging down your door. But they don't do that kind of thing anymore. It's so difficult to be a rebel these days. My friends over in London always pity me asking, 'How are you over in Dublin? Are you okay?' They believe they are living in a very liberal and open society and that London is a great cosmopolitan city, a great mixture of races, whereas Dublin is a sort of backwater. But this isn't a true picture of our two countries today. Living in Ireland today is sometimes like watching the Enlightenment in France in the 18th century happening here. It does have its moments of pure comedy, if nothing else, but also quite a lot else. Right now I would much prefer to live in Ireland than in England, if only for the feeling of belonging to a place where one doesn't belong.

At that point a sardonic smile escaped his pale, round face. Declan Kiberd, the Irish critic and former director of the Yeats Summer School, once wrote that there are only two kinds of post-colonial freedom to aspire to in contemporary Ireland:

The first is the freedom to resume a past pre-invasion identity, still yearning for expression though long denied. This was the meaning of the Irish revival as defined by Yeats, de Valera and others. The trouble with this model is that it asks us to ignore the many things which have happened, for good as well as ill, during the centuries of occupation. The second form of post-colonial freedom is that which allows us to construct an identity out of nothing, beginning from first principles all over again. The difficulty with this is that it is an utterly exhausting process which inevitably offends our deepest sentiment by asking us to forget all the rest of our history as well.[8]

For Toibin, these seem to be spurious alternatives. It is from the tension between historical alienation and commitment, between the outsider's almost clinical observation — reflected in his remarkably sober and simple prose — and the insider's empathy that Toibin's writings, both his fiction and his journalism, derive their strength. It is also, I believe, his way of trying to make sense of what the past may mean in today's post-nationalist Ireland: How to remember without losing one's head; and how not to sacrifice individuality and freedom and still be true to one's 'deepest sentiment' and identify with a remembering community.

The power of place

In 1986 Toibin followed the Irish pilgrims — and poets — to St. Patrick's Purgatory on the sacred Station Island in Lough Derg in the borderland between the Republic and Northern Ireland. He did not go there to do penance or confirm any spiritual ancestry like generations of men and women before him. Basically, he went there because he was curious. And writing a book. Not surprisingly, he arrived feeling a little uneasy lest he should be disclosed as 'an interloper, a fellow who had not come to pray for special intention, a person whose dialogue with the Almighty had become somewhat one-sided'.[9] Nor was his body prepared: Was he able to bear the hunger and the lack of sleep?

It did not, in fact, take long before he started to get bored by the rituals, the constant kneeling, the walking around. He resisted the idea of telling a priest his sins. He found it unbearable to listen to a sermon against the 'moral drought' of the times: the decline of religious practice and the weakened respect for family values. He was irritated by the elaborate instructions in the accompanying leaflet telling him minutely what to do: 'Go to the water's edge; stand. Say five Our Fathers, five Hail Marys and One Creed. Kneel and repeat these prayers'. Standing there on cold stone on his bare feet with an empty stomach and his back to the pilgrims moving around 'like ants in an anthill', he matter-of-factly records, 'I was hungry, I was tired, I was bored'.[10]

Gradually, however, he was beginning to discern a certain aesthetic quality in ritual:

[T]here was something wonderful in the poetry of this, hundreds of people moving on a small piece of ground, quietly praying and coming to the edge of the water to stare towards the shore and pray.[11]

Also, he discovered that he was not the interloper he initially thought he was. Many other pilgrims appeared to have just as ambiguous motives for being on the island as himself. Some had brought things to read. One carried Seamus Heaney's *Station Island*; another former Chrysler president Lee Iacocca's autobiography.

More importantly, Toibin discovered that there was no ban against speaking. Praying took place in the Basilica. Outside, people spent their time talking, building up a community of good will and mutual sympathy: 'Everyone was gentle when they spoke; there seemed to be a kindness building up between us'. He also realized that the observance of ritual did not preclude individual conscience. On the last day, waiting for the boat to take the pilgrims back from the island, he happened to be standing next to a woman from Derry. Talking about the approaching referendum on divorce the same year, they 'both agreed it was wonderful if it were passed, despite the sermon we had listened to on the subject'.[12]

The morning in June 1994 when I visited Colm Toibin, he had the appearance of only a few hours' sleep, his house that of months of uninterrupted work. Which he realized: 'I just finished my new book late last night, or rather in the early morning', he said clearing the sofa of Irish and English newspapers and a handful of books. The script, in loose sheets among a variety of things on his desk, was *The Sign of the Cross: Travels in Catholic Europe*.[13]

One reviewer later described it as a 'novelist's book'.[14] Truly, this is a book which reveals as much about the writer himself as about Catholic Europe today: Toibin begins and ends it with reflections on memories from his hometown, Enniscorthy, in southeastern Ireland; the title essay is a personal — and deeply moving — account of his experiences in therapy by which he hoped to release repressed grief over the early death of his father; and for all Toibin's astute perceptions, anywhere the reader is taken on Toibin's travels she must be prepared to share his personal response to places, like Lourdes, which 'stayed' in his mind.

When Toibin attended the papal Mass at Czestochowa in 1991, the theme of John Paul II's sermon — based on the biblical 'I am', 'I remember', 'I watch' — made a particular impression on him. The words and the atmosphere in the cathedral had a power that appealed to levels below consciousness. They spoke a language that connected the known with the unknown, the conscious with the subconscious:

This was a religion I only half recognized, just as the parts of the body etched into silver seemed part of the the past but hard to locate. There was something about the singing, the colours and the beauty of the words which reminded me of strange, hard won moments of pure contentment I had experienced in the church as a child.[15]

In his early twenties, he admits, he had always 'known' that the interest all around him in security, money, power and status was greater than any love of God or belief in his mercy. 'Religion was consolation, like listening to music after a long day's work; it was pure theatre, it was a way of holding people together'.[16] Throughout the book, he remains the non-believer he proclaims to have been since his late teenage years. An observer and a listener who watches other people express their faith in words and ritual. Still, a remembering and empathetic observer: He tries 'to imagine, or re-member, what it would be like to believe ...'; he gets puzzled at his own 'new' and 'unexpected' 'sense of wonder' at the power of certain places; even when, at Lourdes, he is held down in a tub and others pour cold water over him:

I had expected to be allowed to lower myself into a tub of cold water in my own time. But I had also felt something of the power of the place, the amount of hope and spirit which had been let loose within these walls over all the years. I was confused by this mixture of hatred and fear of the Church's authority with my susceptibility to its rituals and its sheer force.[17]

Toibin's suspicion towards the authority of the Catholic church, and his contempt for its attempts to suppress women and sexuality in Ireland are things which he never hides in his reviews and essays, where he has a fondness for strikingly personal — sometimes sexual reminiscence. The poet Eavan Boland said to me in June 1995 that she thought Colm Toibin was the only well-known male journalist at the time of the referendum on the anti-abortion amendment in 1983 who spoke openly on behalf of women. When I interviewed him in 1994, he remembered it as 'depressing, disappointing and revolting to experience the public debate prior to the referendum'. He said,

'I was personally involved in it as a journalist for *The Irish Independent*. It definitely wasn't very funny to be pushed about and eventually beaten by people that you started out believing to be a minority but ended up realizing was a majority of the population. When I hear people speaking about "Catholic Ireland" and saying that we as a people belong on this island because history has given us a special role to play, it seems to me that they are trying to put the shutters on all the windows to the world outside, which we just recently managed to open in this country. As far as I'm concerned, Ireland is this space here and upstairs, [he said indicating the rooms in which we were sitting]. I don't really have any other Ireland'.

When I reminded him of what he apparently learned about modern Irish Catholics on Lough Derg, he paused for a moment, then said,

'Well, you see, one gets used to people. Many priests and many Catholic people in Ireland may still not be liberal, but they are also my neighbour, also my family. One gets fond of people, personally'.

Besides, the picture of Catholic Ireland is seldom black and white:

'From I was sixteen, I went to a boarding school run by priests, well, actually by a bishop. Normally, Irish people have terrible stories about going to school in Ireland, but my years were pretty happy. This was in 1970 when things were opening up culturally. I was reading Kafka and D.H. Lawrence, and this was actually approved of and encouraged by my teachers as something one should be reading. This school, run by priests, was very liberal, and Ireland was becoming more so in those years'.

Native son

Colm Toibin grew up in Enniscorthy, Co. Wexford, a town rich in historical symbolism. Lying snugly in the verdant Slaney valley below Vinegar Hill, it has a plantation period castle and a neo-gothic cathedral. Symbols of national struggle, colonialism and 19th century triumphant Catholicism. All things of the past.

In his epilogue to *The Sign of the Cross*, Toibin cites his father, who was a secondary school teacher and a local historian, for once having written of Vinegar Hill: 'It is a landmark that symbolizes the spirit of the historic past, a monument to the grim and gallant struggle of 1798'. In fact, to the son of a proud nationalist father, the whole landscape was once a monument over all that is Irish. Now he sees that this monument bore the mark of Irish nationalist historical interpretation:

The names of the towns and villages around us were in the history books and in the songs which we learned in school. They were the places where battles had been fought or atrocities committed.[18]

Not until he was in his twenties, did he learn about the half-truths and complications underneath the official version of history, which in Ireland until the 1950s fundamentally was a collectively lamented rather than a scrupulously studied past: The memory of one place in particular seemed to have been 'erased from what a Catholic child should know about 1798'.[19] This place was Scullabogue, the 'complication in our glorious past', where 'our side took a large number of Protestant men, women and children, put them in a barn and burned them to death', thereby reducing a political and national rising, initially sparked off by local grievances and the ideas of the French Revolution, to sectarian violence.[20]

In the meantime, however, this and many similar erasures from the national memory have been exposed by modern Irish historiography, and history seems slowly to be coming to an end in Enniscorthy. In the decades following the creation of the new independent Irish state in 1922, the Protestant community seemed so settled 'that the rise of violence and sectarian hatred in Northern Ireland from the late 1960s made little difference'. Basically, however, the Catholic and Protestant communities remained separate. Each with its own cultural and institutional characteristics:

Catholic women wore permed hair and highheeled shoes; Protestant women wore straight hair and flat shoes. The names, both Christian names and surnames, were different. Catholics and Protestants played golf and rugby together, but the Gaelic games of hurling and football were, in general, played only by Catholics. On a Sunday morning as you walked back from Mass, you would see the Protestants outside their church after service, a small, tight community oddly separate from our own.[21]

However, by 1994 when the cathedral was badly in need of restoration, the local Church of Ireland offered the Catholic community the use of their church for the duration. It was a truly historic moment in the life of the town when the church was packed for evening Mass on Saturday, 16 April 1994. Most of the Congregation had never been in a Protestant church before. Until the Second Vatican Council Protestant churches had been off-limit for Catholics, even for funerals of friends and acquaintances. For Toibin, too, this was a first experience:

It was strange to be in the Protestant church seeing familiar Catholic faces. We looked around until the Mass began. It was announced that there would be no sermon. There must have been some old ghosts on both sides of what was once a sectarian divide hovering around us, wondering what the hell was going on. My eye wandered to the plaque on the wall to my left. It was to the memory of Archibald Hamilton Jacob, Late Captain of the Loyal Vinegar Hill Rangers, Who Departed This Life, December 1836, Aged 66 Years: 'As a Magistrate, He Was Impartial, As a Subject Loyal, As a Soldier Generous and Brave'. — He must have been up there on Vinegar Hill during the battle in 1798, and he must have been around for the slaughter afterwards, which I had heard so much about when I was a child. We were in his church now; we had been invited. Protestant service as well as Mass would be said here in the morning. No one else was very interested in this plaque, or the sectarian legacy. The plaque was a memorial to a past which we would not repeat. History had come to an end in Enniscorthy.[22]

After getting his Leaving Certificate, Toibin enrolled as a student of English and History at University College Dublin. 'I had great teachers, and I loved being there. Also for the drinking and shouting that was part of being a student', he remembered. This was also the time when the poetry he had started writing as a teenager became a serious preoccupation with him. He decided he wanted to be a writer when everybody else wanted to go into the civil service:

At that time there was virtually no unemployment among graduates. Emigration had died out in 1975, and you could choose either to become a teacher or a civil servant. Being a civil servant at that time was quite an exciting thing to be since you'd be able to shape public policy and have influence, something which mattered a lot. But for me it was a problem that it would probably be a permanent job, which I would never be able to leave.

So the day he did his final exam in September 1975, he left for Barcelona. Two months later, Franco died. The way people reacted to Franco's death made a great impression on him: 'I remember how the city sort of exploded', he said. 'There were wonderful demonstrations and riots, but no killings. It was all very fruitfully moving towards elections and democracy. I just adored it'. But there were other attractions far from 'the living death of the Dublin winter' and the puritan inhibitions of his home country: 'You see, I had never been in a hot country before. I loved the outdoor life; the sense of sex everywhere', he told me in 1994. Earlier that year he had confessed to the readers of the *London Review of Books*,

I was twenty years old and discovering the joys of cruising the Ramblas for the first time. For much of the day and most of the night I was laden down with desire. In those days if you started at Canaletes and you hadn't hit the jackpot by Carre Carme, then you were having no luck. I had a lot of luck.[23]

Toibin had an apartment in the gothic quarter. He tried to write but never really got time for it. After three years he was back in Dublin freelancing for the *Sunday Independent* and writing and editing some of the new magazines which from the late 1970s were becoming the voice of young, urban, anti-establishment Ireland. At that time, he later recalled, 'truth was often stronger than fiction'. There were 'complexities and contradictions behind what the papers said [that] cried out to be explored'.[24] The journalist, the editor and the essayist assumed a role as moderators of anti-nationalist and anti-establishment discourse which had hardly been seen since the days when Sean O'Faolain published *The Bell* 1940-46. Almost everybody from

this new cultural and political vanguard came from the mid-fifties generation: Fintan O'Toole (b. 1955), John Waters (b. 1955), Ferdia Mac Anna (b.
1954), Richard Kearney (b. 1954), Dermot Bolger (b. 1958) and several
others.

Making sense of the past for their own generation, or, as Bolger has it,
'being engaged with understanding both their own and their parents'
past',[25] became a central concern for many 'Dublin Renaissance' writers who
had matured intellectually when the battle over the 'revision' of Irish
history began in the mid-seventies. Partly reacting to the violence in the
North, Irish nationalist history was disclosed by so-called revisionists[26] as
myth, and the continuity that once was seen behind centuries of Irish
subjection broke into fragments or was read as mere fiction.

In his contribution to Dermot Bolger's anthology of *Letters from the New
Island* (1991), Colm Toibin wrote,

The thing we used to call our history, but could more correctly call our mythology,
is a series of short stories, full of moments of great bravery and daring, immense
tragedy with blood everywhere and tears in every eye, but there is no connection
between the stories in the fiction we have been given as our history, no continuity
and no legacy.

Instead,

we were left ... with something broken and insecure, a post-colonial society which
remained in spirit part of the onetime mother country, and part of America, and
part of its own invention.

Even monolithic institutions such as Fianna Fail, the Catholic Church and
the Gaelic Athletic Association that once were guarantors of the nationalist
master story, can no longer 'offer fixity or fusion'. The centre of gravity has
been dissolved, and '[t]here is no society in Ireland as there is elsewhere:
no sense of continuity, tradition, legacy, except one that is jagged, broken'.[27]

'I became a revisionist ... just as the word was coming into vogue', he
remembered two years later when he was asked by the *London Review of
Books* to write a review of a collection of essays by Roy Foster, the Irish
historian and professor at Oxford University.[28] In 1986 Foster provoked lin-
gering nationalist feelings when he adopted what originally had been a
term of abuse: 'We are all revisionists now', he declared in an essay, which
he concluded: 'In a country that has come of age, history need no longer
be a matter of guarding sacred mysteries'.[29] Later, in *Modern Ireland 1600-*

1972, he gave Ireland its first comprehensive national history based on 30 years of academic scholarship.[30]

Toibin does not hesitate to call Foster 'the most brilliant and courageous Irish historian of his generation' and to describe Irish historical scholarship since the 1960s as the product of 'dogged individuals working against the national grain, dealing with complexities rather than the simplicities of Irish history'.[31] But since his student days, 'revisionism' — however loosely and irresponsibly the term may be applied — has been deconstructed. Not by nationalists, who regard the books of Foster and others to be unionism in disguise, or who, like Dr. Brendan Bradshaw of Queens College, Cambridge, 'believe that Irish historiography took a wrong turn in the 1930s'.[32] But by the new generation of young Irish intellectuals to whom Colm Toibin belongs.

If there ever were forbidden 'f' and 'c' words at University College Dublin in 1972, Toibin remembers, they were 'Fenian' and 'colonial'. 19th century history was the story of the constitutional and parliamentary progress of Ireland through men like Daniel O'Connell and David Stewart Parnell, whereas

Young Ireland, the Fenians, even the poor old Land League were presented as non-constitutional headaches for O'Connell and Parnell. Michael Collins was a Treaty negotiator rather than a warlord.[33]

But 1972 was also the year of Derry's Bloody Sunday and IRA's attempt to force Britain out of Northern Ireland by an escalated campaign of violence. The paradox was striking:

Outside in the world there were car bombs and hunger strikes, done in the name of history. Inside we were cleansing history, concentrating on those aspects of our past which would make us good, worthy citizens who would keep the Irish 26-county state safe from the IRA and IRA fellow travellers.[34]

He recalls the elation he felt as a young student when the burden of the past was taken from his shoulders:

I was in my late teens and I already knew that what they had told me about God and sexuality wasn't true, but being an atheist or being gay in Ireland at that time seemed easier to deal with as transgressions than the idea that you could cease believing in the Great Events of Irish nationalist history. No Cromwell as cruel monster, say; the executions after 1916 as understandable in the circumstances;

1798 as a small outbreak of rural tribalism; partition as inevitable. Imagine if Irish history were pure fiction, how free and happy we could be! It seemed at that time a most subversive idea, a new way of killing your father, starting from scratch, creating a new self'.

The whole point was to be 'through with history'.[35]

But, as Toibin makes clear in *The Sign of the Cross* and his second novel, *The Heather Blazing* (1992), the 'killing' of fathers, both the real and the metaphorical, by repressing and silencing painful memories of the past, is only a way to replace the burden of complicity with the burden of ir-remediable loss: with consequences equally grave for the sanity of the individual, the relationship between the generations and the genders, indeed, for society at large.[36]

An event which for him highlighted the limitations and hidden messages of 'revisionist' historiography was, if you excuse the paradox, a non-event: the 75th anniversary of the Easter Rising, one of the nation's remaining 'sacred mysteries' and the bloody birth ritual of the Irish state.[37]

The anniversary was officially marked at a very low key in a brief ceremony in front of the General Post Office, the site of the Rising. Major cultural institutions followed suit: the Abbey Theatre put Sean O'Casey's *The Plough and the Stars* on the stage and the National Museum of Ireland asked the audience to make personal judgments on the basis of a documentary presentation of circumstance and chronology. The general public remained largely indifferent to the occasion.

Interviewed by RTE (state television), Roy Foster said,

'Celebrating 1916, or commemorating it, I think there's a big difficulty there. To celebrate something is, presumably, to say it was wonderful and to, in a sense, reenact it as a communal ritual. I would think that is undesirable'.[38]

The event was regarded as a 'sensitive issue' by the government, Foster later wrote in the book that Toibin was asked to review in 1993. It had 'to be approached in a deliberately restrained way — very different from the unequivocal celebrations of 1966'. And the reaction that followed was only caused by a

small-scale but vociferous old Republican reaction — featuring not historians but out-of-office politicians, freelance journalists, ex-1960s activists ... and the members of the Short Strand Martyrs Memorial Flute Band.[39]

Things were not as simple as that, Toibin protests in his review of Foster.

But nor were they simple for himself, it turns out. He remembers receiving an invitation asking Irish writers to take part in a marathon reading at the General Post Office, and for a moment he thought of reading from Samuel Beckett's *First Love*:

What constitutes the charm of our country, apart of course from its scant population, and this without the help of the meanest contraceptive, is that all is derelict, with the sole exception of history's ancient faeces. These are ardently sought after, stuffed and carried in procession. Wherever nauseated time has dropped a nice fat turd you will find our patriots, sniffing it up on all fours, their faces on fire.[40]

But he decided it would be easier to decline as he did not want any work of his — or of others for that matter — to be

used by the state to replace its own halfheartedness about the past and insecurity about the present. As far I know, I was the only writer who turned down the invitation.[41]

The criticism that Toibin levels against Foster — and other historians of his school — is that underneath his 'brilliant insights', 'real originality' and 'judicious analyses', there is 'an ideology perhaps not as crude as that of any nationalist historian writing school texts in the Twenties, but just as clear'. A certain type of revised history

is precisely what our state needed once the North blew up and we joined the EC, in order to isolate Northern Ireland from us and our history, in order to improve relations with Britain, in order to make us concentrate on a European future. Foster and his fellow historians' work became useful, not for its purity, or its truth, but its politics,[42]

however personally unaware they may have been of their own complicity.

Reading some of their revised versions of the past, Toibin in the late 1980s began to see himself 'a native son', indeed, 'my father's son once more',[43] realizing that one cannot be 'through with history', start from scratch and create a new self. He remembers another invitation he received in 1991 before he finally decided to spend Easter in Seville:

I met a local politician in Wexford whom I knew and liked. He asked me to join other descendants, mostly grandchildren, of the men who had fought in the Easter Rebellion in the town of Enniscorthy, where I was born and where my grandfather had fought, in a march through the town on Easter Sunday to celebrate the 75th anniversary of the Rising. This was closer to home; there would be no quoting of

Beckett in Enniscorthy. No one at any of the meetings to plan the march, I was assured, had expressed the slightest doubt about the Rising; no one knew anything about revisionism; it had filtered from the universities to the middle classes in the cities, but not beyond. People in Enniscorthy were simply proud that the town and their forbears had been involved in the Rising. I would love to have marched with them. I wandered around Seville that Easter wishing things were simpler, wishing that I was not in two minds about everything.[44]

But maybe, it now occurs to him, being in two minds about one's past and cultural heritage is what it is all about. At least it might be one of the ways by which to make sense of the past today without subscribing to past orthodoxies. In this, Toibin agrees with the Foster of the mid-1990s who misses no opportunity to stress connections between cultural and national traditions: 'I know that ambiguity is what is needed in Ireland now. No one wants territory, merely a formula of words ambiguous enough to make them feel at home'. Foster's position is clear, he says:

he wants Ireland to become a pluralist, post-nationalist all-inclusive, non-sectarian place. So do I. But there are other (I hesitate to use the word 'atavistic') forces operating within me too that I must be conscious of. Maybe they come out in odd moments, when I read a book like this ... and know that I am not part of the consensus of which books like these are part. Maybe it would be good if their authors looked again at Catholic Ireland. We, in turn, are learning to talk in whispers. It will take time.[45]

Making sense of the past

Talking in whispers may not exactly be what Toibin did in his first novel, *The South* (1990) but, for all its passion and tragedy, it is, like his second novel, *The Heather Blazing* (1992), a quiet book.

Toibin writes from the conviction that the novel is a social art form that should depict character against the background of a recognizable social setting. He once criticized the American novelist Harold Brodkey for artistic 'indulgence' in his novel *Profane Friendship*:

He does not observe the world or measure himself in relation to others, or talk about last things. Instead, he grandly and humourlessly seeks to find a language to match his feelings and his sensations, to describe in great detail what it is to be himself. So that when he experiences something, the thing is of no interest: what matters is the register of what he feels, how he feels, in all its complexity.[46]

He partly ascribes this to an American tradition in which 'it is almost enough to be American, to experience America in all its newness, to feel interesting and have something to say'. But for a reader like Colm Toibin, it has an effect on the quality of the novel:

Because most of the experience he describes is essentially horseplay between adolescents in the streets of Venice, and because he has no moral sense and no interest in history, there is a real thinness not merely in the overall texture of the book, but in every page, every moment.[47]

When I said to Toibin that reading *The Heather Blazing* I was sometimes reminded of Ishiguro, he expressed surprise: 'When I read *The Artist in the Floating World*, I didn't find it interesting as I felt there wasn't enough density in the book and its society to interest me'. However, he admitted:

I did read it, and I did remark the enormity of the treachery in the main character which one has to gather by one's own effort, because it isn't in the book except only in a few paragraphs. It is very cleverly done by the author. What I have been inspired by are novels like Saul Bellow's *The Dean's December* or the films of Ingmar Bergman. I wouldn't talk of them as influence. Rather, they let me know what can be done. A lot of the late works of Bergman are important for me; *Fanny and Alexander*, for example. I guess it has to do with the fact that I am also living in a country where the sky is always low. Like Bergman, I am interested in ambiguity, in moral ambiguity; in lives which are ostensibly harmless and ordinary, but in fact aren't, when examined under the microscope.

The South is certainly a book about ambiguity in its portrait of a woman's personal conflicts in trying to deal with her own past. And, like *The Heather Blazing*, it is a novel of the kind of treachery against elementary human bonds that self-deception may give rise to.

The novel describes a circular journey in time and space. In 1950 Katherine Proctor decides to leave an unhappy marriage and try to start life all over: to create a new self. This implies not only leaving her husband, Tom, but also her ten-year-old son, Richard, and the places she has known from childhood, a farming estate in the Slaney Valley in the proximity of Enniscorthy. 'I was not clear where I was going', she writes in one of her diary entries which with various letters supplement the narrative's restricted point of view and leave room for the reader to form his own opinions of the main character.[48]

What is clear to Katherine, however, is that a total break with the past must also mean leaving Ireland. Consequently, she leaves the South (of Ireland) for another South: She goes to Spain; first to Barcelona, where she finds a new partner, Miguel, a Catalan painter and anarchist, and later to a small village in the Pyrenees, where they get a daughter, Isona. Having tragically lost both, she returns via Barcelona to Ireland, her original point of departure 15 years before. What first appears to be a traditional story of emancipation and individuation, at the end leaves one with the impression that such mental journeys may only be successful if the individual finds a way to reconcile herself (or himself) with her own history and tries to make sense of the past, however painful the process may be.

In the farming community of Enniscorthy, Katherine and Tom belong to the Protestant minority who, although they are settled and well off in the late 1940s, can still feel beleaguered by their socially inferior, Catholic neighbours; if not haunted by memories from the War of Independence when many of their big houses were burned by 'locals'. Such events sent Katherine's own mother into permanent exile in London, thus leaving husband and daughter behind the way Katherine now leaves husband and son.

She does not leave for the same reasons, however; or so she claims. Her mother once told her she left because she hated Ireland and the people who burned them out in 1921. But this is just something she thinks, Katherine remarks late in life believing herself to be exempt from such self-deception and the legacy of the past. Through with history.

In contrast to Tom, who is not a native of the area, she wants to make peace with the past. When he tells her that he intends to sue one of their neighbours for letting his cattle stray in on their fields, she blames him for his prejudices:

> 'We've always had good relations with our neighbours.'
> 'That's why they burned you out, I suppose,' he said. He stood in the middle of the room as though he might at any moment move to turn off the light.
> 'No one from around here did that. The troublemakers came out here from the town,' she said.
> 'Nobody knows who did it. It could have been anyone.'
> 'That's all over now. It was years ago. You weren't here then.'
> 'We could do without some of our neighbours,' he said.
> 'And they could do without us,' she laughed. He went over to the light.
> 'Don't turn off the light, Tom. I haven't finished. I want this to stop, do you understand? I'm not sure that I've made myself clear. And if my father were alive, he would want it stopped also.'
> 'It's your land, is that what you're trying to say? I have no right to make decisions, is that what you're trying to say?'
> 'You don't understand this place,' she said.[49]

Katherine warns Tom that she will leave him if he goes ahead with his plans. He does. And she does. She makes his intransigence an excuse for leaving a marriage long dead for want of affection. Later, with her mother in London and on her own in Barcelona, 'absorbed in myself', she firmly believes she has made a clean break with the past; to have walked 'out of the cinema leaving it all behind, the big picture'.[50] Not even Richard, her son, makes an inroad to her mind. Anyway, she shirks responsibility for leaving him motherless :

I am not responsible for what I did before ... My son is withdrawn from me, my son will look after himself. There is nothing more I can do for him. No matter how guilty I feel I must look after myself.[51]

So instead, she starts planning, plotting, and dreaming up a future, re-pressing memories of the past:

The past has happened: it is grey and empty like the narrow streets of San Sebastian at four in the afternoon with the shops all closed and their shutters pulled down. The future is wide open.[52]

In Barcelona, Katherine does, at first, experience a new self thaw out of her thirty-two-year-old body which, she feels, has been frozen since her marriage waiting for this moment of freedom.[53] She takes the first steps towards an artistic career, falls in love with Miguel, and makes friends with a joking, drinking, and good-natured Irish exile, Michael Graves, who be-comes their steady companion. Ironically, Graves turns out to be the son of one of the 'locals' back in Enniscorthy (and to bear a striking re-semblance to the writer himself, who once confessed the aubiographical character of parts of the book and his personal love for 'other people's lives').[54]

But Michael Graves's appearance in Katherine's life is not the only thing that begins to remind her of the past. A series of dramatic events in a politically tense Barcelona takes away the control she feels she has finally got over her own life: Miguel barely escapes getting arrested by the civil guards for painting a mock portrait of Franco, and the three of them decide to leave and settle in a small village in the Pyrenees. However, in spite of the beauty and remoteness of the place, this village becomes a fatal point of confrontation with a past that both Miguel and Katherine are trying to flee.

Here at Pallosa Katherine hears for the first time the full story of Miguel's involvement in the Spanish civil war. As a militant anarchist, he took part in many violent activities. Symbolic ones like burning down the local church and the police station, but also such that now haunt his conscience:

> He wanted her to know everything — did she understand that he wanted her to know everything. Yes, she told him, she did. They had bombed a policeman's house and they had burnt his wife and children to death. He stopped for a moment and held her. This was more than ten years ago and there was a war on. He sighed then, and told her that once they had shot a child who had tried to leave the house. He put his arms around her; there was sweat on his hands ...
>
> His story stayed with her for days, as though she had eaten something strange and strong, but vaguely familiar.
>
> She kept away from both him and Michael Graves, went walking on her own, went to bed early, sat apart from them on the small balcony in Michael Graves's room smoking and looking out towards the high mountains to the north. An image came to her constantly of a child running for help, running for her life, being run through with bullets, while the thunderous sound of a fire roared in the background.[55]

The past has caught up with both Miguel and herself. For Miguel the consequences are both mental and physical. He is arrested by the police, who torture him and keep him in custody for weeks. Katherine, having just fled one kind of civil conflict, suddenly finds herself enmeshed in another, which painfully calls forth suppressed memories from her own childhood: the night her parents' house was set on fire. Her growing obsession with the past soon matches Miguel's guiltladen memories of killing a child.

Katherine realizes that she has been cut off from the past by her own mother and writes to her demanding to be told about the night of her own fears.

> 'I want to know about it, so I can think about it. It has become important. If you want me to write to you, I'm afraid you'll have to take me seriously. It's not easy to write like this'.[56]

Being taken seriously means being given the opportunity to remember; learning the truth about a past which was silenced; and which broke the bond between mother and child:

> I am your child. I saw you for holidays and we never talked about what happened that night in all the years.
>
> The locals turned on us. That's what happened. That's what the Troubles were for us. The time the locals turned on us. That's what happened in Ireland in 1920.

I don't remember a fire, but I remember a sound, like a big wind, and being carried. I don't remember seeing the fire, I must have been three years old. I remember staying in Bennett's Hotel in Enniscorthy. I'll never forget the sound of the wind. What do you remember? Please tell me what happened. How did you get out? How did I get out? How many of them came? Why did you leave and never come back?[57]

Now a mother herself for the second time, Katherine may look at her young daughter, Isona, and realize the loss of being cut away from a remembering community:

There is no one here who will understand how much at certain times she looks like my father, how a look comes on her face and she becomes the image of him. Richard had that look when he was her age, although they don't look alike in any other way. We have removed her from the world where that sort of recognition means anything. We are her only roots, no one comes before us.

   She will never know where she came from, where we came from, the accidents that have brought her into the world. I would love her to know the house I come from, the river, the farm. I would love it if we could all meet sometime, Richard, Tom, Miguel, Isona, Michael Graves. I would love to see Richard picking her up and carrying her. I'm afraid I have placed myself beyond all that.[58]

One night having dreamt about the fire of her childhood, it is Katherine's turn to put herself into a historical context. Miguel is puzzled and concludes that she is a victim, a participant. But she denies,

I have failed to explain to him that I am not. I am on my own here without all that weight of history and I differ from him in the way I manage. He's decided I am someone who was on the wrong side of a war. I am sorry I told him anything. I am as innocent as our child.[59]

Katherine's self-claimed 'innocence', her self-deluded conviction of not being a participant in history and of not being 'guilty', i.e. of not being responsible for her past, is her fundamental flaw. As time passes, however, she begins to realize that 'reality rests in being reminded'.[60]

   But there are memories too strong for the mind. Miguel's memories of the war and his own shooting of the child leads him to a tragic end in which he takes Isona with him as a sacrifice in death, driving the car over the edge of a mountain road into a steep incline. This combined suicide and infanticide, veiled as an accident, is witnessed by Katherine and Michael returning from a walk in the hills, and, in its turn, becomes a new painful memory to haunt Katherine.

She moves back to Barcelona and spends five years brooding over her losses and her loneliness; she paints a little but does not know what to do with the rest of her life. Her only solace is her friendship with Michael Graves, who at length convinces her of her need to go back to Ireland. They settle in Dublin, living apart, but as constant companions in suffering, loneliness, and poverty.

It is another lonely person, Katherine's mother, who makes her draw full circle: 'You must go home, if only to see', she tells her.[61] And one cold afternoon in late October, she does return; not only to see, however, but also to get money from the property which she thinks she has a moral right to.[62]

By now, 1971, more than twenty years after she left Enniscorthy, Tom is long dead. Richard has married Deirdre, a girl 'from the town',[63] i.e. a Catholic girl. Together they have refurbished the house according to the norms of Deirdre's own — new Catholic middle — class. Having expected to revisit an unchanged past, Katherine feels uncomfortable at the sight of change and is particularly upset when learning that Richard goes to Mass. At the same time, she is surprised at her own reaction: '[S]he did not know she had prejudices left like that'.[64] In her open contempt for her daughter-in-law and her parents, Katherine, who once blamed her husband for sticking to past prejudices, now fails her own test. Not surprisingly, it is from the son, whom she left when he was a young boy, that she must learn the truth of the weight that choices made in the past may carry for the present:

'You are going to be in Ireland for a while. You are short of money. No, don't interrupt me, your mother tells me you are short of money. You are unhappy in some ways and we want to see something of you, and to help you if we can. There's one thing you need to know for this to happen. You might have guessed but I'm telling you anyway. Until I was ten years old I lived with two people who hardly spoke to each other or to anyone else, and who had no friends. From the time I was ten until I was thirteen and after that during holidays, I had a father who hardly spoke and who had no friends. When I came back here to the farm it was to night after night of silence, of isolation. My father died from isolation and loneliness and I didn't enjoy watching that. And I don't like the cold rooms I was brought up in. I hate everything about the way I was brought up. I like this house now, I like my wife, my daughter, and my wife's family. Will you please not sneer at them?' He looked at her directly. He seemed close to tears.

'I don't know if you remember what happened here. When the house was burned to the ground. These people, the locals ...'

He stopped her. 'I remember other things that happened here,' he said. 'You abandoned me. I remember how I felt then. So how dare you talk about my relations like that? You have no right. The people who burnt this house are long dead.'

'I'm going anyway in the morning,' she said. 'What time is the train?'[65]

Twenty years before, Katherine set out on a journey with the illusion that she could sever her own connections with the past. Now she has ended up as a ghost from the past, hearing her own words to Tom repeated by Richard. But she still tries to flee whenever someone holds her accountable for her life.

Towards the end of the book, there is a muted reconciliation between mother and son and an indication of insight achieved. After years of close companionship, Katherine decides to settle with Michael Graves in Dublin. And occasionally she will return to the Slaney Valley and Enniscorthy to paint and see her son and grandchildren.

Until then, she suffered the 'colonial' illusion that she could make her home anywhere she chose. That she could create a new self from scratch; a self which did not depend on the context of place and past. But towards the end of her life painting the landscapes of her childhood, she begins to realize that one cannot paint a place as though one does not belong to it. Watching with an artist's eye, she becomes aware that making sense of a place is another way of making sense of the past and, ultimately, establishing a sense of belonging

She began to work; she started to paint as though she was trying to catch the landscape rolling backwards into history, as though horizon was a time as well as a place. Dusk on the Slaney. Over and over. Dusk on the Slaney and the sense of all dusks that have come and gone in one spot in one country, the time it was painted to stand for all time, with all time's ambiguities.

In the distance the rebels lie bleeding. In the distance no one has yet set foot. In the distance a car is moving.

In the distance the sanitorium at Brownswood in Enniscorthy.

In the distance Enniscorthy Castle squats at the top of a hill.

In the distance is the light and the darkness falling, the clouds moving, the Blackstairs Mountains above Bunclody, Mount Leinster, the full moon rising.[66]

The concluding chapter describes how the insight Katherine achieves gives her new life as a painter. It also describes her taking Michael Graves, the 'local', to bed. Another achievement of a sort, one might say.

Ambiguity about her moral complicity in the past remains with her to the end. Still, being in two minds about everything, but remembering it all, may be the best way of keeping one's head.

Notes

1. Cf. Heaney's 'Station Island' in which James Joyce admonishes the poet to 'Keep at a tangent./ When they make the circle wide, it's time to swim/ out on your own and fill the element/ with signatures on your own frequency,/ echo soundings, searches, probes, allurements,/ ever-gleams in the dark of the whole sea'.
2. *History Ireland*, Winter, 1993, p. 37.
3. 'The Sense of Place', in *Preoccupations*, (London: Faber and Faber, 1990), p. 132. See also p. 41 and Heaney's poem 'Bogland'.
4. 'Bogland', *Door Into the Dark*, (1969).
5. 'The Tollund Man', from *Wintering Out* (1972).
6. 'A Tale of Two Islands', in P.J. Drudy ed., *Irish Studies*, 1, (London: Cambridge University Press, 1980), p. 17.
7. Interview, June 1994. Quotations from the interview hereafter not annotated.
8. *The Crane Bag*, vol. 8, No. l, 1984, p. 17.
9. *Walking Along the Border*, (London: Queen Anne Press, 1987), p. 37.
10. Ibid.
11. Ibid., p. 41.
12. Ibid., p. 45.
13. London: Jonathan Cape, 1994.
14. Hugo Young, 'Poped', *London Review of Books*, 24 November 1994, p. 17.
15. *Walking Along the Border*, p. 74.
16. Ibid., p. 7.
17. Ibid., pp. 12, 13, 16.
18. *The Sign of the Cross*, p. 290.
19. Ibid., p. 291.
20. Ibid., p. 290.
21. Ibid., p. 293.
22. Ibid., pp. 294-95.
23. 6 January 1994, p. 21.
24. *The Trial of the Generals: Selected Journalism 1980-1990*, (Dublin: Raven Arts Press, 1990), p. 197.
25. Dermot Bolger, ed., *The Picador Book of Irish Fiction*, (London: Picador, 1993), p. xvi.
26. Originally, a term of abuse used about historians who do not hold orthodox nationalist views of Irish history.
27. 'Martyrs and Metaphors', in Dermot Bolger, ed., *Letters from the New Island*, (Dublin: Raven Arts Press, 1991), pp. 45, 47.
28. *Paddy and Mr Punch: Connections in Irish and English History*, (London: Allen Lane, 1993).
29. *The Irish Review*, No. 1, 1986, reprinted in *The Field Day Anthology of Irish Writing*, vol. 3, (Derry: Field Day Publications, 1991), pp. 583-86.
30. London: Allen Lane, 1988.
31. 'New Ways of Killing Your Father', *London Review of Books*, 18 November 1993, p. 3.
32. *History Ireland*, Spring 1993, p. 53.

33. *London Review of Books*, 18 November 1993, p. 3.
34. Ibid.
35. Ibid. Toibin refers to a poem by Derek Mahon, 'The Snow Party' in which one of the characters is allowed to be 'through with history'.
36. Cf. e.g., *The Sign of the Cross*, pp. 125-38 and *The Heather Blazing*, (London: Picador, 1992), pp. 180, 227-28.
37. 'New Ways of Killing Your Father', *London Review of Books*, 18 November 1993, p. 3.
38. Quoted by Toibin, ibid., p. 5.
39. 'History and the Irish Question', *Paddy and Mr Punch: Connections in Irish and English History*, (Harmondsworth: Penguin Books, 1995), p. 17.
40. Quoted by Toibin in 'New Ways of Killing Your Father', p. 6.
41. Ibid.
42. Ibid., p. 5.
43. Cf. 'A Native Son', *The Sign of the Cross*, pp. 1-16, and 'New Ways of Killing Your Father', p. 5.
44. 'New Ways of Killing Your Father', p. 6.
45. Ibid.
46. 'Insiderish', *London Review of Books*, 26 May 1994, p. 7.
47. Ibid.
48. London: Picador, 1992, p. 7.
49. Ibid., pp. 42-43.
50. Ibid., p. 51.
51. Ibid., p. 14.
52. Ibid., p. 10.
53. Ibid., p. 46.
54. 'Diary', *London Review of Books*, 6 January 1994, p. 21.
55. *The South*, pp. 84-85.
56. Ibid., pp. 90-91.
57. Ibid., p. 90.
58. Ibid., pp. 113-14.
59. Ibid., p. 115.
60. Ibid., p. 166.
61. Ibid., p. 180.
62. As a woman who had chosen to separate from her husband, she had no legal right over that property at that time. This has been changed by recent legislation.
63. *The South*, p. 185.
64. Ibid., p. 199.
65. Ibid., pp. 204-05.
66. Ibid., pp. 220-21.

'The Canadian Winter is a Real Blessing' or How Canada was Sold to Danish Emigrants in the 1920s

Jørn Carlsen

It was not until after World War I that Canada *really* emerged in the minds of prospective European emigrants as a land of great opportunities and as an alternative to the United States. Two facts in particular helped to turn the flow of emigrants towards Canada: 1) After 1900 there was no more free land for homesteading in the United States, a fact and a magnet that had pulled hundreds of thousands out of the old world; and 2) after World War I restrictive quotas for the number of immigrants were introduced in 1921. In all fairness it should be said that a strong and aggressive Canadian recruitment effort and the efficiency of Canadian owned and government-supported transportation systems were also important factors responsible for the increase in the number of immigrants to Canada.

Soon after Confederation in 1867 both federal and provincial governments began to take an active part in attracting immigrants to Canada. Shipping lines were encouraged financially more or less openly to use Canadian ports for disembarcation, that is, Halifax in Nova Scotia, St. John in New Brunswick and Quebec City. By the 1920s immigrant transportation in Canada had long been big business, in fact a huge well-oiled machine that needed a constant flow of fuel in the form of immigrants.

The most important company was the privately owned Canadian Pacific Railway (CPR), which often spoke and acted with the authority of a government. The CPR is closely connected with the history of Canada. After surmounting obstacles of legendary proportions the CPR had completed the construction of the trans-continental railway across Canada in 1885. The importance of this railway can hardly be overstated. It linked together this vast country and played a key role in the development and settling of the Canadian West. Among other remunerations, the CPR was granted huge tracts of arable land along its lines — 25 million acres, or an area about twice the size of Denmark. In the following years numerous Danish settlers bought land from the CPR.

By the 1920s the CPR had established itself in Europe, and thus one of the largest transportation empires in the world had come into existence. A huge network of CPR offices and agents sold tickets to their own Atlantic liners and their railways in Canada.

This paper will cover a period, that is the 1920s, in the history of Danish emigration to Canada when the 'push' factor, that is of social deprivation in the mother country, had by and large given way to the 'pull' factor. In the 1920s letters from and visits by successful family members or friends to the old country along with the very efficient work by agents and their distribution of tens of thousands of free emigration pamphlets became the prime mover of emigrants.

Up to World War I the preferred destination was the United States. According to the yearbook of Danish Statistics no less that 255,000[1] Danes left for the United States from 1868-1914, many of them from North Schleswig. In the same period a mere 11,618 emigrated directly to Canada. We know, however, that many Danes came to Canada by way of the United States. But the open border between the two countries makes a count impossible.

After World War I this pattern changed. In 1927[2] 3,835 Danes emigrated to Canada. For the first time since European mass emigration started in the 1850s and 1860s more Danes left for Canada than for the United States. In 1928 3,891 and in 1929[3] 2,982 emigrants left Denmark for the agricultural areas in western Canada. Then a drastic reduction occurred, and in 1933[4] only 23 Danes were registered as emigrants bound for Canada. No statistical material quotes numbers as regards the opposite flow from Canada back to Denmark. There can be no doubt that during the 1930s, with the Canadian stop for immigration except for close relatives, many more Danes returned *from* than left *for* Canada.

It is a puzzling fact that at a time when the number of immigrants from Denmark was the highest ever, Canada already had severe financial problems in the agricultural sector. These were intensified by the Wall Street crisis in 1929 when Canada, along with the rest of the Western world, was plunged into the Depression of the 1930s. It is also a fact that very many of the Danish immigrants mentioned above came to experience social conditions in Canada that they would never have found in Denmark during the 1930s. In 1933 when the Canadian Government had virtually stopped all immigration into Canada almost one fifth of the Canadian labour force were without jobs. During the so-called Dirty Thirties the Canadian West was hit by natural catastrophies, such as drought that turned arable land in southern Saskatechewan and parts of Alberta into a sand desert. As a result numerous farmers received food-help from the federal government for several years.

How come that so many people, all of them able to pay their own passage and in many cases wealthy enough to buy their own farm, thought of leaving Denmark in the late 1920s? There were many reasons. The Danish economy was very weak after World War I. It was difficult to find employment throughout the 1920s. In 1924 100,000 Danes or 30% of the workforce were unemployed. Danish farmers had done extremely well during World War I when high prices for agricultural products had led to expansion. As a neutral country, Denmark could export to both the UK and Germany. However, many found themselves in difficulties when land and food prices fell back to normal after the war.

The ominous sounds from the Weimar Republic in a state of dissolution also did much to destroy the hope for a worthwhile future in Europe. Most important, though, was the fact that Canada during the 1920s had caught the imagination of numerous Danes and had become the promised land of hope and prosperity. All newspapers, national as well as local, reflect this interest. Articles about Canada and the great opportunities in that country abounded and so discussions for and against emigration did. Especially in the latter part of the 1920s newspapers would send journalists to visit Danish immigrants already in Canada and let them report back. Also a spate of popular books on Canada appeared, written by eye witnesses and self-proclaimed experts.[5] In terms of volume, however, the greatest and most constant suppliers of information on Canada were the Canadian Pacific Railway and the Canadian National Railways (CNR) and their representatives in Denmark.

When we look at the available material on Canada we find that the image established from these sources is one of a new, strong, healthy and free country with equal opportunities, hardly any taxes, a minimum of red tape and with the certainty of success, if only you were prepared to work hard enough.

From the beginning of mass emigration, horror stories of exploitation would at intervals appear in Danish newspapers. The shipping lines and their agents all over the country would be accused of lying about the opportunities in the new world and of being too aggressive and ruthless in their sales drive.[6] However, in the 1920s complaints would now and then appear in Danish papers accusing agents of dishonest practices when it came to selling tickets and persuading people to emigrate. For a number of years a Danish parliamentary committee worked on a bill that was eventually passed in 1930. This act made it a criminal offence to advertise for emigration and to encourage people to emigrate. As soon as the committee began its work in the mid 1920s the CPR and CNR stopped their literal and outspoken propaganda for emigration.

As late as in 1930 Aksel Sandemose pointed out in a newspaper article[7] that the 'lines' got round the law by financing certain Danish-Canadian visitors to Denmark who should by their mere presence illustrate the opportunities in Canada and nourish the American/Canadian success myth. But on the whole the time of the old rough sales methods was over, and the pamphlets were left to speak for themselves.

However, all the Danes that emigrated from 1925 and to the early 1930s must have had easy access to the widely distributed pamphlets published by the CPR and the CNR in Danish. At that time both the CPR and the CNR had their own offices in Copenhagen. The CPR office was a sales office at the head of a network of agents found in all major towns in Denmark. The CNR had an information office only; their tickets were sold through travel agents all over the country.

The following is a reconstruction of the picture of Canada that these pamphlets offered Danish emigrants in the late 1920s.

The surviving material is by no means impressive. Even though Danish printing firms were obliged to supply the two central libraries, i. e. the Royal Library in Copenhagen and the State Library in Aarhus, with a free copy of all that was printed, these two institutions did not have an authorized policy in the 1920s for how to deal with ephemera like those pamphlets. In Aarhus it all ended in the waste paper basket. In Copenhagen just a few items have been preserved, and that by sheer accident.

My research material comes mainly from the Danes Worldwide Archives at Aalborg and from Mr. Marius Holmgren, a former (now retired) CPR agent in Denmark. The archive at Aalborg began as a private collection of emigration memorabilia predominantly from the United States, first of all letters but also the odd emigration pamphlet. Today the Archives are sponsored by the town of Aalborg.

At my disposal I had five CPR (1921-30) and three CNR (1926-29) pamphlets. Apart from a change of cover the CNR pamphlets are identical. The CPR editions from 1927-28-29 are identical apart from a new cover on the 1929 edition. The 1930 edition has been revised and supplied with new pictures and extended from 72 pages to 104 pages; out of these 104 pages only 15 pages are covered with pictures, which leaves us with a substantial amount of text. In the following I shall concentrate on the 1930 CPR pamphlet[8] that was the last to appear.

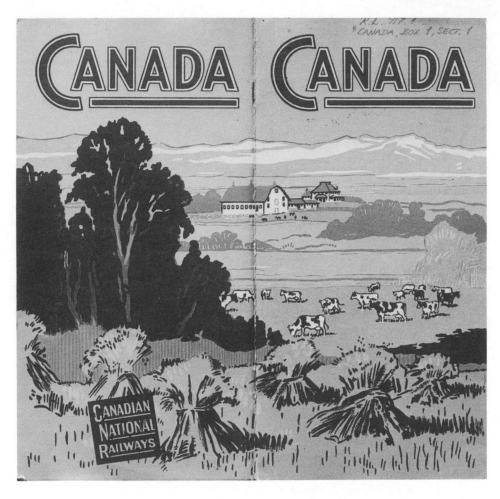

In the preface, CPR's manager in Denmark Mr. M.B. Sørensen says that his pamphlet has been compiled because not all travel agents in Denmark can be expected to have full information about Canada and the conditions over there. He emphasises that the CPR alone is responsible for the contents of this pamphlet, which is based upon facts supplied by the Canadian Government. We are also told that the CPR is the biggest company in Canada and that its position and prestige is of such a nature that it can be relied upon. In a brief introduction it is emphasised that the pamphlet has not been produced to encourage emigration and to cause dissatisfaction with the conditions in Denmark. 'Far be it from us to play down the difficulties you encounter in a new country. Let it be said that Canada is not for the weak and unstable, it is a question of will power and will power again. — The people Canada needs are those who won't eat bread that they

Tens of thousands of emigration pamphlets from the two big railway lines with covers like the ones reproduced above and on the facing page were distributed all over Denmark. The pastoral idylls on the jackets did not prepare the immigrants for the realities of prairie farming in the Canadian West. (Reproduced with the permission of the Danes Worldwide Archives, Aalborg, Denmark).

haven't paid for, people with pride, the kind of pride that will bring a free and honest man through fire and water for the sake of his independence'.

A preventive statement and warning like the above reflects the debate and the accusations of a too rosy and romantic presentation of Canada brought forward by the Danish newspapers at regular intervals. Compared with earlier editions the demand for hard work has been intensified and might seem to be in agreement with the realities in Canada in 1930. This kind of realism is not found in the following description of Canada, however. The description of the Canadian society and its economic life is similar to the one found in earlier pamphlets based on Canadian statistical material from 1923-24. Optimism abounds and the huge growth potential is emphasised.

After a brief discussion of the political system in Canada and the close relations to the U.K., a panoramic view of Canada is given underlining the variety not only in scenery but also in agricultural and industrial products. We are told that Quebec produces 25 million pounds of tobacco (p. 7). Then we find a new reference to the trustworthiness of the CPR and a rhetorical question: Why is the CPR interested in an increase of the population in Canada? (p. 8) We are told that the CPR owns a lot of land along their railway lines and that the company wants to sell to hardworking farmers who will guarantee an increase in traffic, which is basically what the CPR is interested in. 'For the settlers there is no better guarantee for the future than that the CPR expects to profit by them' (p. 8).

Again the company warns off the lazy and the ones who expect to find the roads paved with gold. 'Never trust luck but only your own hands'.

Don't expect any high wages if you don't know anything about farming and don't know the language, be prepared to be 'an apprentice', be reliable and hard working.

'What kind of job can you get in Canada?' one of the headlines asks. 'Above all we want farmers and farmhands for the western part of Canada', 'During spring and summer you will be paid between $30-$45 per month, and $25 is an average winter salary'. 'During harvest you can earn up to $6 per day if you know something about farming'. Bearing in mind that the pamphlet addresses prospective emigrants of 1930 it can be said to be more than over-optimistic in the figures it quotes for wages. Immediately afterwards the Danish settlement, Standard,[9] in Alberta is pointed out as the embodiment of success and wealth.

It is mentioned that the CPR runs labour exchanges in all major towns but that the competition is hard. Women, however, have great chances on the labour market; they will be paid between $25-$45 per month for housework. It is pointed out that there is a surplus of men in Canada (p. 12) and that numerous settlers are forced to stay single.

The pamphlet includes paragraphs on Canadian agriculture, especially wheat production. We are also introduced to the mysteries of townships, sections, quarter sections and school sections. Then each of the provinces from Nova Scotia to British Columbia is described. This is a stock survey of the population and the opportunities that can also be seen in all earlier pamphlets. It is very optimistic in tone; dynamic development is represented as going on everywhere, and nowhere more than in the prairie provinces where the CPR still has fertile land to sell at reasonable prices. The possibility of owning a homestead, which used to take up a lot of space in emigrant pamphlets and is now only mentioned in passing; the land available is now really on the periphery, more than 30 miles away from any railway line (p. 61). Clearly, homesteading based on free land is not of prime interest to the CPR any more.

The surveys of Manitoba, Saskatchewan and Alberta offer not only brief geographical descriptions of these provinces but also sections of the climate, on what crop to raise, and on irrigation. There are also sections on domestic animals, and on where CPR land is available for settlers. At that time (1930) CPR wanted settlers in the Lloydminster and Battleford districts, in areas round Calgary and Edmonton, and in the great irrigation block that the CPR had started in the south-eastern part of Alberta. The sales conditions, which are described in detail, seem fair and advantageous to the settler.

The section on the climate in Canada is typical of all the pamphlets printed in Denmark. Even in 1930 the CPR writes about 'The White Man's Climate' (p. 12) which is a reminiscence of an argumentation found in earlier pamphlets that the climate in Canada, which is 'exceedingly healthy and bracing', is the right climate for the Nordic race. A CNR pamphlet from 1926 offers a veritable eulogy on the Canadian winter. Under a headline, *The Canadian Winter Is a Real Blessing*, we learn that it is healthy and that here you find the lowest mortality rate in the world; it is a positive health factor for man and beast, and you have the advantage that the food you can buy cheaply in big quantities will keep during the winter.

The CNR brings in an authority, Mr. Maddison Grant, anthropologist, and they quote his 'remarkable' book *The Racial Basis of a European History*, to provide the fact that the Nordic race becomes lazy in a southern climate and even gives up procreation. In a 1921 brochure CPR points out that western Canada is for the white race (p. 7) and in 1927 it says that a southern climate is 'nearly always destructive', that is to the white man (p. 12). A CNR pamphlet from 1927 emphasises that the climate is the right one for 'the dynamic and energetic Nordic race'. We also read that 'more than 90% of Canada's population are of North European descent, less than 1% are Orientals, and only 0.2% [sic] are negroes' (p. 16). That North Europeans belong to the preferred category of immigrants is also seen in an advertisement by the White Star Dominion Line from 1921 where it is underlined that Scandinavians and British people have their own dining-room during the Atlantic crossing.

The Canadian winter is praised for being very helpful in establishing friendships and for winter sports. Among the many positive aspects of the Canadian winter is the 'remarkable' chinook, the warm wind that will bring a spell of spring right in the middle of winter (CPR 1930, p. 45; CNR 1929, p. 27). A full page is given over to a discription of this phenomenon, and placed as it is at the end of the description of the Canadian winter it has a truly temperature raising effect on the reader.

At the end of the section devoted to the prairie provinces the pamphlet includes miscellaneous information. There is a paragraph dealing with heating in which we are told that there is plenty of cheap coal in Alberta, 'in places the farmer can just help himself'. The outstanding hunting and trapping possibilities are mentioned. The school and health situations are described. Immediately before a very brief survey of British Columbia we find a page full of sensible advice to the settler.

You should bring along with you a couple of thousand dollars, but don't buy right away — go as a hired hand for a couple of years. Learn the trade and the geographical peculiarities and then buy.

The immigrant is also advised to bring all his old clothes along (p. 69).

The CPR (1930) includes a brief description of major Danish settlements in Canada. Standard, Alberta, and New Denmark, New Brunswick, receive most attention, and are pointed out as model settlements. You find a list of Danish clergymen in charge of Danish churches in Canada. The Danish Immigration Aid Society that had been founded in 1927 by Danish clergymen has been given a page (p. 85) where they state the purposes of the society. Apart from offering reliable information about Canada, one important purpose was to maintain and further Danish culture and language in the Danish settlements.

CPR's general agent in Denmark, Mr. M.B. Sørensen, says in his postscript (pp. 86-87) that he has tried to collect from the best possible sources of information. He stresses that he used to be employed by the Canadian Department for Agriculture until he got his present job as CPR's chief representative in Denmark. 'If you ask me whether there are opportunities in Canada my answer is: Yes, but only for the farmer and if you are prepared to work hard' (p. 87).

The remaining pages consist of letters to Mr. Sørensen and the CPR in

Copenhagen. They all in some way or other express gratitude. The passage was well organized and comfortable etc. No one had been promised more than they found; there are even a couple of real success stories. Only one of the 20 letters is signed. This does not mean that they are fabrications, but that they have been published without the knowledge of the writers. It seems that Mr. Sørensen asked his customers to write to him about the conditions after some time in the new country. The 1930 edition includes more letters than the 1926 edition.

The illustrations included are all photographs. It is in the selection of these photographs that you really become aware of a discrepancy between what is shown in the pamphlet and what the emigrants would eventually find. The selection is entirely lopsided. There are harvest scenes, happy domestic animals in ideal surroundings, and beautiful and well-kept farm houses set among trees and flowers. Throughout, a cozy and successful atmosphere exudes from the vistas. The pictures illustrating the section on the prairie provinces show agricultural machines at work. They do not give you any idea of the prairie landscape.

Bearing in mind that the prime target for the companies was to bring settlers to the three prairie provinces it is perhaps hardly surprising that the visual idea you get of the prairie is one of harvest activity and bumper crops only. Needless to say, Danish villagers who settled on the prairie and who had relied on CPR pamphlets for factual information would have been in for a great surprise. Not due to the hard work demanded, but to the immensity and emptiness of the prairie landscape, its lack of objects that would break the view, the treelessness of vast areas and the capricious and ferocious climate. These were elements that the settler was not prepared for in the pamphlets, with their preponderance of photographs representing civilized and garden-like idylls from Eastern Canada. *There is among the CPR pamphlets not a single photograph indicating that winter and snow are Canadian facts of life.*

When it comes to the choice of photographs the last CNR brochure (1929) is more balanced. Along with pictures suggesting a garden quality in the Canadian landscape, CNR has included pictures illustrating the primitive life and houses of the pioneers near Manville, Alberta (p. 39). There are also winter scenes. Apart from the choice of photographs, the CPR and CNR pamphlets are remarkably alike. Both try to bring settlers to districts which are served by their railway lines. Both underline with racist overtones that Scandinavians are badly wanted. Their constant emphasis on the virtues of hard work is identical. The CNR (1926) quotes a Saskatchewan premier for the following statement: 'Canada is the land of milk and honey, but only for those who want to milk the cows and keep bees' (p. 9). Even at that time the automatic linkage between success and hard work was highly problematic; during the 'dirty thirties' a vast number of settlers in the prairie region were up against natural and man-made forces which rendered the concept of success through hard labour alone an illusion.

Notes

1. Due to more widespread poverty and deprivation in Norway and Sweden more than 10 times as many emigrated in the same period from these countries.
2. *Statistisk Aarbog*, 1928.
3. *Statistisk Aarbog*, 1930.
4. *Statistisk Aarbog*, 1934.
5. In 1924 the Danish-Norwegian writer Aksel Sandemose was sent by the *Berlingske Tidende* as part time correspondent to the Canadian West, where he stayed for 7 months. He wrote 36 articles which appeared in different Danish newspapers. In 1928 Sandemose published a novel *Nybyggerne i Alberta* (Ross Dane) based on his Canadian experiences.
6. This is discussed in detail in Kristian Hvidt, *Flugten til Amerika eller Drivkræfter i Masseindvandringen fra Danmark 1868-1914*, Aarhus 1971.
7. *Morsø Folkeblad*, Jan. 7, 1930 (Aksel Sandemose is careful enough not to mention any specific lines).
8. Printed at Trier's, Copenhagen 1930. All quotes in the text are from this edition in my own translation.
9. Standard, north east of Calgary, was founded in 1911 by Danish settlers who came after staying for one generation in Iowa, U.S.A.

Jack London: 'Impassioned Realism' and the Marketplace

Earle Labor

> He had striven to be something more than a mere writer
> of magazine fiction. He had sought to equip himself with
> the *tools of artistry*. On the other hand, he had not sacri-
> ficed strength ... Nor had he departed from his love of
> reality. His work was realism, though he had endeavored
> to fuse with it the fancies and beauties of imagination.
> What he sought was an *impassioned realism*, shot through
> with human aspiration and faith. What he wanted was
> life as it was, with all its spirit-groping and soul-reaching
> left in.[1]

This quotation, which sets forth the literary credo of Jack London's
autobiographical hero Martin Eden, serves nicely to represent London's
attitude toward his own craft as well — with one crucial addition: what he
also wanted was that his work should pay. To put it as succinctly as
possible, Jack London was a professional literary artist.

Unlike such critics as Christopher Wilson, I use the label 'professional'
in a purely ameliorative sense; furthermore, I see the concept of professionalism as being in no way incompatible with that of literary artistry. In
fact, I understand professionalism as complementing rather than vitiating
the integrity of the literary artist. Professor Wilson explains that he uses the
term

in its more modern, sociological sense: as a later stage within which prose writers
... came to see their craft predominantly as a product of technical expertise rather
than inspiration, viewed the market as an arbiter of literary value, and were
guided principally by an internalized sense of responsibility to their public.[2]

When I call London a professional, I mean to suggest that he deliberately
chose writing as the principal means of making his livelihood; that he
underwent rigorous training to acquire the special expertise of his chosen

field; that he wrote with the full expectation of being paid well for his investment; that he maintained the discipline of steady application of his time and energies to his vocation; and, finally, that, once having become secure in his literary virtuosity, he regarded it with a confidence sometimes bordering on contempt. None of this is meant in any way to suggest that he was willing to prostitute his artistic principles merely to sell his work.

Unfortunately, London's own pronouncements on the subject of success in the literary marketplace — if not examined with exceeding care — make it altogether too easy to dismiss him as something of a commercial hack. For example, after an interview with London in January 1905, Julian Hawthorne wrote the following report in the *Los Angeles Examiner*:

When I wanted to know whether he derived no pleasure from the act of creative imagination, [London] said no; but afterward explained that, while the mere conception might be agreeable, the drudgery of writing the thing down took the good taste out of the mouth. Besides, looking at the product subsequently, in the cold day light, — in the reaction from the creative glow, — it was apt to look like poor stuff, which one was sorry to have fathered. It was best to let it alone, if one could afford to do so, and get out of this fleeting existence something real, personal, positive. But if one could not afford to take this attitude, then let him write his stuff as well as he could, sell it in the most favorable market, and forget it.

He did not care much what became of it, otherwise, nor even was disturbed by suggestions from editors as to modifications of the text. Let them ditch the indiscreet words and phrases, if they liked; it was all one to him. They might change the very title of the stories, should that be their fancy. He had no paternal tenderness for his literary progeny. They were mothered by necessity, not by love.[3]

This statement should be taken with at least two grains of salt: first, it was scarcely representative of London's typically optimistic state of mind, having been made during what was probably the unhappiest period of his life — the time between his separation from his first wife Bessie and his decision to marry Charmian Kittredge and move from the city into the Valley of the Moon, a period he later referred to in his autobiographical treatise *John Barleycorn* as 'the Long Sickness'; second, it *was* characteristic of London, even in his best moods, to present himself in the popular image of the writer as businessman — or, in his own words, as 'brain merchant'.

Time and time again throughout his career, London openly confessed that he wrote for money; and in defense of this attitude I should like to reiterate Dr. Johnson's famous dictum that 'No man but a blockhead ever wrote except for money' (I mention this somewhat reluctantly as I apprehend the implications for those of us in my own profession). Moreover, as I have explained elsewhere,

London was forever playing the role of the American Adam. As in the case of Fitzgerald's Gatsby — and London's own Martin Eden — the obsession to get money was materialistic and vulgar only in the most superficial way; fundamentally, the conception was ideal. In this ideal sense, money — though essential — was the means to an end, never an end in itself'.[4]

It was, in short, a vital component of the American Dream. Money was the coin of the New Realm — the essential means to happiness, social esteem, the Good Life. 'More money means more life to me', London wrote to Cloudesley Johns in 1900;[5] and this statement was the key to his meteoric career, just as it is a key to our understanding of the larger myth in which all of us participate — even those of us in the academic profession (as David Lodge's *Small World* attests with such brilliant hilarity). Or, as London wrote in the September 1902 issue of *The Critic*, 'The deepest values of life are today expressed in terms of cash ... This being so ... it is only fair that literature be expressed in terms of cash';[6] and, again typically, in a 1914 letter to a young literary aspirant, he wrote,

The test of a thing is its saleability. I bring my knowledge of literature, my knowledge of the magazines and what they buy, to bear, to back me up in my contention that your story is not a literary product — what I mean is, that I'll bet ten to one right now there is no first-class or second-class magazine in the U.S. that could be induced to accept and publish your story. You've got to do more work; you've got to learn the trick employed by the other fellow who does succeed — in short — and here comes the fundamental difference between you and me, — you've got to study formula.[7]

One of the ironies of this advice is that, contrary to Christopher Wilson's contention that London 'adopted [a] technique of mimicry' and that his work has an 'often-formulaic feel',[8] London, the mature writer, seldom practiced what he preached in this regard (this may be what he means by 'the fundamental difference between you and me' in his letter to Bozeman). It was during his frantic pre-Klondike writing ordeal that he tried so desperately to break into the literary marketplace by writing according to what he perceived the right formula to be and by producing, in the process, a great quantity of third-rate stuff, some of which he later managed to get published, in the same manner as Martin Eden, and most of which he wisely trashed after multiple rejections.

The truth is, the best of London, the creator of tales, is never written by formula — nor written merely to appeal to either contemporary popular tastes or editorial prejudices. While there is scarcely time or space enough in this essay to elaborate the complex process by which London composed his best work, I might mention briefly that a great proportion of this work is based upon fact, much of it derived from actual historical events that London had overheard (as in many of his Klondike stories) or had read in the newspapers. His remarkable talent enabled him to reweave this factual material into genuine art, and his unconscious penchant for myth raised much of that art into timeless literature. I need only cite his great classic *The Call of the Wild* as an outstanding case in point. However, I should also like to mention that there are no stories in our literature that anticipate such originals as 'The Night-Born', 'Told in the Drooling Ward', and 'The Red One'. The first of these three — 'The Night-Born' — is an extraordinary triple-frame story taking its title from a Thoreau quotation and based upon a newspaper story which leads London, the mythopoeic artist, into a story of female individuation; archetypally speaking, it is one of the richest pieces of fiction in our literature. The second — 'Told in the Drooling Ward' — is based upon London's own personal observations of the inmates of the Sonoma State Home for the feeble-minded, adjacent to his ranch in Glen Ellen. Don Graham is evidently one of the few academic critics aware of this unique literary gem: 'If London's story reminds us of almost nothing from the past', he observes,

in style, comedy, and realism it seems to foretell certain fictional experiments with the feeble-minded to come, in such works as the Benjy section of *The Sound and the Fury*, the portrayal of Lenny in Steinbeck's *Of Mice and Men*, and above all, the inverted world of the complete insane-asylum novel, Ken Kesey's *One Flew Over the Cuckoo's Nest*. Even ranked in this company', Graham concludes, 'London's story is still a most impressive revelation of the comic and serious potentiality of the feeble-minded persona.[9]

Even higher acclaim than this has been accorded 'The Red One': Philip José Farmer calls this his 'favorite', hailing it as a 'long-lost' classic which

conceals beneath its blood-sweat-dirt-beauty tale of South Seas adventure the 'impenetrable', the unconquerable mystery of things beyond man's ken.[10]

Dale Walker praises it as 'an extraordinary, greatly neglected science-fiction-fantasy tale of shuddering impact'.[11] Gorman Beauchamp rates it as a

minor masterpiece of science fiction, more teasingly ambiguous yet more com-
pelling than anything else that London ever wrote in this form ... [a story in
which] his art soars infinitely far above his wonted Naturalistic theories and
achieves an imaginative purity of vision all too rare in his other work.[12]

Andrew Sinclair calls it 'the most haunting' of London's last stories, comparing it favourably with Conrad's 'Heart of Darkness'.[13] Thomas Clareson
acclaims it as a forerunner of mid-twentieth century science fiction, pointing
out that

One has only to shift from Guadalcanal [the setting for 'The Red One'] to *Mare
Crisium* on the Moon to find its re-enactment in a different idiom in Arthur C.
Clarke's 'The Sentinel' [the germinal piece for Stanley Kubrick's *2001*]. While their
attitudes toward man and science differ, their stories contain the same sense of
wonder, the same sense of cosmic loneliness.[14]

And James Kirsch, founder and former president of the Society of Jungian
Analysts of Southern California, in a pioneering essay on 'The Red One',
has interpreted the story as 'an accurate picture of American psychology
and of Western man as a whole'.[15] Finally, apropos of such as Dr. Kirsch's
reading of 'The Red One', I ought to point out that London was the first
writer deliberately to incorporate the theories of C.G. Jung into his fiction.
A half-dozen of his last stories, culminating in his unforgettable dramatic
dialogue between the voices of rationality and the collective unconscious
titled 'The Water Baby', are truly like nothing written before or since. Like
most great literary artists, Jack London sometimes wrote better than he
knew; and he knew a great deal more than most literary critics have given
him credit for.

   However, to return to the main subject of this essay: London was, before
all else, a professional. To affirm that he wrote in order to sell does not
necessarily imply that he was willing to sell out. He detested hack work
and asserted that

the confirmed hack writer is a melancholy spectacle — a gibbering spectacle of a
once robust manhood; while lucrative mediocrity typifies in these latter days those
ancient, muck-wallowing swine who were once brave men in Ulysses's band.[16]

As I have explained before, London's work was basically governed by a
clear-cut professional code, a code comprising a mystique, a practical esthetic, and an ethic.[17] The mystique was that of imaginative or 'impassioned
realism', the realism described in *Martin Eden* as 'shot through with human

aspiration and faith ... life as it [is], with all its spirit-groping and soul-reaching left in', a truthful compromise between what London describes as 'the school of god' and 'the school of clod', charged with vitality and with 'humanness'.[18] The impassioned realist 'must seize upon and press into enduring art-forms the vital facts of our existence', and, while he will always endeavour to fuse his realism with imaginative beauty and with the true spirit of romance and adventure, he must never shun the terrible and the tragic in favour of the illusion of life's 'sweet commonplaces'.[19] The true realist will be as forceful as he is honest — for, as London rhetorically asks, 'what more is the function of art than to excite states of consciousness complementary to the thing portrayed? The color of tragedy must be red'.[20] In sum, the supreme fiction will be truer than phenomenal reality because the writer's imagination will have seized upon the cosmic essence, thereby making it 'LIVE, and spout blood and spirit and beauty and fire and glamor'.[21]

London's esthetic, informed by this same spirit of vital realism, manifested itself in functionalism: 'Art, to be truly effective', he wrote in 1900, 'should be part and parcel of life and pervade it in all its interstices'.[22] Only so much beauty does an object possess as it has utility:

What finer beauty than strength — whether it be airy steel, or massive masonry, or a woman's hand? ... A thing must be true, or it is not beautiful, any more than a painted wanton is beautiful, any more than a sky-scraper is beautiful that is intrinsically and structurally light and that has a false massiveness of pillars plastered on outside.[23]

In writing, then, vigorous content is essential: 'What is form?' London demanded in an early letter to his fellow writer Elwyn Hoffman. 'What intrinsic value resides in it? None, none, none — unless it clothe pregnant substance, great substance'.[24] Furthermore, as he asserts in his essay on 'The House Beautiful', 'There is no utility that need not be beautiful ... construction and decoration must be one' in literature as well as in architecture.[25]

London's ethic was predicated upon what he called 'sincerity'. In his 1903 essay on 'Getting into Print', he advised aspiring young writers as follows: 'The three great things are: *good health*; *work*; and *philosophy of life*. I may add, nay, must add, a fourth — *sincerity*. Without this, the other three are without avail; with it you may cleave to greatness and sit among the giants'.[26] In 1907, reacting to the suggestion by Macmillan President George P. Brett that publication of his disreputable tramping experience might damage the sales of his other works, London asserted:

In *The Road*, and in all my work, in all that I have said and written and done, I have been true. This is the character I have built up; it constitutes, I believe, my big asset ... I have always insisted that the cardinal literary virtue is sincerity, and I have striven to live up to this belief.[27]

To be sincere was to tell the truth as he saw it in relationship to his philosophy of life; it was to be true to his artistic self as that self had been shaped by experience; and it meant that he must in his fiction articulate the basic, cosmic realities — it was, in short, to remain committed to the principle of 'impassioned realism'.

Because London discovered early in his career that writing fiction paid better than writing literary criticism, he published no more than a handful of essays on the art of fiction; but in those few essays the principles upon which his professionalism was based may be clearly seen. The most revealing of these is titled 'First Aid to Rising Authors', published in the December 1900 issue of the *Junior Munsey Magazine*. In this seminal essay London divides writers into two major categories. The first group consists of those for whom writing is a part-time, secondary activity: *for example*, the specialist (doctor, lawyer, professor, etc.) who writes in order to disseminate the knowledge of his profession; the social gadfly who writes merely to get his name into print; the dilettante who writes for diversion and pleasure. The second major group comprises the serious authors for whom writing is a way of life: *that is*, the true poet 'who sings for the song's sake' and 'because he cannot help singing'; the didactic 'heavenly, fire-flashing, fire-bringing' soul who has — or thinks he has — 'a message the world needs or would be glad to hear' and whose 'ambition is to teach, to help, to uplift'; and, finally, the ambitious, practical man who is driven by what London calls 'belly need' and by an obsession to achieve the good life. Of course London places himself in this last category:

We are joy-loving, pleasure-seeking and we are ever hungry for the things which we deem the compensation of living ... [And because] we want these things, ... we are going to rush into print to get them ... We have chosen print because we were better adapted for it; and, further, because we preferred it to pulling teeth, mending broken bones, adding up figures, or working with a pick and shovel.

Yet even though one writes to satisfy his 'belly need', the true professional must exercise artistic discretion: he should avoid the inanely vapid sort which amuses the commonplace public, and the melo-dramatic messes which tickle the palates of the sensation mongers ... Of course it pays; but ...

and here is a key to the seeming contradiction of London's attitude —

because we happen to be mercenarily inclined, there is no reason why we should lose our self-respect ... Though the dreamers and idealists scorn us because of our close contact with the earth, no disgrace need attach to the contact. The flesh may sit heavily upon us, yet may we stand erect and look one another in the eyes; and in this connection we may well take a lesson from those same dreamers and idealists,

he concludes (and here we may appreciate London's own fine sense of playful irony):

Let us be fire-bringers in a humble way. Let us have an eye to the ills of the world and its needs; and if we find messages, let us deliver them. Ah, pardon me, purely for materialistic reasons. We will weave them about with our fictions, and make them beautiful, and sell them for goodly sums.[28]

What he is saying, in other words, is what D.H. Lawrence cautioned a generation later: 'Never trust the artist. Trust the tale'. This admonition, better than any, should direct our reassessment of Jack London's relation-ship to the literary marketplace and — even more importantly — of his proper relationship to the literary canon.

Notes

1. London, Jack, *Martin Eden*, (New York: Macmillan, 1909), pp. 231-32; my italics.
2. Wilson, Christopher P., *The Labor of Words / Literary Professionalism in the Pro-gressive Era*, (Athens, Ga.: University of Georgia Press, 1985), p. 204.
3. Hawthorne, Julian, 'Jack London in Literature', *Los Angeles Examiner* 12 Jan. 1905, p. 1.
4. Labor, Earle, *Jack London*, (New York: Twayne, 1974), pp. 82-83.
5. London, Jack, *The Letters of Jack London*, ed. Earle Labor, Robert C. Leitz, III, and I. Milo Shepard. 3 vols, (Stanford: Stanford University Press, 1988), p. 164.
6. London, Jack, *No Mentor But Myself / A Collection of Articles, Essays, Reviews and Letters, by Jack London, on Writing and Writers*, ed. Dale L. Walker. Foreword by Howard Lachtman. (Port Washington: Kennikat, 1979), p. 49.
7. Unpublished letter to 'friend Bozeman', 12 Nov. 1914, Huntington Library.
8. Wilson, op. cit., p. 95.

9. Graham, Don, 'Jack London's Tale Told by a High-Grade Feeb', *Studies in Short Fiction*, 15 (1978), p. 433.

10. London, Jack, *Curious Fragments / Jack London's Tales of Fantasy Fiction*, ed. Dale L. Walker. Foreword by Philip Jose Farmer. (Port Washington: Kennikat, 1975), p. VIII.

11. Ibid., p. 198.

12. Beauchamp, Gorman, *Jack London*, Starmont Reader's Guide 15, (Mercer Island: Starmont House, 1984), p. 85.

13. Sinclair, Andrew, *Jack: A Biography of Jack London*, (New York: Harper & Row, 1977), pp. 230-310.

14. Clareson, Thomas D., ed. *A Spectrum of Worlds*, (Garden City: Doubleday, 1972), pp. 87; 90.

15. Kirsch, James, 'Jack London's Quest: 'The Red One', *Psychological Perspectives*, 11 (1980), p. 153.

16. *No Mentor*, p. 21.

17. *Jack London*, pp. 84-89.

18. *Martin Eden*, p. 232.

19. London, Jack, *Revolution and Other Essays*, (New York: Macmillan, 1910), p. 224.

20. London, Jack, *Jack London Reports: War Correspondence, Sports Articles, and Miscellaneous Writings*, ed. King Hendricks and Irving Shepard, (Garden City: Doubleday, 1970), p. 334.

21. *Revolution*, pp. 231, 224.

22. *Letters*, p. 976.

23. Foner, Philip S., ed. *Jack London / American Rebel / A Collection of His Social Writings Together with an Extensive Study of the Man and His Times*, (New York: Citadel, 1947), p. 429.

24. *Revolution*, p. 166.

25. *Letters*, p. 234.

26. *Revolution*, p. 164.

27. *No Mentor*, p. 57.

28. *Letters*, p. 675.

29. *No Mentor*, pp. 24-29.

30. Lawrence, D.H., *Studies in Classic American Literature*, First publ. 1923, (New York: Viking, 1968), p. 2.

Conceptions of Mystery in Eudora Welty and Flannery O'Connor

Karl-Heinz Westarp

> It is the business of fiction to embody mystery through manners, ... The mystery [Henry James] was talking about is the mystery of our position on earth, and the manners are those conventions which, in the hands ot the artist, reveal that central mystery./ [The fiction writer is] concerned with ultimate mystery as we find it embodied in the concrete world of sense experience.
> (Flannery O'Connor)[1]

> The sense of mystery in life we do well to be aware of. And, of course, I think we do try to suggest that mystery in writing a story, not through any direct or cheap way but by simply presenting the way things happen.
> (Eudora Welty)[2]

In these two statements about the importance of mystery for their understanding of fiction, Eudora Welty and Flannery O'Connor seem to be largely in agreement. Welty talks about the 'sense of mystery in life' that is suggested in a story, O'Connor about 'the mystery of our position on earth' that is 'embodied in the concrete world of sense experience'. O'Connor seems to add a further epithet in that she expects fiction to '*reveal* that *central* [or 'ultimate'] mystery' [emphasis added]. I take this slight change of emphasis to be symptomatic of the two writers who knew and respected each other, though they were well aware of their differences. Welty told Jan Nordby Gretlund, 'I can't imagine ... three more different writers than Katherine Anne Porter, Flannery O'Connor and myself'.[3] Also O'Connor saw the differences: 'I am not one of the subtle sensitive writers like Eudora Welty'.[4] In another interview Welty was very generous in her tribute to O'Connor: 'Of course I think she is just tremendous. I think she was a fantastically gifted writer. I have enjoyed everything she has done. I love it'. Yet she also acknowledges that 'there are a lot of things I realize are a closed book to me in her work because of the Roman Catholic Church of which I'm ignorant'.[5] At one point even, when her brother was ill, Eudora Welty was gracious enough to invite Flannery O'Connor to replace her at the University of Chicago.[6] O'Connor herself counted Welty among the 'best Southern writers'[7] and in 1962, when they had been at a conference together, O'Connor wrote, 'I really liked Eudora Welty — no presence whatsoever, just a real nice woman'.[8] Yet later O'Connor became a little more apprehensive about some of Welty's work. She wrote to her friend 'A': 'You are right about the Welty story. It's the kind of story that the more you think about it the less satisfactory it gets'.[9]

Both writers differ widely in their upbringing and in their personal attitude to, for example religious practice. Welty was baptized a Methodist but is not a church-going person. Jan Nordby Gretlund concludes in his study *Eudora Welty's Aesthetics of Place*: 'Welty's own religious inclinations are singularly undramatic. In her fiction she does not offer religious hope',[10] and he quotes from Welty's autobiographical *One Writer's Beginnings*: 'I painlessly came to realize that the reverence I felt for the holiness of life is not ever likely to be entirely at home in organized religion'; but she adds:

It was later, ... that the presence of holiness and mystery seemed, as far as my vision was able to see, to descend into the windows of Chartres, the stone peasant figures in the capitals of Autun ... in the shell of a church wall in Ireland still standing on a floor of sheep-cropped grass with no ceiling other than the changing sky.

I'm grateful that, from my mother's example, I had found the base for this worship — that I had found a love of sitting and reading the Bible for myself and looking up things in it.[11]

O'Connor was a believing and active Roman Catholic, but she gratefully acknowledged:

The fact that the South is the Bible Belt is in great measure responsible for its literary pre-eminence now. The Catholic novelist can learn a great deal from the Protestant South.[12]

Both writers are, as representatives of the fiction writing American South, well-known for their strong sense of place and concrete narrative detail in their short stories and novels. Critical response to their work has differed widely, but many critics seem to agree that a sense of mystery is almost absent in Welty, whereas most critics have focussed on its presence in almost all of O'Connor's writings. It is the prime aim of this essay to present Eudora Welty and Flannery O'Connor's differing and parallel conceptions of mystery and to show the use of mystery in two of their fictions, that is, in Welty's long novel *Losing Battles* (1970) and in O'Connor's novellette 'The Lame Shall Enter First' (1962).

What is 'Mystery'?

Before we enter into a discussion of the texts I shall make a few introductory remarks about the concept of 'mystery'. In Longman's *Dictionary of Contemporary English*, (London 1995, p. 939) 'mystery' is defined as follows — according to frequency of usage: 1. Something 'impossible to understand or explain'. (2. is the verbal form of 1.) 3. 'a quality that makes someone or something strange, secret or difficult to explain'. 4. 'a quality that something has that cannot be explained in any practical or scientific way'. 5. 'a story about a murder'. The bulk of Welty and O'Connor's work does not fit the category 'murder' story, though 'The Demonstrators' by Welty and 'A Good Man Is Hard to Find' by O'Connor would qualify. To both writers the idea of the Greek 'mystærion', that which is not said or seen, comes close to what they are doing in their stories. Flannery O'Connor leans in her treatment of the inexpressible or the inexplicable in the direction of St. Paul, who uses the term 'mystery' for a 'sacrament', in which an outward sign — say water in connection with baptism — is indicative of the inward and spiritual reality of grace, in the same sense as Jesus in the incarnation is the physical sign of the spiritual godhead — 'and the word became flesh' [Jn 1,14] — that is, the spiritual or internal reality is hidden behind the visible or the external, as Welty calls it, or in O'Connor's terminology, 'mystery' is revealed through 'manners'.

Mystery as understood by Welty and O'Connor

To Welty 'fiction isn't the place for philosophy' at least not 'when put in as philosophy'.[13] As Shelby Foote said in a conversation with Welty, 'I've never known Southerners do anything but tell stories',[14] they have — and these are Welty's own words — 'inherited, a narrative sense of human destiny'.[15] Or as O'Connor put it: 'When a Southerner wants to make a point, he tells a story; it's actually his way of reasoning and dealing with experience'.[16] Particularly in connection with *Losing Battles*, which Welty wanted to be a 'novel-as-drama' — with some 90% dialogue[17] — in which all should 'be shown forth, brought forth, the way things are in a play, ... The thought, the feeling that is internal is shown as external'.[18] I see this as a clear authorial statement that the surface, the story, 'manners' is not all, that we have to look for something underlying, or in other words that *Losing Battles* is not only the story or the stories of a family's 'multifront' battles but that they have a deeper dimension of 'mystery' as well. In 1972 Welty told Charles T. Bunting,

The sense of mystery in life [, which 'is often lost sight of by reductive criticism']¹⁹ we do well to be aware of. And, of course, I think we do try to suggest that mystery in writing a story, not through any direct or cheap way but by simply presenting the way things happen.[20]

Mystery is omnipresent in the story, in the place and in the characters. In *The Eye of the Story* Welty states that all the arts are connected with place and 'all of them celebrate its mystery'.[21] 'From the dawn of man's imagination, place has enshrined the spirit'.[22] Against this background Cleo's teasing question in connection with Gloria's wedding gains greater depth: 'Do you all worship off in the woods somewhere?'[23] Welty also commented on mystery in relation to her characters:

They know something else is out there. It's just an awareness of spaciousness and mystery of — really, of living, and that was just a kind of symbol of it, a disguise. I do feel that there are very mysterious things in life, and I would like just to suggest their presence — an awareness of them.[24]

In the same way Flannery O'Connor sees the depth dimension of the character as the novelist's central concern: 'A story always involves, in a dramatic way, the mystery of personality'[25] and characters lean 'toward mystery and the unexpected'.[26] Welty and O'Connor seem to agree that:

If the writer believes that our life is and will remain essentially mysterious, if he looks upon us as beings existing in a created order to whose laws we freely respond, then what he sees on the surface will be of interest to him only as he can go through it into an experience of mystery itself.[27]

Michael Kreyling has summed up Welty's presentation of deeper dimensions: She

displays in the time- and place-bound particulars of Banner, Mississippi, the timeless combatants of a larger battle, one that can genuinely be termed cosmic ... Welty views her people and their condition with the depth and breadth of the philosopher who sees the universal in each moment.[28]

In *Losing Battles* Judge Moody quotes his old teacher Julia Mortimer, who wrote in her last letter, with clear overtones of the blessings of the Fall: 'The side that gets licked gets to the truth first' (*LB*, 298). This statement is reminiscent of the title of O'Connor's story 'The Lame Shall Enter First', which again reminds us of the biblical promise 'The last shall be the first' [Mt 19,30]. Following another of Julia's pieces of advice to her pupil Gloria, that 'every mystery had its right answer — we just had to find it. That's what mysteries were given to us for' (*LB*, 252), I'll suggest what answers there might be to the mysteries in *Losing Battles* and in 'The Lame Shall Enter First'.

Mystery in *Losing Battles*

Losing Battles has been interpreted in many different ways as the clash between the agrarian past of the Beecham-Renfro families and the future as taught by Julia Mortimer. Both Gossett and Heilman place central importance on young Jack as a biblical figure.

For his family, Jack is a radiant innocent, a 'blessed mortal', and a good Samaritan [Lk 10, 30-37]. He is an incorruptible Prodigal Son [Lk 15,11-32] prodigally received with a feast and rejoicing and forgiving.[29]

But Gossett is only partly right. It is true, Jack helped Judge Moody's car back to the road (*LB*, 79) as an act of a Good Samaritan, and later, when Moody is looking for roadside assistance, Jack says,

'But you got a Good Samaritan right here!' ... 'I'm not asking for a Good Samaritan, I'm asking for a man with some know-how', called Judge Moody (*LB*, 125).

Welty uses this image as an epithet for Jack several times (*LB*, 80, 82, 84, 126, 149, 163), yet the comparison halts, since Jack is not — as in the biblical parable — the alien, 'saving' Moody's Buick, he is one of the family — and is even the remote cause of the Buick's suspension off Banner Top. Moody himself is also seen as a Good Samaritan, though he 'was one and didn't know it' (*LB*, 196) in that he 'saved' Gloria and her daughter Lady May's lives. In characteristic Welty mode the image is satirized when Mrs. Moody, herself a Presbyterian, comments on a group of hungry Methodists coming from Sunday service 'headed home for dinner' (*LB*, 133) passing the site of the accident without offering help. 'I'd just like to see a bunch of Presbyterians try to get by me that fast!' (*LB*, 134) she says.

Brother Bethune, the Baptist preacher, calls Jack a 'Prodigal Son' (LB, 105, 107), but again the comparison does not hold true. Jack is a Prodigal Son, since he didn't turn up at the previous year's family reunion, which he couldn't, since he was in prison at Parchman; but he did not leave the family on his own account, as did the youngest son in the New Testament story. After all, he had carried off Curly Stovall's safe in an attempt to defend and restore his family's honour. Nevertheless, I think Welty uses the narrative elements from the stories of the Good Samaritan and the Prodigal Son quite to the point. This is just one instance, which proves Welty's ample knowledge of the Bible. Welty's answer to John Griffin Jones in a 1981 interview corroborates this: 'I love to read the Old Testament. The Old Testament has the best stories. The King James Version stays with you forever, rings and rings in your ears'.[30] There is little surprise therefore that a close reading of Losing Battles proves that Welty's prose is permeated with the English of the Bible.

The family Bible itself is of pivotal importance for the life and history of the 'God-fearing' (LB, 344) Vaughn-Beecham-Renfro families: apart from the births, marriages and deaths recorded in it, it contained Ellen's now fatally lost gold ring (LB, 24, 266), Ellen's hair in 'Chronicles' (LB, 266), Grandpa's spectacles 'deep in the crease of First Thessalonians' (LB, 266) and, close to it, Sam Dale's postcard to Rachel Sojourner (LB, 266). More important than this physical presence of the Bible is its spiritual influence on the different layers of language and narrative. Welty's love of Old Testament stories can be seen in her use of story elements and names. The information about Julia Mortimer's death makes Gloria cry, 'as if she had been struck in the forehead by a stone out of a slingshot', as Goliath from David's slingshot (LB, 157, [1 Sam 17,49]). Also in connection with Julia's death Judge Moody said, 'It could make a stone cry' (LB, 306, [Hab 2,11]). In the morning after the reunion, which Brother Bethune described as 'Belshazzar's Feast without no Handwriting on the Wall to mar it' (LB, 177, [Dan 5,1-5]) and where 'Mr. Renfro ... rose with the long halves [of the first watermelon] facing outward from his arms, like the tablets of the Ten Commandments' (LB, 195, [Ex 31,18; 32,15]), Miss Beulah compares Jack to Samson. In turning over Moody's car Jack is even better than Samson, because he shows judgement, and after the act he 'still got [his] strength' (LB, 435, 434), whereas Samson got killed together with his enemies: 'Reminds me of Samson exactly!' (LB, 394, [Judg 16,29-30]) is Miss Beulah's comment.

Robert B. Heilman has drawn attention to a number of casual allusions to the Bible:

To Lucifer (*LB*, 81), the Crack of Doom (*LB*, 129), the book of Romans (*LB*, 183), the Flood (*LB*, 250), Job (*LB*, 404, [also 293]), the parting of the Red Sea (*LB*, 406) [as the street between Ora Stovall's Methodist and Brother Bethune's Baptist churches in Banner], Solomon [whose wisdom Jack senses in Gloria (*LB*, 432)].[31]

But he left out references to 'Noah's Ark' for the school bus (*LB*, 4, [Gen 6,14]) and for Moody's Buick (*LB*, 135); the 'Walls of Jericho' (*LB*, 5, [Josh 6,2-5]); 'the cherubs of Heaven' (*LB*, 9); 'Damascus' (*LB*, 49), the city of Saul's conversion [Acts 9,1-19]; the 'Creation' (*LB*, 62, 250); and 'The Day of Judgment' (*LB*, 83, 212, [Jn 5, 25-29]).

Michael Kreyling has observed the eponymous overtones of Moody and Mortimer.[32] He says for example that 'Mortimer's name suggests death for the "primitive men" of Banner'.[33] Added could be Comfort's name, where Aycock's Buick-balancing act is a welcome comfort; but I think most striking is Welty's use of biblical names and their significance. The family farm was built by Jacob Jordan, grandfather to Granny, whose 90th birthday is the occasion for the family reunion. Jacob means 'supplanter', that is, for Esau [Gen 25, 25-26] and 'Jordan' is the Hebrew for 'flowing down', since he is the oldest source of the family river, which continues through Granny, the last of her generation (Miss Thurzah Elvira Jordan, *LB*, 179), and Jack, who both bear the middle name of Jordan. Further Old Testament names are: 'Nathan' which means 'gift'. It was a gift — though also a sin — that he stood up for the family against the exploitations of Dearman and that, through repenting and cutting off his hand in accordance with the biblical advice in Mt 5, 30: 'If your right hand causes you to sin, cut it off and throw it away', he reminds the family that 'Destruction is at hand' (*LB*, 115, [Lk 21,20]). He is the gift of a sign for his family and others to warn them of what is to come. Therefore Miss Beulah can say of him: 'We've lost him ... to the Book of Revelation' (*LB*, 348), in which the main theme is the Day of Judgement, as it is in Nathan's life. The warnings on his posters show this: 'Destruction is at Hand' (*LB*, 115), 'Where will you spend Eternity?' (*LB*, 404) and 'Live For Him' (*LB*, 434). 'Noah', which means 'wandering', has been to southern Mississippi to find his new wife, Cleo. 'Samuel' in Sam Dale, whom the entire family regards as the perfect son (*LB*, 221), means 'heard of God', that is, he is already united with God in death. Finally the name 'Beulah', which means 'married', fits the position of the hostess of the reunion very well.

As already mentioned, Jack's middle name, Jordan, links him to the old family, but his first name 'Jack' or John, which means 'gracious', indicates that he also belongs to the new dispensation, as did John the Baptist through his double link with the Old and the New Testaments. 'Gloria', as sung by the angels announcing a new beginning in the birth of Jesus [Lk 2,14], does not want to have anything 'to do with the old dead past' (*LB*, 361). Gloria means 'praise, adoration, pride', all epithets fitting her character, which Miss Beulah describes as follows: 'Gloria's got a sweet voice when she deigns to use it, she's so spotless the sight of her hurts your eyes, ...' (*LB*, 69). Finally 'Lady May', born in December (*LB*, 64) and the hope for the future, is short for Mary, which means 'rebellion'. In drawing attention to these names I am not claiming that Eudora Welty was aware of their overtones, but they are certainly a further indication of the fact that biblical material is almost second nature to her.

Sin *versus* Forgiveness

One of the larger battles fought in *Losing Battles* is the recognition of evil and the individual's losing this battle in sin, and the necessity of forgiveness, which — on a different level — is also a form of losing. Welty accepts the presence of evil in her fiction, but does not seem to acknowledge 'sin'. In his first interview with Eudora Welty (1980) Gretlund suggested: 'You do not seem to be interested in the concept of "sin" or in the idea of "evil."' To which Welty answered:

'I am, though. Not in "sin" — not from a Roman Catholic point of view like Flannery O'Connor, because I am ignorant of that religion. But I do believe that there is "evil." I believe in the existence of "evil," or else your reaching for "good" could not mean anything. I do feel there is "evil" in the world and in people, very really and truly. I recognize its power and value. I do!'[34]

Therefore Gretlund concludes that Welty 'makes no attempt to hide the fact that inexplicable evil exists among [the Mississippi farmers]'[35] and that 'there is no attempt to explain away the tale of [Miss Lexie's] premeditated evil',[36] which is later atoned for because Miss Lexie is 'converted' to helping Jonas Hugg (*LB*, 377). Yet Gretlund is not willing to accept, as some critics do, 'that only the presence of unexplained evil will give Welty's fiction its full depth'.[37] I have little doubt that evil and sin loom large in *Losing Battles*. Uncle Noah says that Jack didn't sin simply because he didn't steal:

If a boy's brought up in Grandpa Vaughn's house, and knows drinking, dancing, and sport-card playing is a sin, you don't need to rub it into his hide to make him know there's something a little bit the matter with stealing (*LB*, 44).

Awareness of sin is even present in little Elvie's skipping song: 'Yield not
to temptation for yielding is sin, ...' (*LB*, 137/8). Welty lets Judge Moody
define 'sin' as follows:

I suppose it just aggravates whatever's already there, in human nature — the best
and the worst, the strength and the weakness ... And of course human nature is
dynamite to start with (*LB*, 319).

In that sense almost all members of the reunion sense the presence of sin.
Uncle Curtis remembers Grandpa's last sermon in connection with the
previous reunion: 'Oh, he thundered! He preached at us from Romans and
sent us all home still quaking for our sins' (*LB*, 183). It is Uncle Nathan's
mission, as his posters show, to raise consciousness of sin, which is a
necessary presupposition for a growing understanding of forgiveness. As
'the car is salvaged only after it has fallen; similarly, the family must accept
its fall, its doom of death, before its members can be saved'.[38] Since the
theme of Brother Bethune's reunion sermon is forgiveness, there is a pro-
gression from Grandpa's last threatening sermon based on St. Paul's letter
to the Romans to Bethune's admonition, based on John the Baptist, to 're-
pent, for the kingdom of heaven is at hand' [Mt 3,2]. He says, 'Forgiveness
would suit us all better than anything in this lonesome old world' (*LB*, 209,
also 208-13 passim, 321, 372, 427, [Lk 24,47]). Forgiveness is so much in the
air on the Beecham-Renfro farm that Judge Moody can say, 'Forgiving
seems the besetting sin of this house' (*LB*, 319). Even Nathan's homicide can
be forgiven. When he had confessed to Julia, she told him — says Beulah,
who heard it — : 'Nathan, even when there's nothing left to hope for, you
can start again from there, and go your way and be good' (*LB*, 344; [Cf. Is
1,18; Jn 8.11]). Even though Nathan has changed to a life of atonement, Jack
takes on vicarious suffering for Nathan in that he considers himself a
deputy for Uncle Nathan in going to the pen: 'As long as I went and took
my turn, maybe it's evened up, and now the poor old man can rest' (*LB*,
431; [Cf. Mt 25,40]). In spite of all the sufferings the family has to endure,
there is hope for a new beginning. Welty told Bunting,

'I wanted to show indomitability there. I don't feel it's a novel of despair at all.
I feel it's more a novel of admiration for the human being, who can cope with any
condition ...'[39]

'I wanted to take away everything and show them naked as human
beings',[40] a statement that reminds me of Lear's remark to Poor Tom
[Edgar] in *King Lear* III,iv,104 'Thou art the thing itself; unaccommodated

man is no more but such a poor, bare, forked animal as thou art'. Daniele Pitavy-Souques concludes about Welty's description of the human condition that there is a

depth of the tragedy of human relations behind the brilliant surface ... Man's dignity and heroism is this endless fight against death and all forms of evil, which are forms of death[41].

'Ultimately what Welty shows us is that man has within him the capabilities of being both godly and sinful'.[42] However, there is in *Losing Battles* an unmistakable movement from evil and sin to forgiveness and being good. One of the most striking images of this is the 'procession' of helpfulness and forgiveness with the school bus pulling the Buick and the van assisting with its brakes on their united way to Banner (*LB*, 407). Seymour Gross comes to the conclusion that *Losing Battles'*

spiritual ebullience is the result of Welty's grand understanding of the joys and griefs of her large cast of characters who, do what they will to tip the world, cannot upset its balance. There is something in the world which does not like a fall — call it the life force or the natural order or whatever.[43]

Gloria is the most prominent representative of innovation and life force. Again and again she underlines (*LB*, 111, 171, 314, 359, 361, 429, 431, 434) that she wants independence for Jack, her daughter Lady May and herself. 'Oh, if we just had a little house to ourselves, ...' (*LB*, 271). Though she is forced to pronounce herself a Beecham (*LB*, 269) or even may have Beecham blood in her, she is 'standing [her] ground' in the family, against whom Julia Mortimer had warned her (*LB*, 250). Her last words to Jack are: 'And some day, some day yet, we'll move to ourselves. And there'll be just you and me and Lady May' (*LB*, 435).

Life's Pilgrimage

What kind of future can there be for Jack, Gloria and Lady May? I see an answer to this question in Welty's use of central images from Bunyan's *Pilgrim's Progress*. In Bunyan's allegorical narrative Christian leaves the City of Destruction, is refreshed on the Delectable Mountains and travels through the country of Beulah on his way to the Celestial City. His wife Christiana follows after, accompanied by her neighbour Mercy. They are escorted by Great-heart, who overcomes Giant Despair, before they reach the Gates of the Celestial City. I have already mentioned the central

position Miss Beulah holds in the novel and I've mentioned Welty's idea
that this is not a narrative of despair. Three times reference is made to the
design on Granny's quilt 'The Delectable Mountains' (*LB*, 222, 287, 347, also
used in Welty's first novel *Delta Wedding*), which could be seen as an image
of the mountains of Banner country. 'The Gates of Beyond' (*LB*, 110) are
used by Gloria both about Lady May's sleep but also about Jack's being
beyond the borders of Mississippi and behind the bars of Parchman. In the
context of Bunyan's allegory they are also a hint at life after death. In her
essay on Welty's 'Angelic ingenuity' of balance, Seymour Gross[44] has stated
that Julia's last words 'What was the trip for?' (*LB*, 241) resemble Lady
May's first words ever: 'What you huntin', man?' (*LB*, 368), which are
possibly a remembrance of Aunt Nanny's earlier words to Lady May: 'Who
you hunting' (*LB*, 64)? Both quest formulations are in line with the *homo
viator* theme of *Pilgrim's Progress*. Mrs. Moody has a simple answer to this
question: 'All I know is we're all put into this world to serve a purpose'
(*LB*, 306). Julia's purpose here on earth was to bring knowledge, which was
her 'Heaven' (*LB*, 299) and she 'was ready to teach herself to death for you'
(*LB*, 240, [Joh 15,13]) as Uncle Curtis puts it, but this altruism was not accepted; on the contrary Uncle Dolphus says, '[Julia] was our cross to bear'
(*LB*, 240, [Mt 16,24]). Julia's final instruction in her post-mortem letter is:
'And then, you fools [i.e. you, who did not want to learn] — mourn me'
(*LB*, 292), upon which Brother Bethune quotes from the Bible 'Whosoever
shall say, Thou fool, shall be in danger of hell fire' [Mt 5,22]! Julia lost her
battle as teacher of the Banner community, as many critics have observed,
but she was aware of the spiritual dimension of losing a battle: 'The side
that gets licked gets to the truth first' (*LB*, 298).

After Julia's funeral Jack and Gloria notice Sam Dale and Rachel's
graves. The narrator comments that Rachel's sliding grave is 'ready to go
over the edge of the bank, like a disobedient child. The small lamb on its
headstone had turned dark as a blackened lamp chimney', whereas Sam
Dale's rubbed name 'shone out in the wet' (*LB*, 427/8). Maybe Rachel,
whose name means 'ewe' [Gen 29,6], was really the black sheep of the family. Her mystery (*LB*, 251, 253, 259, 265) was linked to Sam Dale, as his
card to Rachel, so carefully kept in Granny's Bible, reveals (*LB*, 266/7). As
Beulah observes, Gloria 'might have been Rachel's secret' (*LB*, 256). Maybe
the graves hint at Rachel and Sam Dale's Doomsday chances.

I think it is important to notice Welty's carefully arranged similarity of
tone at the end of Part III of the novel, which after Brother Bethune's
sermon ends in forgiveness, and at the end of Part VI, where forgiveness

is actually lived out by all parties involved. At the end of Part III the members of the family sing (*LB*, 223):

> Gathering home! Gathering home!
> Never to sorrow more, never to roam!
> Gathering home! Gathering home!
> God's children are gathering home.

There can be no question of the eschatological overtones of this hymn.[45] Similarly at the end of the novel Jack sings (*LB*, 436):

> Bringing in the sheaves,
> Bringing in the sheaves!
> We shall come rejoicing,
> Bringing in the sheaves!

Both songs have the joyful overtones of returning home with a good harvest, but also returning home with life's harvest through 'The Gates of Beyond'.

Mystery in 'The Lame Shall Enter First'

In a characterization of her own work Flannery O'Connor said:

To insure our sense of mystery, we need a sense of evil which sees the devil as a real spirit who must be made to name himself, and not simply to name himself as vague evil, but to name himself with his specific personality for every occasion. Literature, like virtue, does not thrive in an atmosphere where the devil is not recognized as existing both in himself and as a dramatic necessity for the writer.[46]

She summed up her views in the well-known statements: 'My subject in fiction is the action of grace in territory largely held by the devil'.[47] 'Often the nature of grace can be made plain only by describing its absence'.[48] Preoccupation with the mysteries of evil and grace is clearly present in O'Connor's novellette 'The Lame Shall Enter First'.[49] The narrative structure of the story seems simple and straightforward: Mr. Sheppard — a consciously chosen eponymous name, because he wants to be a good shepherd — is a recently widowed social worker and City Recreational Director, who lives with his ten-year old son Norton, who is still deeply affected by the recent death of his mother. On Saturdays Sheppard works gratis in a boys' reformatory to show his concern for the poor. Here he shows special concern for fourteen-year-old club-footed and highly intelligent [I.Q. 140] Rufus Johnson, who when outside the reformatory lives with his religious grandfather, because his father is dead and his mother is in a penitentiary. His record is: 'senseless destruction, windows smashed, city trash boxes set afire, tires slashed' (CS, 449). Sheppard's concern has a double function: he wants to educate his own spoiled son, Norton, who is 'selfish, unresponsive, greedy' (CS, 449), by showing him his own affluence through the contrast with Rufus, who picks his food out of garbage cans, but more importantly, in his humanistic optimism he wants to 'save' Rufus Johnson by dragging him out of the morass in which he has ended through no fault of his own.[50] Sheppard spares neither effort nor expense to help Rufus and Norton: he buys both a microscope and a telescope to let the boys gain insight into the micro- and macrocosmic dimensions of the world. He also has a new shoe made for Rufus Johnson's club-foot, which Rufus, however, refuses to put on. Sheppard is truly an outstanding example of unselfish concern, it seems; though he is not quite perfect, because at a crucial point he does not trust Rufus Johnson's word of innocence and wrongly hands him over to the police.

This mistake only increases Rufus Johnson's aversion: he doesn't want any of Sheppard's concern. Right from the beginning Rufus hates Sheppard's do-gooding. Upon being asked who made him commit all those crimes, Rufus says: 'Satan. He has me in his power' (CS, 450). Instead of accepting Sheppard's demythologized technological optimism — Sheppard foresees that Rufus will go to the moon one day — Rufus counters: 'When I die I'm going to hell' (CS, 461). The mysteries of Satan and hell are concrete realities to the fundamentalist-educated boy Rufus, but to Sheppard they are empty concepts, part of the bag of lies, against which he wants to protect his son Norton. Rufus, the evil boy whose club foot is a sign of the devil's stigma, believes in Jesus and the Bible, so much so that, in imitation of the Prophet Ezekiel, he eats a page of the Bible. He sees through Sheppard's emptiness and tells Norton: 'He thinks he's Jesus Christ!' (CS, 459). Later, when O'Connor describes him as 'a small black figure on the threshold of some dark apocalypse' Rufus twice spits into Sheppard's face: 'The devil has you in his power' (CS, 478). Finally, after his relapse into crime, Rufus returns to Sheppard with the police only 'to show up that big tin Jesus!' (CS, 480), who is 'a dirty atheist' because he said 'there wasn't no hell' (CS, 480). Sheppard makes a final attempt to 'save' Rufus by saying: 'You're not evil, you're mortally confused. You don't have to make up for that foot ...' (CS, 480); but Rufus retorquates:

'I lie and steal because I'm good at it! My foot don't have a thing to do with it! The lame shall enter first [Mt 19,30]! The halt'll be gathered together. When I get ready to be saved, Jesus'll save me, not that lying stinking atheist' (CS, 480).

Taken at face value, evil is victorious at the end of the story: Rufus is back on the path of crime, and Norton has committed suicide in an attempt to be united with his mother in heaven — a heaven he believed to be at the far end of the telescope, where he thought he saw his mother. Yet, what is more important, the mystery of evil, in the shape of Rufus, has functioned as a means of bringing Sheppard to the point of anagnorisis or self-recognition and possible conversion. Towards the end of the story he reflects:

He had stuffed his own emptiness with good works like a glutton. He had ignored his own child to feed his vision of himself. He saw the clear-eyed Devil, the sounder of hearts, leering at him from the eyes of Johnson (CS, 481).

He comes to recognize that he did 'the right deed for the wrong reason', as Eliot's Becket confesses in *Murder in the Cathedral*. In the final analysis, evil is not victorious; on the contrary, Sheppard comes to realize his sin of pride and thus, I think, reaches a moment of grace.

Mystery through Manners

In my *tour de force* of quotes I hope to have shown that both Welty and O'Connor are writers who vividly describe manners, but also that they allow us to sense mysteries beyond manners. For both writers fiction deepens the mind's 'sense of mystery ... by contact with reality, and its sense of reality ... by contact with mystery',[51] as O'Connor put it. The interplay between internal and external, between mystery and manners, defines fiction as 'incarnational art' since it deals 'with all those concrete details of life that make actual the mystery of our position on earth'.[52] Though mystery is undeniably present in *Losing Battles*, Welty's novel and her other work has a more open-ended structure. In O'Connor's novelette, as in her other work, I sense a tendency towards closure and a final acceptance of an 'ultimate' mystery which remains inexplicable:

The fiction writer presents mystery through manners, grace through nature, but when he finishes there always has to be left over that sense of Mystery which cannot be accounted for by any human formula.[53]

Notes

1. O'Connor, Flannery, *Mystery and Manners*, eds R. & S. Fitzgerald, (New York: Farrar, Straus & Giroux 1980), pp. 124-25.
2. Welty, Eudora, *Conversations with Eudora Welty*, ed. Peggy Prenshaw, (New York: Washington Square Press, 1985), p. 62.
3. Ibid., pp. 243-44.
4. O'Connor, Flannery, *The Habit of Being*, ed. S. Fitzgerald, (New York: Farrar, Straus & Giroux, 1979), p. 141.
5. Welty, *Conversations*, p. 22.
6. *The Habit of Being*, p. 316.
7. Ibid., pp. 98 and 121.
8. Ibid., p. 471.
9. Ibid., p. 537.
10. Gretlund, Jan N., *Eudora Welty's Aesthetics of Place*, (Odense: Odense University Press, 1994), p. 332.
11. Welty, Eudora, *One Writer's Beginnings*, (Cambridge, Mass.: Harvard University Press, 1984), p. 49.
12. O'Connor, Flannery, *Conversations with Flannery O'Connor*, ed. Rosemary Magee, (Jackson: University of Mississippi Press, 1987), p. 87.
13. Welty, *Conversations*, p. 65.
14. Rubin, Louis D., 'Growing up in the Deep South — A Conversation' in Rubin, Louis D. ed., *The American South*, (Washington: United States Information Agency, 1991), p. 60.
15. Welty, *Conversations*, p. 87.
16. O'Connor, *Conversations*, p. 49.
17. Welty, *Conversations*, p. 273.
18. Ibid., p. 50; see also pp. 85, 208, 303.
19. Welty, Eudora, *Critical Essays*, ed. Peggy Prenshaw, (Jackson: University Press of Mississippi, 1979), p. 271, note 1.
20. Welty, *Conversations*, p. 62.
21. Welty, Eudora, *The Eye of the Story*, (New York: Vintage International, 1990), p. 119.
22. Ibid., p. 123.
23. Welty, Eudora, *Losing Battles*, (New York: Random House, 1970), p. 49, hereafter cited as *LB* in the text.
24. Welty, *Conversations*, p. 342.
25. *Mystery & Manners*, p. 90; see also p. 198.
26. Ibid., p. 40.
27. Ibid., p. 41.
28. Kreyling, Michael, *Eudora Welty's Achievement of Order*, (Baton Rouge: Louisiana State University Press, 1980), pp. 143-44; see also p. 152.
29. Welty, *Essays*, p. 345; see also p. 292.
30. Ibid., p. 362.
31. Ibid., p. 292, note 3.
32. *Eudora Welty's Achievement*, pp. 149-50.

33. Ibid., p. 149.
34. Welty, *Conversations*, p. 253.
35. *Eudora Welty's Aesthetics of Place*, p. 11.
36. Ibid., p. 279.
37. Ibid., p. 276.
38. Welty, *Essays*, p. 361.
39. Ibid., p. 52.
40. Ibid., p. 54.
41. Ibid., p. 267.
42. Ibid., p. 366.
43. Ibid., p. 327.
44. Ibid., p. 329.
45. Notice also the similarity to O'Connor's 'Judgement Day' story, which in the 1963 version had the title 'Getting Home'.
46. *Mystery and Manners*, pp. 117 and 168.
47. Ibid., p. 178.
48. Ibid., p. 204.
49. O'Connor, Flannery, *Collected Stories*, (New York: Farrar, Straus & Giroux, 1980), pp. 445-82, hereafter cited in the text as *CS*.
50. The characters here and their relations are reminiscent of the situation in O'Connor's novel *The Violent Bear It Away* (1955) with humanist Rayber and his son Bishop trying to 'save' Tarwater from his back-woods grandfather's Old Testament attitudes. Indeed, in a letter to John Hawkes, O'Connor called Rufus Johnson 'one of Tarwater's terrible cousins' (*HB*, 456).
51. *Mystery & Manners*, p. 79.
52. Ibid., p. 68.
53. Ibid., p. 153.

The Critical Perspective

Criticism and Aesthetics: The Status of the Example

Hans Hauge

> The great critics do not contribute, they interrupt.
> (George Watson, *The Literary Critics*)

> O, la, la! the Aesthete!
> I've met one in the street ...
> I'm glad there's someone still who 'yearns'
> And dotes on Dowson and on Wilde.
> (Isis, 1922)

Criticism *versus* Aesthetics

George Watson, former Liberal MP, begins his *The Literary Critics* (1962) thus: 'the ultimate condition of a literature without criticism is one that modern England has happily never known'. His book bears the subtitle 'A Study of English Descriptive Criticism'. He divides criticism into three kinds. The oldest he calls legislative criticism which he identifies with rhetoric. The second is theoretical criticism or literary aesthetics. It began when Hobbes turned to the study of the creative act itself instead of the nature of poetry. 'By the eighteenth century, aesthetics is a mania among the English'.[1] This came to a stop, he claims, with Coleridge. The English abandoned aesthetics, and hence theoretical criticism, to the Germans. Aesthetics surfaced again with Pater and Wilde. The last kind is descriptive criticism, which is defined as 'the analysis of existing literary works'. The father of this type of criticism is John Dryden. It began as talk 'and survived as talk that someone has thought worth writing down'. Descriptive criticism is falsifiable. It is particular, and Watson elaborates, it is 'about one thing, a given text to which critic and reader may appeal equally for confirmation'. Criticism, further, presupposes an open society and Watson defends criticism against those who make the claim that it is inferior to or parasitical upon creative writing. Criticism is merely of another logical order than poetry. Watson concludes his first chapter by citing

Thomas Mann and Baudelaire to the effect that *Kunst wird Kritik* and *tous les grands poétes deviennent naturellement, fatalement, critiques.*

In Watson's historical scheme theoretical criticism or aesthetics belongs to the past or to the Germans. Descriptive criticism is certainly English. Watson was quite optimistic, since he was convinced that Marxist as well as the New Criticism had had their time. Watson's ideal critic was the poet-*cum*-critic; the poet who in a crisis in his career begins to write criticism 'to define more closely what he is about'. His final words are: 'At all events it will hardly do to belittle how much such crises of critical doubt and reappraisal have done for the awareness of Western Man'.

Watson here appears to be apologetic. It is true that criticism had been criticized in the late fifties. Watson himself mentions both T.S. Eliot's 'The Frontiers of Criticism'[2] and Helen Gardner's 'The Limits of Criticism', both from 1956.

Three years after Watson's book William Wimsatt wrote in the Introduction to a collection of essays, *Hateful Contraries*, about the existence in America of a movement against criticism or even an emancipation from it. Wimsatt refers to the New Amateurism as that which began as a campaign in newpapers by what he calls the school of anti-criticism or 'the old-guard resistence to criticism in America'.[3]

René Wellek voiced similar concerns. In 1961 he wrote: 'The New Criticism, and actually any criticism, is today on the defensive'.[4] If criticism was on the defensive what was it defending itself against? What was criticism trying to preserve? In Watson's case surely theoretical criticism or aesthetics was no threat, neither were Marxist historicism nor New Criticism. Watson's enemy was method. He favoured a wise eclecticism.

Anyone, indeed, who supposes that there is one method apt to every critical adventure must be vastly underestimating the immense variety of the thousands of documents called English literature. There could be no one way.[5]

On this premise he attacks every attempt to subsume the individual, particular, singular work under general categories. Criticism should be essentially concerned with particular concrete texts: 'with the example'. Watson's book created some controversy because he was so critical of F.R. Leavis. He quotes the following from Leavis:

No treatment of poetry is worth much that does not keep very close to the concrete: there lies the problem of method ... In dealing with the individual poets the rule of the critic is, or should (I think) be, to work as much as possible in terms of particular analysis.[6]

Watson in fact agreed with Leavis; he just did not think Leavis actually did keep close to the concrete in practice.

Helen Gardner said pretty much the same as Watson in her lecture 'The Limits of Criticism'. Here she praised the English critic Mary Lascelles for leaving 'her reader with no theory, no scheme of thought, but with a sense of the great tides of thought and feeling which swirl through the play'.[7] She quotes Dr. Johnson's words that the conclusion is that there is no conclusion. Helen Gardner defended openness and fluidity. Both Watson and Gardner agreed that the purpose of criticism is, in Watson's words, discrimination and judgment, and in Gardner's, evaluation. This would also be Wimsatt's and Wellek's idea of criticism. In his 'The Frontiers of Criticism' from 1956 Eliot emphasized how he now considered understanding and enjoyment to be the purpose of criticism whereas his attack upon impressionistic criticism in 'The Function of Criticism' from 1926 held the elucidation of works of art and the correction of taste to be criticism's main goal. He warned against the tendency to place too much emphasis upon understanding, for then 'we are in the danger of slipping from understanding to mere explanation. We are in danger of pursuing criticism as if it was a science, which it never can be'.[8] Eliot of course alludes to the distinction between *Verstehen* and *Erklären*.

It is now possible on the basis of what I have quoted from Watson, Gardner, Wimsatt, Wellek and Eliot to form some sort of an idea of the dangers facing criticism in the late fifties. All seemed to agree to its being threatened by something: amateurism on the one hand, and science, concepts, and method on the other. All agreed that the purpose of criticism was some kind of judgement, evaluation or discrimination, and finally that criticism should deal with particular, individual, singular texts. Several saw aesthetics as the one potential threat to criticism. By the end of the decade, in 1960, Gadamer published *Wahrheit und Methode*. Hermenuetics was as critical of aesthetics and method as English descriptive criticism always had been.

I.A. Richards's *Principles of Literary Criticism* from 1924 opened with a repudiation of all aesthetics. Richards did not believe in a distinct kind of 'mental activity present in what are called æsthetic experiences' nor in something of the nature of a 'peculiar æsthetic value' inherent in the object. Works of art, Richards contended, did not possess qualities but they caused effects. Richards, like almost all Anglo-American New Critics, was also an apologist for the value of poetry against the threats of popular culture, mass culture or commercialism. 'We have not yet fathomed the more sinister potentialities of the cinema and the loud-speaker', he said. Richards, in short, wanted to 'habilitate' the critic — in 1924. Both he and Eliot were more rigid, scientific and principled then than later, because they were also fighting the aesthetes or neoaesthetic so-called girl-men or sun-children that swarmed all over Oxford in the twenties. The anti-aesthetic attitude, which pervades Richards, is almost a constant in Anglo-American criticism. John Crowe Ransom commenced his famous essay 'Criticism as Pure Specula-tion' with these words: 'A chasm, perhaps an abyss, separates the critic and the aesthetician'; yet Ransom's intention was to bridge the gap. In his book, *The Verbal Icon,* from 1953, Wimsatt stated explicitly that he had undertaken the role of 'defending the domain of poetry and poetics from the encircling (if friendly) arm of the general aesthetician'.[9] Northrop Frye continued the tradition in his *Anatomy of Criticism.* Aesthetics, he said in a foot-note, should

get out from philosophy, as psychology has already done. Most philosophers deal with aesthetic questions only as a set of analogues to their logical and meta-physical views.[10]

Even today the critical attitude towards aesthetics seems to have continued in Paul de Man and Terry Eagleton's writings against aesthetic ideology and we find it in an anthology about postmodern culture which is also identified with the anti-aesthetic.

Perhaps with the exception of Northrop Frye much of what I have said and many of the statements I have quoted appear terribly dated. It is as if I have been talking about a lost world. Yet it was that world of literary criticism I first met in the late sixties and early seventies. So, it is in many ways a world I have lost. Going back and re-reading Eliot, Richards, Leavis, and Wimsatt has been like being on a *recherche du temps perdu.* One feels slightly nostalgic reading it. Many of the quotes are no more than five or ten years older than, say, some of Derrida's first influential texts. Some of them are contemporaneous with some of Jakobson's. Who, today, could seriously and honestly claim, with Eliot, that the purpose of criticism is 'to promote the understanding and enjoyment of literature'? Or to judge, evaluate, discriminate and correct taste? However much we publicly regret that we do not have any values or that we need values, no-one, I am sure, would go to literature or literary criticism to find them. Yet evaluation was the business, and the only business of criticism from Richards to the New Critics. The only reason why one bothered to explicate, understand, eluci-date and analyse was in order to criticize: to judge — not to judge texts as such but to judge poetry.

We still use the word criticism but we no longer identify it with judgement. We have become critical of judgement; we critique judgement. Contemporary criticism is a critique of the idea of judgement. Most of the critics I have mentioned were on the defensive. They all perceived criticism to be under threat. Has criticism always been threatened? Is that, perhaps, its mode of existence? The threats were, as far as one can guess, aestheticism, impressionism, method, theory, amateurism, and mass-culture. What happened between the late fifties and the late sixties? Why have we given up evaluation, judgement, and even defences of criticism? For literary criticism has not, on the whole, become methodical and scientific. It could not have been linguistics and structuralism that constituted the enemy to these people. Part of the change, I think, has something to do with the status of the example. Literary criticism no longer deals with the concrete, particular, individual text. Neither does aesthetics. The example never played any role in aesthetics. Despite the lip-service much aesthetic theory pays to the particular and the singular; however much followers of Adorno say that an aesthetic thought is an oxymoron because thought subsumes the object under general categories (Eagleton: 'But if thought is conceptual, and so general, how can "aesthetic thought" be anything but an oxymoron?'); the individual, concrete, particular, singular, unique literary text has disappeared; it is simply no longer interesting.

Watson referred to the immense variety of those one thousand documents called 'English literature'. Here we are at the heart of the matter. Watson could be fairly confident in 1962 because that immense variety only comprised a thousand documents. Only a thousand. The thousand even had a name: English literature. Not only have the one thousand documents become many thousands, they have also lost their name. The text in general, the generalized text, is nameless and uncountable. The concrete text has become general. Why undertake textual analysis, close reading, explication or elucidation of the text when the work of art has become text — when the text is without interest?

Let me illustrate this loss of the example with an example — with a tang of nostalgia. I am conjuring up a world of literary criticism which is (well) lost. Once upon a time literary critics had these problems:

Thomas Hardy, for example

Richard Blackmur was one of the New Critics who was rather difficult to characterize. He both belonged and didn't. In Stanley Edgar Hyman's classic study from 1955, *The Armed Vision: A Study in the Methods of Modern*

Literary Criticism, Blackmur was described as a critic who tended to 'use on each work the special technique it seems to call for'.[11] He always used concrete examples. Blackmur himself defined criticism as 'the formal work of an amateur' to express his conviction, which he shared with many others, that criticism can never be a science. Yet it could and must have principles, so he also said that he wanted criticism to be

constantly confronted with examples of poetry, and I want it so for the very practical purpose of assisting in pretty immediate appreciation of the use, meaning and value of the language in that particular poetry.[12]

Here is respect for the example, for poetry and particularity. Let us see him pratice then.

Blackmur's *Form and Value in Poetry* (1957) begins as follows:

Both for those who enjoy the bulk of Thomas Hardy's poems and for those whose genuine enjoyment of a few poems is almost overcome by a combination of depression and dismay at the bulk, the great need is some sort of canon — a criterion more for exclusion than for judgement.[13]

Many things are taken for granted here. First that there are readers of Thomas Hardy, second that these readers can be divided into two groups. There exist readers who enjoy Hardy's poems and he appeals to his readers who could all see how great the need was for a canon; a criterion of exclusion. I wonder if I could have done anything but quote this. Imagine that I had started this essay, now, today, even to professional critics and aestheticians in a similar vein? If English literature still consists of, say, a thousand documents, then Hardy's poems — he wrote around a thousand — form only a tiny fraction of these thousand documents. Let me postpone my further comments and add some other Hardy examples. In 1958 there was a Johns Hopkins Poetry Festival — evidently quite an event. One lecture was by Mark van Doren on the poetry of Thomas Hardy. The fact that it took place at Johns Hopkins intrigues me somewhat. Eight years later there was another — not festival but conference — on the human sciences at Hopkins. In 1958 the big names were MacLeish, Marianne Moore, John Crowe Ransom, e.e.cummings, Robert Frost, and Blackmur; in 1966 the big names were Lacan, Barthes, Derrida, Girard with de Man and Hillis Miller in the audience. Something happened between the late fifties and the late sixties. No one talked about Hardy's poems eight years after; but they did in '58.

Van Doren — poet-critic-educator — also discussed the large number of Hardy poems. I enter his text here:

the modern reader cannot do so either [i.e. arrange his poems in a rational order] nor can the modern critic decide with readiness which poems of Hardy's are the best, let alone the most characteristic. No poet more stubbornly resists selection.[14]

Van Doren takes for granted that a modern critic will want to decide which poems are the best. He even knows there is a modern reader of Hardy's poems who would like to know which are the best.

Finally I turn to F.R. Leavis, 1952, comparing three poems — one of them by Hardy — with the intention of showing why Hardy was better than, in this case, Alexander Smith and Emily Brontë, because that was the whole idea of criticism. Hardy had, Leavis concluded, a 'greater advantage in reality'.[15] If so, even if he had this greater advantage, we have ceased discussing which of Hardy's poems are his best. The discussion smacks too much of Matthew Arnold's 'the best that has been said and thought'. Let us leave Hardy and Hopkins, November 1958, and move south-west from Baltimore to Bloomington and back in time to spring. We will find Roman Jakobson, the Russian, talking about poetics, yes, and linguistics while Richards was present.

From I enjoy Hardy to I like Ike

From Jakobson's famous talk — 'Poetics and Linguistics' — we remember just one example plus of course six linguistic functions. We have learnt from it how to describe poetry phenomenologically and structurally. Poetry, for Blackmur, was the meaning of meaning. For MacLeish and Richards it didn't mean; it was. For Jakobson poetry could be visualized with the image of projecting the axis of selection into the axis of combination. This was hardly the formal work of an amateur, as Blackmur said about the critic's work. Two years earlier Eliot had sermonized at the University of Minnesota: 'We are in danger even of pursuing criticism as if it was a science' and 'we need to be on guard against the purely explanatory'. The same year saw Ike's re-election and the Montgomery bus boycott — the beginning of Afro-American blues criticism. The pastor there dwelt in his sermons on examples taken from Socrates, Aristotle, Shakespeare, Hegel and Gandhi — he had a dream, was a Harvard Ph.D. and we remember him as Martin Luther King.

Who doesn't remember, too, by heart, Jakobson's example: 'I like Ike'? This was poetry anno 1958 — probably more discussed by literary theorists in the years that followed than 'Arma virumque cano'. Eliot had said, just after World War II, that whatever definition of a classic we agree upon it must not exclude Virgil. 'I like Ike' is a modern classic. Jakobson used examples; he stayed close to the individual text but of course he subsumed the individual under general categories. He did not judge, discriminate nor evaluate. The example had lost its function the moment poetics defined the poetic function because the poetic function was no longer confined to poetry.

Up in Toronto, Canada, Northrop Frye's *Anatomy of Criticism* was already beginning to be the model for a sweet, progressive science of literature. The most controversial thing about Frye's whole theory was his rejection of value-judgements:

The demonstrable value-judgement is the donkey's carrot of literary criticism, and every new critical fashion, such as the current fashion for elaborate rhetorical analysis [he means New Criticism], has been accompanied by a belief that criticism had finally devised a definitive technique for separating the excellent from the less excellent; but this always turns out to be an illusion of the history of taste.[16]

Frye, however, had examples, indeed many. He did not do close readings but the opposite: he praticised the stand-back method. He classified, categorized, subsumed, generalized. If Jakobson and Frye can be said to have judged — in the Kantian sense — they did so by means of the determining judgement, not the reflexive or aesthetic one, even though Frye took all his concepts from literature itself. Perhaps Jakobson's linguistics was derived from poetics, too. In George Watson's terms it could seem as though both Frye and Jakobson had returned to theoretical or aesthetic criticism; but how can we not describe them both as descriptive, inductive? Indeed, we cannot but do so, but they did not 'do criticism' despite of Frye's use of the word; and they were not, incidentally, or is it incidental, English.

Were they aestheticians? Was criticism, in other words, being replaced in the English-speaking world by aesthetics?

Frye observes:

Of course literature is only one of the many arts, but this book is compelled to avoid the treatment of aesthetic problems outside of poetics. Every art, however, needs its own critical organization, and poetics will form part of aesthetics as soon as aesthetics becomes the unified criticism of all the arts instead of whatever it is now.[17]

Frye was foreseeing a future where aesthetics would become the same as criticism. It depends, of course, on what we mean by aesthetics now, whatever it is now, and was then. Is there in both Jakobson and Frye a kind of mimeticism or even naturalism? Frye's categories and genres and modes are somehow natural, grow like nature, originate in nature and mime nature; and Jakobson after all rejected the theory of the arbitrary sign — and would this not be an instance of aesthetic ideology in Paul de Man's sense? Further, it could easily be shown that the focus upon the message for its own sake is much closer to Kantian disinterestedness than to semiotics.

Frye and Jakobson were contemporaries of Wimsatt (who criticized them both), Brooks, Blackmur and the rest, yet we feel closer to the first two in time and temperament. None of them showed any sign of defensiveness or threat. They were fairly offensive and confident. Literature had lost its borders in Jakobson's theory. Just about anything could be poetic or aesthetic. This was what he had brought with him from his encounters with the Prague avantgarde poets. Poetry was *labile*, but the poetic function was *stable*, objective or at least phenomenological; but it could settle everywhere — any linguistic act could become dominated by the poetic function. If literature had become limitless or borderless in Jakobson, it lost its voice with Frye. It became mute. George Watson related how criticism began with and as talk. Were we to characterize criticism as a genre, talk would be its radical of presentation, to use Frye's words. If criticism is basically or originally talk then there is something dialogical about it. I am aware that dialogue or dialogic is an honorific word today. It was significant for Watson that the first piece of genuine English criticism was a dialogue in form — he was thinking of John Dryden. It has kept this characteristic in Frye's theory. Criticism for him is also talk, though not, I should think, in Watson's sense. Frye says that criticism talks while literature is silent, mute, voiceless. Without criticism literature would have no voice. It gives literature its voice. Frye was methodical and a former methodist preacher. Much method and little truth? But did he have any followers apart from certain Canadian poets and then Margaret Atwood? Could Frye be applied? He probably could and was, but the result always turned out to be unfruitful, disappointing and mechanical — like all structuralism: Only Frye could apply Frye. However, the single most significant aspect about *The Anatomy,* is that *it is itself an anatomy*. It is an example of one of the four prose genres which the text itself established. It is even the best modern example of an anatomy — Frye's word for a Menippean satire. *The Anatomy of Criticism* is literature. And Frye's precursor is Oscar Wilde. When criticism somehow lost contact with the example it became an example or literature itself.

Criticism in the classroom

Critic, novelist, and professor of American literature, Malcolm Bradbury introduced an anthology from 1970. He called it 'The State of Criticism Today'. What was the state like when Bradbury looked back on the sixties? First:

Today any devotee of bookshops will know that there is probably more new criticism appearing than new creative writing; and criticism has become a discipline, like sociology or biology, the skills and techniques of which are in perpetual transmission through the classrooms of schools and universities.[18]

Indeed, yes — in the sixties criticism entered the classrooms. There was more criticism in the class than class in criticism. Women, too, entered the classroom and were exposed to the perpetual transmission of techniques and skills — they came, the women, before there was an active women's movement. Thousands of students began reading the thousand documents. Did they learn the skills and techniques?

The English still lived, said Bradbury, in the (cold) climate of New Criticism. We don't, most certainly today. There was a proliferation of description and interpretation, rather than judgement. Then Bradbury refers to a rather interesting statement which Malcolm Cowley made when commenting on the American scene right after World War II. Cowley had said that 'many of the new literary energies were to be found not so much in creative writing as in criticism'. This could be a comment which would be accurate today, too; but just when did this process actually begin? It is difficult to say. In England, at least, the tendency can be traced back to Matthew Arnold and certainly to Oscar Wilde. This tendency was, in fact, what Eliot objected to in the twenties in his essay on the function of criticism. I have a feeling that this is where we are going to end: that literary energy is found in criticism or in theory — also today — also in the classroom. Bradbury goes on:

Cowley saw this situation as an almost unprecedented cultural evolution; a new era of classicism in which the old desire for the literary academy has been institutionalised on campus.[19]

Bradbury relates how the critic had outstripped the creator and finally

this produces the paradox that, when many critics are claiming that conditions of literary production are declining and that the age of the book is over, they hardly seem to share the sense of literary concern. They hardly need to: the audience for *criticism* is assured.[20]

This was what Ransom called Criticism Inc.

There is no need for us to complain. We have an audience. Criticism, or theory, or aesthetics, the words don't really matter, have taken over the literary energies of not only the producers but also the readers. We still live in this era of classicism. So we don't need to worry much about whether there is a text in our class. Bradbury was slightly worried and why? Precisely because the 'critical analysis then tends to lose its point of reference in literary texts'. I believe this sums up the situation. Criticism or theory has lost its point of reference. This point of reference is the example. There are no examples to refer to — there are too many — like Hardy's poems. We have no criteria for selection or exclusion. We don't want to select let alone exclude. Exclude who, whose, what? Why not? Because selection and exclusion have become ethical categories instead of critical, evaluative aesthetic. At least they appear to be ethical but are in fact moralistic.

Criticism lost its point of reference the moment we began including. process can also be called bursting the canon; but there is another interpret all this: literature isn't dead, it's just that a new genre h into existence. We have seen this happening before. Did it not take at least two hundred years or more before the novel was inclu erature?

So much for the state of criticism in 1970. My final Jakobson and Frye is Terry Eagleton; but first this:

Literature has become institutionalized as much audience for it is as assured as criticism's. This is nothir It has always, nearly always, been like that in the West school there would have been no literature. Homer transmitted in the classrooms since I don't know whe exist, they would have disappeared. The era of cl room — and outside are the romance and the ro beyond or above sits what Curtius with Walte Beautiful'.

So one wonders how radical it really is wh Barthes defined literature as what is taught i Catholic like Terry Eagleton surely knows how powerful it can be. We can drop, h

are
can
exam
way
as ha
cultura
more a

What, t

once and for all [does he mean for all?] the illusion that the category 'literature' is 'objective', in the sense of being eternally given and immutable. Anything can be literature, and anything which is regarded as unalterably and unquestionably literature — Shakespeare for example — can cease to be literature.[21]

Shakespeare, for example.

I began by quoting George Watson to the effect that England had never known the ultimate condition of a literature without criticism: now, or then, or when — let's say now: England and many other nations have criticism without literature — aesthetics without examples. All literature can cease to be literature, even Shakespeare; so perhaps literature becomes literature because it can cease to be literature; but what happens to literature after it has ceased to be literature? Is there a kind of limbo for it? Can it return? Or does it mean total oblivion and annihilation? I never thought death had undone so many. Of course literature lives because it is maintained by the institution; and the institution can resurrect literature from the dead. If anything can be literature then even Terry Eagleton's statement that anything can cease to be literature is or can become literature, if it hasn't already become it. Eagleton can say as he does; he can unmask an illusion because he is inside the institution. His text is a testimony to the literary institution's power and is made possible by the institutionalization of criticism.

My final example(s)

When there is a proliferation of theories, says Hillis Miller in *Hawthorne and History*, 'the relation of "theory" to "example" is fundamentally changed'. The many conflicting theories mean that theory 'tends to become a primary means of access to the works read. These works now tend to become re-defined as "examples" demonstrating the productive effectiveness of this that theory'. These examples, he goes on,

no longer so often drawn from an established canon arranged in traditional nical ways, for example by genre and historical period. The result is that the ples are likely to be subordinated to theory [...] What is taught is a universal f reading [...] not the works of an agreed-upon canon read in canonical ways ing established meanings and as transmitting from the past agreed-upon values. The place of those established meanings and enshrined values is d more taken by theory itself.[22]

en, does Hillis Miller do? He says: 'The example I have chosen is

canonical'. His example is Hawthorne's 'The Minister's Black Veil'. He draws his example from the established canon, now, when universality has just been said to reside in ways of reading and when established meanings and enshrined values belong to theory. If Hillis Miller is a deconstructive critic, and if deconstruction is criticism, then we are in a position where we can describe the relation between example and deconstruction. Hillis Miller reads canonical works in a noncanonical way instead of doing what most avantgarde critics do today: they read non-canonical works in a traditional way. Deconstruction has not lost its point of reference in the text. It hasn't even put the canon into question. This sounds like a paradise lost, paradise regained story. Theory has found and made contact with the text again. Hillis Miller's book, *The Linguistic Moment*, even has an analysis of poems by — guess who — Thomas Hardy. And Harold Bloom was always a faithful defender of the unrivalled greatness of Hardy, the poet. It is also true, however, that theory has become the primary access to the example. Hence these examples never meet us unattended or unaccompanied. They never come alone. We read example plus theory. Heidegger and Hölderlin or Heidegger's Hölderlin; Heidegger and Van Gogh's shoes; De Man and Rousseau; Hartman and Wordsworth; Hillis Miller and George Eliot or George Eliot because of Miller. The question is whether all this can be called literary criticism. It seems to me the situation or the state of criticism now is something like this:

First we have theory plus example. Second we have autonomous literary criticism with no contact with the example. Oscar Wilde's critic as artist has been finally realized. In such criticism the poem, as Wilde said, is just the occasion for good, creative criticism. Criticism can be more aesthetically fascinating than so-called contemporary creative writing. As Wilde said: 'The tendency of creation is to repeat itself. It is to the critical instinct that we owe each new school that springs up'. Third we have a new kind of cultural criticism; its novelty stems from the combination of theory and old cultural criticism. In this kind of criticism — which includes many individuals and schools — literature as such has ceased to be the exemplary. Literature as such is regarded as too exclusive a category. What goes on in most literature departments can only be described as cultural criticism. Texts are treated as culture and culture as a text. The literary critic is, as Harold Bloom has recently said, surrounded by professors of hip hop and that garbage called cultural criticism.

What is needed in the future is a new deal. If literary studies develop into cultural studies, literature will really cease to exist. Literary studies and cultural studies are two incompatible paradigms. The poetry-lover confronted with Hardy's poems needed a criterion for exclusion and selection; we need similar criteria in literary studies for exclusion. However, the concept of culture may also cease to exist. Many things indicate that culture as concept is being replaced by the concept civilization. It is too early to say what the role of literature will be in the civilization studies to come. At least the notion of civilization reduces the many thousands of cultures to five world civilizations of which Western civilization is one of the examples.

What happened to judgement and evaluation in all this? None of the three kinds of criticism does it. Can such acts of evaluation simply disappear? Of course not. We perform them all the time. Everyone performs them. Listen to how young students talk about music and film. They do nothing but judge, but they do it outside the classroom. The New Critics excluded and selected texts by means of aesthetic criteria. They knew perfectly well that when one performs an act of evaluation the act is not cognitive. It tells us nothing about the work of art only something about the person who evaluates. There have not existed aesthetic criteria since aesthetics was invented in Germany in the late eighteenth century. Aesthetic selection or exclusion — think of the Hardy example — was replaced by ethical selection and inclusion. Why was this slave narrative excluded; why this woman's diary; why this early Trinidadian novel? The old New Critic would have said because it isn't good. The new cultural critic will respond it isn't good to exclude at all whilst chanting 'ho ho ho Western Culture's got to go' — a song they sang at Stanford and are now singing in Algeria. Evaluation has left the institution. Is there evaluation in this class? No, but we do it outside. Why do we evaluate? Because acts of evaluation create community. This was what Arnold and Leavis both knew. They knew that evaluation is a social act, an act of collaboration — more than an aesthetic, ethical or cognitive act. Leavis once said:

For standards (which are not of the order of the measures in the Weights and Measures Office) are "there" only in and by the collaborative process that criticism essentially is.[23]

Why have we excluded this collaborative process from the institution?

Notes

1. George Watson, *The Literary Critics*, 2nd edn., (Harmondsworth: Penguin, 1973), pp. 1-9.
2. T.S. Eliot, 'The Frontiers of Criticism' in *On Poetry and Poets*, (London: Faber and Faber, 1969); Helen Gardner, 'The Limits of Criticism' in *The Business of Criticism*,

(1959) (Glasgow: Oxford University Press, 1966). This book Donald Hannah told us to read in 1967.

3. William K. Wimsatt Jr., *Hateful Contraries*, (Lexington: University of Kentucky Press, 1966), pp. xiv and xvii.
4. René Wellek, *Concepts of Criticism*, (New Haven: Yale University Press, 1967), p. 6.
5. George Watson, op. cit., p. 219.
6. Ibid., p. 200. Watson quotes from Leavis's *Revaluation*.
7. The play in question is *Measure for Measure*, Helen Gardner, op. cit., p. 152.
8. T.S. Eliot, op. cit., p. 115.
9. William K. Wimsatt, *The Verbal Icon*, (London: Methuen, 1970), p. 221.
10. Northrop Frye, *The Anatomy of Criticism*, (New York: Athenemu, 1968), p. 357 n.
11. (New York: Vintage Books, 1995), p. 197.
12. Ibid., p. 214.
13. R.P. Blackmur, *Form and Value in Modern Poetry*, (New York: Doubleday Anchor Books, 1957), p. 1.
14. Mark Van Doren, 'The Poems of Thomas Hardy' in *Four Poets on Poetry* (ed.) Don Cameron Allen, (Baltimore: The Johns Hopkins Press, 1959), p. 84.
15. F.R. Leavis, 'Reality and Sincerity' in *A Selection from Scrutiny*, (Cambridge: Cambridge University Press, 1968), p. 251.
16. Northrop Frye, op. cit., p. 20.
17. Ibid., p. 15.
18. Malcolm Bradbury, 'Introduction: The State of Criticism Today' in *Contemporary Criticism 12*, Stratford-Upon-Avon Studies, (London: Edward Arnold, 1970), p. 12.
19. Ibid., p. 19.
20. Ibid.
21. Terry Eagleton, *Literary Theory*, (Oxford: Basil Blackwell, 1983), p. 10.
22. J. Hillis Miller, *Hawthorne and History: Defacing It*, (Cambridge, USA: Basil Blackwell, 1991), p. 47.
23. F.R. Leavis, 'Mr Pryce-Jones, the British Council and British Culture' in *A Selection from Scrutiny*, op. cit., p. 183.

On the Dynamics of Harold Bloom's Agonistic Canon

Lars Ole Sauerberg

> Whatever the Western Canon is, it is
> not a program for social salvation.[1]

To Harold Bloom canon formation is 'ultimately a society's choices of texts for perpetuation and study',[2] and in this there seems to be no basis for quarrel between Bloom and the great majority of canon defenders; but with Bloom's principle of agonistic misreading there are certainly differences in the premises that lead us to this conclusion, since the canon is essentially an *'achieved anxiety'*.[3] The literary tradition in Bloom's perspective is not a handing down of similarities and friendly borrowing from past masters. On the contrary, it is brought about as the result of fierce fights for self-assertion on the part of younger writers in relation to their forebears. In Bloom's critical universe the stakes are ruggedly existential in a Darwinian struggle for survival, and the tradition-making struggle is no more merciful and humane than the rest of creation in a Darwinian world:

Out of the strong comes forth strength, even if not sweetness, and when strength has imposed itself long enough, then we learn to call it tradition, whether we like it or not.[4]

Bloom does not find in the setting up of the canon a process or a result with wide-ranging and positive significance for something vaguely known as society, culture or mankind. When writers gain for themselves a place in the canon — which anyway it takes at least two generations to determine[5] — it is a very private and selfish showdown with a beloved but also paradoxically hated precursor. To the reader the only ethical value of the canon is its constant reminding of the imposition of limits,[6] forcing the reader ultimately to face the final limit — of death.[7] This is one reason why Bloom calls himself an 'elegiac' critic in *The Western Canon* (1994), the other, the rather more readily appreciable one, is that he sees himself as the last agonist taking his stand against approaches to literature making it serve ends different from the aesthetic.

Bloom, however, shares with less radical canon theorists a concept of the valid literary tradition as an extremely fastidious selection in terms of a process which is dialectical within an overall logic of spiral circularity. Bloom is metonymical in terms of ever oblique contiguity, whereas Eliot is metaphorical with intertextual substitution as the principle both of his own writings (explicit and implicit reference and allusion). Eliot strives to define a tradition of objectively defined textuality — a classical tradition — purified of personal elements, whereas Bloom arrives at a — romantic — tradition characterized exactly by the presence of productive personalities strong enough to assert themselves by their violent and patricidal individualism. So, according to Bloom's own dogma, by his very opposition to Eliot, he may be considered his true heir.[8]

The number of poets to have merited the sustained critical interest of Bloom makes up an exclusive canonical list. Compared with the astounding scope of Frye's literary frame of reference, Bloom's steady and narrow focusing most recently on Shakespeare and previously on the romantics proper — Blake and Shelley having both been given book-length attention — and two romantic modernists — Yeats and Stevens, also treated at considerable length — appears to ignore many of the standard major as well as almost all the standard minor writers who go into conventional literary history.

Bloom's literary history is a history consisting of unique individuals and unique texts related paradoxically to each other by their intertextual tensions, producing in effect an inevitable sadness or melancholy, an anxiety deriving, in the examplary case of Thomas Mann in relation to Goethe, from the knowledge that 'one cannot write a novel without remembering another novel'.[9] Artistic creation thus contains an enormous negative charge gathered by the artist's terrible anxiety of being smothered by his forebears, and his equally terrible urge to destroy them. One is entitled to query where the pleasure traditionally associated with art is in this negative and gloomy approach to literary art. Only very sporadically does Bloom admit to joy or pleasure in connection with poetry, and then only as a corollary of defence in the Freudian sense of the term: '[T]he beautiful necessity of defense'.[10] In his description of the dynamics of poetic response, Bloom sees the encounter of a poet with the precursor poem as a process which 'takes the poet back beyond the pleasure principle to the decisive initial encounter and response that began him'[11]. The 'high unpleasure' or the 'more difficult pleasure'[12] characteristic of the canonical text is derived for the investment into it of its author's 'cognitive acuity, linguistic energy, and power of invention' which 'fuse in an ontological passion that is a capacity for joy'.[13] As the final, difficult and authentic pleasure,[14] it gives to the idea of literary pleasure another dimension than the mere appreciation of harmonious sound pattern or even the Coleridgean unity-in-variety condition. The nature of pleasure or joy in connection with literature is hence something that Bloom never really considers to be a subject of its own, but always integral to the very canonicity of a given work. The object of pleasure, poetic beauty, appears as the presence of the structural order emerging from the application of an assumed interpretative pattern. In the early criticism, the appreciation of Blake's apocalyptic endeavour gives to Blake's works such beauty,[15] later on beauty is seen to depend on the extent to which the principle of strength applies.

Bloom's focus is almost invariably on the semantic side of the poetic text to the exclusion of its formal aspects. Poetry, to Bloom, is constituted by what a more conventional poetics would call the content or substance aspect.[16] In the early work he follows Emerson — who in this respect is in agreement with Shelley, Wordsworth and Coleridge — in suggesting that the poetic is a question of the nature of the idea seeking expression. Bloom quotes Emerson to the effect that

it is not meters, but a meter-making argument that makes a poem, — a thought so passionate and alive that like the spirit of a plant or an animal it has an architecture of its own, and adorns nature with a new thing. The thought and the form are equal in the order of time, but in the order of genesis the thought is prior to the form.[17]

The example adduced is a sweeping interpretation of what in Hardy constitutes this metre-making argument, that is, a 'skeptical lament for the hopeless incongruity of ends and means in all human acts ... the truest name for the human condition is simply that it is loss'.[18] Bloom, despite his insistence on the 'idea-ness' of the poem, never really engages with the problem of the phenomenology of poetic constructs. The closest he comes is in the Peirce-inspired rejection of New Criticism supposedly favouring an approach to poems as monads, whereas a triad concept, with reference to Peirce's suggestion of a sign relation termed 'thirdness', being a relational mediation between a 'sign, its object, and the interpreting thought',[19] is much more appropriate, since to Bloom a poem is a 'mediating process between itself and a previous poem', a 'relational event',[20] which is interpretation itself.[21] Bloom's view of the mode of existence in a literary work of art is, then, if we consider Wellek and Warren's Ingarden-derived structure of norms, the distillation of New Criticism poetics, different in so far as the work of art can never be made to stand still for the observation of a specific norm level. The poem is a troped rendering of an idea, the trope however being the rhetorical abstraction of a poetic image.[22] As soon as the image is taken in by the reading consciousness, in the act of interpretation that the act of reading necessarily is, the image-realized-as-trope changes into a psychic defence. In *The Western Canon* the image, in the light of the strong focus on Shakespeare, appears in the *Gestalt* of the character, since according to Bloom the achievement of originality is most difficult and therefore most important in

everything that matters most: representations of human beings, the role of the memory in cognition, the range of metaphor in suggesting new possibilities for language.[23]

However, Bloom has not succumbed to any A.C. Bradleyan approach to literature, but his critical attention has been directed to the lodging of the image potential in character, which is different from reading literature (drama) as the verbal transscription of human action.[24]

Recognition of an image as a reaction to an earlier image in the act of reading — the poet's and the reader's — constitutes the moment of truth, the moment when the poem comes into its own. That moment is not to be considered any 'right' reading of a text, since there are no such right readings of texts, only strong and weak readings, but a reading imposing itself by its immediate strength, setting a whole system of texts in motion, as it were.

It follows that any discussion about influence must ignore not only issues that have to do with 'verbal resemblances between one poet and another'[25] but also the traditional tracing of motifs and themes that academic comparative criticism specializes in. The critic must dive down into what Bloom somewhat vaguely calls the 'depths'[26] which is, supposedly, more or less the subconscious — the Freudian id — where primal-scene love-and-hate battles are fought.[27]

It goes without saying that such an approach to literary history relies on a mediating critical consciousness different from the one able to make out the textual and conceptual similarities on which conventional literary history is based. The mediating critical consciousness in Bloomian literary history is one able to make out textual traces of resistance and opposition to other texts. This requires will to interpretation in terms of a scheme designed to bring out not only differences rather than similarities, but also of a nature that naturalizes such interpretation in a framework larger than literature itself, a framework within which literature can be read as a symptom of an ongoing, never-ending struggle for dominance and power. Such a framework Bloom has devised by a combination of psychoanalytic and kabbalistic concepts and terminology.

Although perhaps not his best book, *The Anxiety of Influence: A Theory of Poetry* from 1973 is Bloom's articulation of his central poetics, standing in the same kind of relation to both his theoretical and practical work as Frye's *The Great Code* does to his. Bloom's work prior to *The Anxiety of Influence* — the studies of Shelley (1959), Blake (1963 and Erdman 1965) and Yeats (1970) — points forward to it for a theoretical resolution, and it forms the matrix for what has followed, regarding his elaboration of the hermetic framework, in *A Map of Misreading* (1975) and *Kabbalah and Criticism* (1975),[28] and of his practical, interpretative criticism, of which *Wallace Stevens: The Poems of Our Climate* (1977) stands out as a singular triumphant critical achievement of a deliberately strong critic. With *The Western Canon* (1994) the focus is somewhat changed, but the lens remains the same. In this bid for twenty-six canonical writers, with Shakespeare as the central figure with whom all later writers have to struggle and by whom all previous writers are judged, Bloom makes clearer some of his main issues, and deliminates his ground against what he loosely and wryly terms the School of Resentment, which includes most structuralist and poststructuralist criticism.

Bloom's central distinction between weak and strong poets rests on an ability to decide the manner in which a poet has managed his anxiety of influence as 'creative misunderstanding'.[29] In a poet like Oscar Wilde, this anxiety is all too visible as the poet's consciousness of having absorbed and recycled the poetic past, and in the process lost his own personality, the net result, despite a show of idealization, being a sense of loss, of dilution. Strong poets — and they are the ones who make poetic history[30] — overcome their anxiety of influence by reacting against those supposed to be capable of exerting influence, in order to free themselves of any fetters whatsoever.[31] The main objective for strong poets is to create 'imaginative space'[32] for themselves, and this involves deliberate or instinctive evasion of influence, usually appreciable not as evasion but as opposition. By this logic, the study of poetic influence, which has to do with 'imaginative priority[33] that is the (strong) poet's will to creation, with due attention paid to the kind or degree of anxiety of influence, turns into the study of poetic misprision, involving the study of the 'life-cycle of the poet-as-poet'.[34]

That this complex argument is not without difficulties, even contradictions, I shall return to below, but first the term 'misprision' deserves
attention, since it is one of Bloom's key terms and in itself is a demonstration of a strong person's appropriation of a word away from its usual
line of derivative influence for his own — idiosynchratic — purposes.

'Misprision', according to the OED, is an Old French word ('mesprison')
meaning mistake or error, whence it has entered English legal language in
the sense of judicial misdemeanour, a failure of duty on the part of a public
official. In the special sense related to treason or felony, 'misprision of
treason' came to mean the concealment of a person's knowledge of treason-
able actions. In popular parlance the term took on the more general
meaning of 'mistake' or 'misunderstanding'. An obsolete sense of the term
is 'malformation of nature'. The OED lists as another, and archaic, sense of
the term, derived from a slightly different French root ('mespris'), 'contempt, scorn', or 'failure to appreciate or recognize as valuable'. No doubt
all these overtones appeal to a critic keen on tracing influence as anxious
anti-influence in terms of evasion and opposition, in other words as
treason — contemptuous or not — against a well-protected sense of literary
history as a process of imitation and adaptation.

Although constituted by Nietzsche's appropriation of the antithetical and
by Freud's theory of defence as analogous supports for the revisionary
ratios on which Bloom's elaboration on intra-poetic relations rely, there is
nonetheless a need for modification.[35] It is true that in the development of
his theory of poetic misprision in terms of radical revisionism, Bloom approaches the stance of Shelley — the subject of his first and in retrospect
tentative major study — attributing to poets — Shelley's *vates* or *hierophants*
— and to poetry more power than conceded by Nietzsche or Freud; but at
the same time Bloom considers the power of the imagination or phantas-
magoria exaggerated in their teachings. The reason is that Bloom finds
Nietzsche somewhat wide of the chosen mark by his idealism, for which
he wishes to substitute the literal, and in his preference for the rational,
which must yield place to divination. Indeed, even though Shelley is more
than just a hovering shadow in this situatedness of poets as strong literalists
with intuitive access to what in *The Anxiety of Influence* is still only vaguely
hinted at, there is no embracing of the romantic poet's neo-Platonic burning
fountain as the *ne plus ultra*. So Bloom's invocation of Nietzsche and Freud,
with a view to the antithetical and mechanisms of defence respectively, only
brings him to the point of highly tentative analogues, as he readily admits[36]
to the dynamics of the six revisionary ratios[37] — clinamen, tessera, kenosis,
daemonization, askesis, apophrades[38] — instrumental for the understanding

of intra-poetic relationships as influential anxiety. Bloom himself provides a capsule definition of the first five in the following manner:

For *clinamen* and *tessera* strive to correct or complete the dead, and *kenosis* and *daemonization* work to repress memory of the dead, but *askesis* is the contest proper, the match-to-the-death with the dead.[39]

The sixth ratio, *apophrades*, is then the return of the dead in the poetry of the living, to such an extent that it even appears as if the precursor imitates the later poet. In *A Map of Misreading*, the six ratios are correlated within a dialectic of revisionism in which the antithesis of 'limitation' and 'substitution' receive their synthesis in 'representation', a dialectical operation covering the relation between every successive pair of two ratios. To the six ratios correspond six (Freudian) psychic defences. Between, on the one side the revisionary ratios and their corresponding psychic defences and on the other the three dialectic pairs, we find the textual categories in which these are manifested, both described by the proper rhetorical trope — irony, synecdoche, metonymy, hyperbole/litotes, metaphor and metalepsis — and by the kind of imagery to which the tropes apply. 'What I have called "revisionary ratios" are tropes and psychic defenses, both and either, and are manifested in poetic imagery'.[40] It should be added that to complete Bloom's 'strong' appropriation of Freud we need to take into account that the process of poetic misprision is considered (almost) identical with the sublimation on the part of writers and readers of aggressive instincts.

Misprision in literary history is, however, a phenomenon with a double edge. On the part of the poet, misprision, the necessary revolt against the precursor, is experienced as a sin, in its rejection of an earlier authority.[41] No wonder that the 'ephebe' or the newcomer feels at a loss at what must be felt as treason of one most dear to him. Yet at the same time, looking beyond the personal situation of the individual poet, the commitment of misprision is a sign of health. In a kind of antithetical Darwinian process, the survival of the fittest poet is a matter not of adaptability but of the exact opposite: poetic survival is granted to the poet most able to stand out.

In Bloom's view, Freud is not a sufficiently strong 'poet' since it is the very nature of his notion of defence mechanisms that they provide a 'second chance'. Defence mechanisms are essentially remedial, taking the pressure out of primordial urges, thus always aiming at the restoration of a balance as a secondary stage. This goes right against Bloom's axiom that '[p]oets as poets cannot accept substitutions, and fight to the end to have their initial chance alone'.[42] Strong poets show their strength exactly in their intuitive bull's-eye hit. They do not need, indeed they scorn any attempt at rationalistic or trial-and-error workings-out of trajectories. Only the power of divination will suffice to provide the necessary condition for the strong poet to produce his literal 're'-creation.

Caught in an all too human propensity for defence reaction (Freud) and the intuitively realized need for refusing to let go into defence, the strong poet instinctively opposes (Nietzsche's antithesis) to subliminally defend his own being, thereby creating the necessary space. The ultimate point of opposition is death, in Hartman's phrase quoted by Bloom,[43] a natural priority opposed to spiritual authority.

In Bloom's view, the motive force in every new poet's effort is the rebellion against the necessity — the priority — of death — 'a poem is written to escape dying',[44] — later on modified into the 'final antagonist, which is not death but time and time's "it was"'.[45] This realized, the fight is foredoomed, since death will assert itself indiscriminately of poetic endeavour. The grandeur of Wordsworth's 'Immortality Ode' rests exactly in the persistence of its antithesis to death, and its comparative failure is in its assumption of the defence mechanism of successful sublimation, a characteristic it shares with its stronger precursor poem, Milton's 'Lycidas'.

Bloom's main tenet, then, is the assumption that a poet will inevitably try to rebel against the fact of death, the basic natural priority. This he will do by forcing the natural into the poetic. The success of the poet — his strength — is in his relative success of offering opposition to the existentially unavoidable without it petering out into sublimation — mere verse.

In mapping out the theoretical foundations, Bloom offers for illumination a capsule literary history, which, relying on an implicit cyclical perspective, again reminds the reader strongly of Shelley.

It is hardly surprising that Bloom turns to romantic poetry for this theory. On the one hand it provides him with a poetics — the distillation of which is in Shelley's 'Defence of Poetry' more than anywhere else[46] — which celebrates the intuitive leap of the specially gifted seer. On the other it forms the conceptual background to the theorizing of both Nietzsche and Freud, in Bloom's shape of things comparatively weak romantic latecomers, but useful for heuristic purposes. But one should not be led into the error of categorizing Bloom as a mere idolator of romanticism. Rather, romanticism is to be seen as an especially pedagogical example of the strong poets' rebellion, first and last against death.[47] The greatness of Wordsworth's 'Intimations of Immortality' ode is to be found in its high aim of attempting to negate what Hartman terms nature's priority, by the imposition of cultural authority. This is an impossible venture, doomed to failure, but marks will be given for trying hard. In Wordsworth's case the desperation stemming from the realization of the ultimate impossibility of merging nature with culture is added to by the circumstance that the ode not only attempts to evade death but also attempts to overcome the anxiety of influence from Milton's 'Lycidas', a poem which, according to Bloom, re-fuses even harder not to succumb to that arbiter between natural necessity and cultural possibility, sublimation.

The gist of Bloom's anxiety theory then, is to be found in a view of poetry as always more or less attempting to deny death, and not just in the trivial sense of a poem becoming 'immortal' by entering the literary canon. A degree of defence, as sublimation, is always present, because this is culture reacting against nature, and poetry, except for the very first poem ever written, reacts both in relation to the poet's awareness of death and in relation to earlier attempts at containing death, hence the anxiety of influence.

It is not romanticism as a period which is attractive to Bloom, but the rebellion against and the denial of the natural by insisting on its cultural transformation into an ideal merger — Hulme's derogatory 'circumambient gas' — which romanticism espouses. The greatness, the strength, is in the insistence and the ultimately ensuing tragedy of vast and irrevocable failure. Romanticism, in this sense of an existential attitude, not an epoch, is to be found throughout literary history, but with the progress of time as an increasingly diluted version of the essential struggle against nature, since the poet's reaction in terms of anxiety of influence will lead further and further away from the real thing. When Bloom deplores the weakening of English poetry[48] since the renaissance up through the enlightenment, romanticism, modernism and post-modernism, it is a regrettable but in-evitable fact in view of culture's, that is poetry's, accumulating and re-peatedly anxious evasion of nature. So poetry is bound to diminish in existential importance with time because increasingly weighed down by its past strength. In Bloom's view, then, the project of romanticism, as trendy modern critics would call it, was bound to fail, because the burden of the past cannot be shed but keeps on growing. The favourite romantic image of Prometheus, the giver of fire to mankind, must yield his place to blinded Oedipus, ignorant of the Sphinx as his muse.[49]

This defeatist view of cultural history with, presumably, the renaissance and antiquity as the golden ages of poetry would presumably lead to a necessarily decreasing critical interest in poets since Shakespeare.[50] Yet Bloom's analytical tool of the six revisionary ratios applicable to individual poets at any time redeems certain poets by the degree to which they can be shown to fight against their anxiety and thus to enter into the tradition — the canon — of great strugglers which makes up Bloom's Parnassus. For that purpose the blindness and the ignorance of Oedipus may be turned into an asset. Again here, the solution is the intuitive leap of 'romantic' man. Oedipus, Bloom asserts, 'was on the path to oracular godhood',[51] and by the same oracular short-circuit 'strong poets have followed him by transforming their blindness towards their precursors into the revisionary insights of their own work'.[52]

Bloom tends to be dismissed as one of the major excentrics of contemporary literary criticism. Admittedly, his unpreparedness to consider critical positions other than his own, his general arrogance in his writings, which completely lack any traditional note and reference apparatus, and the esoterism especially in his early work (for which he draws heavily on Kabbalah and Gnosticism) make him formidably forbidding; but that we have to deal with a man deeply absorbed in and equally deeply in love with literature is beyond the merest shadow of doubt. Bloom's refusal to comply with the conventions of the academic treatise is a deliberate move to demonstrate his internalization of literature: if literature has a meaning and a function, it must be part of the mental make-up of author and reader alike. If you cannot quote from memory — and we do not need to bother about any total recall — literature has not sufficiently imprinted itself, for only the strongest literature merits a place in the mind.

Notes

1. Bloom, H., *The Western Canon: The Books and the School of Ages*, (New York: Harcourt Brace, 1994), p. 29.
2. Bloom, H., *A Map of Misreading*, (New York: Oxford University Press, 1975), p. 200.
3. *The Western Canon*, p. 526; Bloom's italics.
4. *A Map of Misreading*, p. 200. The best ultra-short accounts given by Bloom himself about his poetics are found in Bloom, H., *Kabbalah and Criticism*, (New York: The Seabury Press, 1975), pp. 88-89 and Bloom, H., *Wallace Stevens: The Poems of Our Climate*, (Ithaca and London: Cornell University Press, 1977), pp. 393-94. A longer, but still condensed version is offered as the first chapter of Bloom, H., *Poetry and Repression: Revisionism from Blake to Stevens*, (New Haven: Yale University Press, 1976), pp. 393-94 and in the more roaming introductory chapters of Bloom, H., *Agon: Towards a Theory of Revisionism*, (New York: Oxford University Press, 1982), pp. 3-90. A good and brief introduction to the key concepts and their relations in Bloom's poetics is John Hollander's in his edition of essays and chapters by Bloom: *Poetics of Influence: Harold Bloom*, (New Haven: Henry Schrab, 1988), pp. xi-xlvi.
5. *The Western Canon*, p. 522.

6. Ibid., p. 35.

7. Ibid., pp. 32 and 200.

8. Following this kind of logic through, it makes sense that Bloom, despite acknowledging Johnson and Coleridge (and the critic W. J. Bate) as among the 'great affirmers' of the anxiety of influence, and Nietzsche and Emerson as among the 'great deniers', has learnt more from the latter than from the former (Bloom, H., *The Anxiety of Influence: A Theory of Poetry*, (New York: Oxford University Press, 1973), p. 50). Somewhat further on in his 'tessera' chapter, Bloom extends the list of affirmers to including Ruskin, and the list of deniers to including Goethe, Mann, Thoreau, Blake, Lawrence, Pascal, Rousseau and Hugo (Ibid., p. 56).

9. Ibid., p. 55.

10. *Kabbalah and Criticism*, p. 82.

11. *A Map of Misreading*, p. 18.

12. *The Western Canon*, p. 30.

13. Ibid., p. 46.

14. Ibid., p. 443.

15. Bloom, H., *Blake's Apocalypse: A Study in Poetic Argument*, (London: Victor Gollancz Ltd., 1963), p. 9.

16. Cp. '[T]he kind of ideas that poems are' *Kabbalah and Criticism*, p. 55.

17. Quoted in *A Map of Misreading*, p. 20.

18. Ibid.

19. Peirce quoted in *Kabbalah and Criticism*, p. 56.

20. Ibid., pp. 57 and 106.

21. Bloom suggests that 'meaning in belated texts is always wandering meaning' (Ibid., p. 82).

22. Bloom's careless attitude to definitions is very much in evidence in his discussion about the ontology of the poem, cp. e.g.: '[T]he verbal image (however you want to define an image)' (Ibid., p. 65).

23. *The Western Canon*, p. 10.

24. Falstaff is very much at the centre of interest in *The Western Canon*, where that character is related — agonistically — to Chaucer's Wife of Bath (115). Bloom goes so far as to suggest a parallel of character, in which he professes his interest over plot (112), to 'virtual reality' (105).

25. *A Map of Misreading*, p. 19.

26. Ibid., p. 21.

27. Cp. '[T]he deepest or most vital instances of influence are almost never phenomena of the poetic surface' (*Kabbalah and Criticism*, p. 66).

28. The three works from 1973 and 1975 are a trinity of Bloomian poetics, with the first to sketch the theory of anxiety of influence in terms of six revisionary ratios, elaborating on the Freudian and the Kabbalistic aspects respectively in the two later works. The first coherent articulation of the theory is in the introduction to *Yeats* (New York: Oxford University Press, 1970), pp. 3-22. Bloom has returned to theoretical issues of his poetics from time to time since 1975, notably in *Agon: Towards a Theory of Revisionism* from 1982, and in *Ruin the Sacred Truths* from 1989, but here repeating rather than developing his views.

29. *Kabbalah and Criticism*, p. 62.

30. *The Anxiety of Influence*, pp. 5-7.
31. Cp. 'There is no anxiety of representation for a strong poet, ... because that anxiety was met and overcome already for the strong ephebe by the precursor (and for the Kabbalists by God)' (*Kabbalah and Criticism*, p. 82).
32. *The Anxiety of Influence*, pp. 5-7.
33. Ibid., p. 72.
34. Ibid., p. 7. Bloom recognizes the existence of ideas and images taken over by succeeding generations of poets, and also the justified work of criticism to trace such influences, as they belong to discursiveness and to history (Ibid., p. 71).
35. Bloom suggests a relation of Kabbalah to Freudian theory in the proposition that '[a]s a psychology of belatedness, Kabbalah manifests many prefigurations of Freudian doctrine' (*A Map of Misreading*, p. 43).
36. *The Anxiety of Influence*, p. 8.
37. Inspired by Cordovero, whereas the triad of dialectic revisionism is derived from Luria.
38. For an exemplification of the interaction of these for the reading of any strong crisis poem — the master text for Bloom — cp. *A Map of Misreading* pp. 95-104 and the reading of Browning's 'Childe Roland' poem, Ibid., pp. 105-22. For an application of the six behinah of the sefirot in general cp. *Kabbalah and Criticism*, pp. 66-71. In the later — post-1977 — theory this is supplemented by troping into the analytical device of 'poetic crossings'.
39. *The Anxiety of Influence*, p. 122.
40. *A Map of Misreading*, p. 89.
41. *The Anxiety of Influence*, p. 78.
42. Ibid., p. 8.
43. Ibid., p. 9.
44. *A Map of Misreading*, p. 19.
45. *Wallace Stevens*, p. 11. The parallel of Bloom's theory of poetic misprision to Kabbalistic usage is well worth noting: 'In its degeneracy, Kabbalah has sought vainly for a magical power over nature, but in its glory it sought, and found, a power of the mind over the universe of death' (*Kabbalah and Criticism*, p. 47), and further on: 'Let us say (following Vico) that all religion is apotropaic litany against the dangers of nature, and so all poetry an apotropaic litany, warding off, defending against death' (Ibid., p. 52). Also Bloom links psychic defence closely to the fear of dying, cp. Ibid., p. 84.
46. In addition to the great amount of indirect evidence for the prominence of Shelley's poetics in Bloom's critical works, the debt is duly acknowledged from time to time, e. g.: 'In Shelley's *A Defence of Poetry*, which Yeats rightly considered the most profound discourse upon poetry in the language' (*The Anxiety of Influence*, p. 39).
47. Bloom does not even feel sure about the exact nature of romanticism. The impression from the first chapters of *The Anxiety of Influence* of romanticism as strong prophecy is later on problematized as perhaps only an 'intensity of repression' (Ibid., pp. 111-12).
48. Ibid., p. 10.
49. L.c.
50. Shakespeare already here — before *The Western Canon* — presents a special case

in Bloom's view, since he is the only English poet to have absorbed his source of influence, Marlowe. Also, Shakespeare belongs to a time when the anxiety of influence was not 'central to poetic consciousness' (Ibid., p. 11), and since his form was dramatic rather than lyric, the 'shadow cast by the precursors' (Ibid., p. 1) was less dominant.

51. Ibid., p. 10.
52. L.c.

Notes on Contributors

Michael Böss is an Associate Professor of American and English Studies at the Faculty of Modern Languages, the Aarhus School of Business. He is also a free lance broadcaster with Radio Denmark. He graduated from the University of Aarhus in 1977 and was afterwards encouraged by Donald Hannah — 'who made lecturing an art' — to stay on and teach English literature while completing his B.A. in religion.

Jørn Carlsen is an Associate Professor at the Department of English, University of Aarhus. Although his present work is concerned with Canadian literature and culture it was Donald Hannah who, in 1959, inspired his study of modern British literature. Since 1965 he has benefited from being one of Donald's colleagues.

Inger Hunnerup Dalsgård holds a *cand. mag.* in English and Religious Studies from the University of Aarhus, and in 1994 she completed her M.A. thesis on *Frankenstein* under Professor Hannah's supervision. She has taught at the universities of Aarhus and Odense and has spoken on a variety of topics at universities in Britain and the United States. She is currently a doctoral researcher at the Department of English, King's College, University of London, preparing a thesis on technological warning myths in the novels of Herman Melville and Thomas Pynchon.

Niels Bugge Hansen read English at Aarhus from 1957 to 1959 and graduated from the University of Copenhagen in English and Latin in 1965. After postgraduate studies at Merton College, Oxford he was appointed to a post at the Department of English in the University of Copenhagen where he is now an Associate Professor in English literature. In the first year at Aarhus Donald Hannah joined the staff of the Department of English, and his fine lectures on modern novelists and the personal contacts in his tutorials for undergraduates (five in the class of 1957!) became the source of a lifelong inspiration for the study of English literature.

Hans Hauge commenced his studies of English at the University of Aarhus in 1967 with Donald Hannah as his professor of literature. He is now an Associate Professor at the Department of English with literary theory as his special field. In 1993 he completed his Danish Doctorate on the Danish philosopher and theologian K.E. Løgstrup.

Seamus Heaney is one of the best known Irish poets of today. For his numerous volumes of poetry published over the last 30 years Seamus Heaney was in 1995 honoured with the Nobel Prize.

Earle Labor, Wilson Professor of American Literature at Centenary College of Louisiana, is considered a leading authority on Jack London, having published eight books on this world-famous author (including the Stanford editions of London's letters and short stories). Professor Labor's friendship with Donald and Inge Hannah has flourished for more than two decades, beginning in 1973, when Earle was a Fulbright lecturer at the University of Aarhus, and subsequently highlighted with visits to Louisiana and Denmark by the Hannah and Labor families.

Lee Morgan is Brown Professor of English and Chairman of the Department of English at Centenary College of Louisiana, where he has taught since 1954. An eighteenth-century specialist, Professor Morgan has co-edited two anthologies, co-authored a widely used textbook on critical-interpretive approaches to literature, and published reviews and articles on eighteenth-century subjects. He has just completed a biography of Henry Thrale, friend and benefactor of Dr. Samuel Johnson. In 1977, Professor Morgan was Guest Professor of English at the University of Aarhus. It was at this time that he first met Donald Hannah, who later became a Visiting Professor at Centenary. The Morgan and Hannah families have remained close through the years.

Claus Bratt Østergaard was a student at the Department of English from 1964-73, where he also taught phonetics and grammar from 1971-73. As a student he attended Donald Hannah's lectures on the English novel and he wrote his master's thesis on D.H. Lawrence under Hannah's supervision. Hannah's literary impulse worked long-term and underground, and it surfaced in Østergaards Danish Doctorate on the English Novel. Østergaard now teaches among other disciplines European literary history from Homer to Beckett at the Department of Literature at the University of Copenhagen.

A student back in the early sixties, *Per Serritslev Petersen* was taught his literary appreciation and English literature by Donald Hannah, who also supervised his master's thesis on the impact of Flaubert's fiction on Henry James's aesthetics. Since 1971 Per Serritslev Petersen has been Donald Hannah's colleague in the Department of English at the University of Aarhus — and also his chairman (1979-92).

Lars Ole Sauerberg is Professor of Literature in English at Odense University, to which he came after undergraduate and graduate studies in English at the University of Aarhus (1969-73) and a period as teaching assistant at the university's Department of English (1973-7). His love for and specialization in modern English-language literature owes much to the years of study and 'apprenticeship' in Aarhus profiting greatly from the learned and stimulating presence of Donald Hannah.

Michael Skovmand graduated from the Department of English in 1971; since 1976 he has been an Associate Professor in English at the University of Aarhus. Donald Hannah is his teacher and adviser, colleague and indiscriminate co-reader of all manner of literature, and friend, a kindred spirit in matters human and Toscanan and in something as old-fashioned as literary appreciation.

Knud Sørensen is Professor Emeritus of English Philology at the University of Aarhus and former colleague of Donald Hannah. His interests are English grammar and style, the history of the English language, English influence on Danish. Recent publications are: *Charles Dickens: Linguistic Innovator* (1985), *English Past and Present* (1988), *English and Danish Contrasted* (1991), *Engelsk i dansk. Er det et must?* (1995).

A 1964 freshman essay on Yeats' 'The Second Coming' was *Karl-Heinz Westarp*'s first contact with the experienced and helpful teacher Donald Hannah. Later Donald Hannah supervised his M.A. thesis on Joyce, and since his own appointment at the Department of English in 1969, innumerable formal and informal contacts let a close and cherished friendship grow.

Tabula Gratulatoria

Aalborg Katedralskole
Aalborg

Aalborg Studenterkursus
Aalborg

Engelsk Bibliotek
Aarhus Universitet
Aarhus

Engelsk Institut
Handelshøjskolen
Aarhus

Engelsklærerne
Langkær Gymnasium
Mundelstrup

Engelsklærerne
Dronninglund Gymnasium
Dronninglund

Det Humanistiske Fakultet
Aarhus Universitet

Rektor Henning Lehmann
Aarhus Universitet

Nørresundby Gymnasium
Nørresundby

VUC
Aarhus

Ea Cecilie Aidt
Aarhus

Hanne Albinus
Ribe

Lone Albrecht
Aarhus

Joan Alexandersen
Aarhus

Ulla Amsinck
Frøstrup

Carsten Kjær Andersen
Rønde

Christian Andersen
Anne Sofie Møller
Aarhus

Karsten Gramkow Andersen
Aalborg

Tony Søndergaard Andersen
Risskov

Karsten Andreasen
Løsning

Hans Arndt
Althea Ryan
Mørke

Annemarie Backmann
Højbjerg

Kirsten Sass Bak
Højbjerg

Søren Hattesen Balle
Aarhus

Else Barlach
Risskov

Knud Børge Bendtsen
Risskov

Ann Benkjær
Aarhus

Helle Bergstein
Horsens

Peter Billund
Ribe

Sheila and Jørgen Bissenbakker
Odense

Gitte Bjerre
Aarhus

Niels Bjøreng
Nørresundby

Michael Böss
Tvis

Annemarie Slej Boje
Skive

Heidi Bojsen
Højbjerg

Lise Windfeld Bornerup
Egaa

Lotte Borre
Aarhus

Rikke Bramming
Aarhus

Else Brendholdt
Skive

Poul Bruun
Højbjerg

René Bühlmann
Espergærde

Chris Bunt
Texas

Ole Bønnerup
Aarhus

Birgit Bennike Carlsen
Taastrup

Jonna and Jørn Carlsen
Aarhus

Dale Carter
Aarhus

Tim Caudery
Mundelstrup

Anna Marie Tams Christensen
Malling

Christina Christensen
Aarhus

Dorte Rafn Christensen
Aabenraa

Helen P.W. Christensen
Egaa

Ingeborg Christensen
Aabyhøj

Jørgen Riber Christensen
Aalborg

Trine Christensen
Randers

Ole Christiansen
Silkeborg

Pia Christiansen
Risskov

Peter Nyborg Clausen
Aarhus

Sonja Clingman
Aarhus

Hanne Dalgård
Odense

Inger Hunnerup Dalsgaard
Aarhus

Peter Dau
Risskov

Line Bülow Davidsen
Aarhus

Anne-Marie Dibbern
Aarhus

Birthe and Steen Diederich
Aarhus

Charlotte Diehn
Lystrup

Karen Dyrholm
Randers

Birthe Hollesen Ekmann
Thisted

Anne Elliot
Aarhus

J.E. Engelbrett
Holstebro

Christine Eie Eriksen
Aarhus

Anne Mette Finderup
Copenhagen

Marianne Bartholdt Fisker
Aarhus

Henrik Fogde
Ringkøbing

Mogens Fredberg
Rønde

Signe Frits
Aarhus

Gunner Frøberg
Frederiksberg

Peder Gammeltoft
Henne

Elisabeth Thomsen Gjesse
Aarhus

Gro Glans
Hjørring

Bente Elkjær Gram
Rønde

Olaf Baun Grarup
Hellerup

Yrsa Søgaard Gregersen
Aarhus

Jan Nordby Gretlund
Odense

Mads Grøftehauge
Aarhus

Ragna Grøngaard
Aarhus

Inge Vibeke Hahn
Skive

Ida and Niels Hald
Aarhus

Nanette Louise Hale
Copenhagen

Mette Hampen
Aalborg

André Wang Hansen
Aarhus

Annette Hansen
Viby J.

Bent Hansen
Inger Mølgaard
Middelfart

Bente Hansen
Copenhagen

Birthe Dalby Hansen
Aarhus

Kenneth Søndberg Hansen
Aarhus

Line Hansen
Aarhus

Mette Mølgaard Hansen
Aarhus

Niels Bugge Hansen
Hellerup

Ole M. Hansen
Aarhus

Rikke Mølgaard Hansen
Middelfart

Lone Hasring
Copenhagen

Inger Hastrup
Slagelse

Vibeke Hattel
Copenhagen

Winni and Hans Hauge
Aarhus

Kirsten Have
Randers

Seamus Heaney
Dublin

Einar Pihl Helleland
Brabrand

Svend Erik Henningsen
Viborg

Cathrine Kyø Hermansen
Aarhus

Inger Heyerdahl-Jensen
Aalborg

Lisbeth Gry Hjørlund
Randers

Troels Hoffmann
Aarhus

Rikke Holdgaard
Aarhus

Claus Krohn Holm
Aarhus

Kirsten Holsegård-Rasmussen
Aarhus

Gertrud Horsbøl
Copenhagen

Martin Horsted
Nykøbing Mors

June Horup
Copenhagen

Inger Houmøller
Thisted

Elsebeth Hurup
Aarhus

Kirsten Husted
Randers

Tanja Huus
Aarhus

Povl Hvidkilde
Tønder

Michael Boÿe Hvorslev
Spøttrup

Anne Dorrit Hølholm
Charlottenlund

Eskil Irminger
Nykøbing Falster

Anne Karoline Iversen
Risskov

Hanne Iversen
Varde

Inger and Anders Iversen
Risskov

Susanne Ørbæk Jacobsen
Frederiksberg

Ib Jarlskov
Aabybro

Benedikte Sinkjær Jarlstrøm
Randers

Karen Nocis Jensen
Brædstrup

Klaus Bruhn Jensen
Copenhagen

Lene Nørholm Jensen
Aarhus

Ruth Jensen
Højbjerg

Bente Skibsted Jespersen
Aarhus

Larry Paul Jorgenson
Bjerringbro

Gerda Jørgensen
Kerteminde

Helle Dreyer Jørgensen
Aarhus

Maja Jørgensen
Ranum

Lars Kaastrup
Skanderborg

Hanne P. Kjeldsen
Hjørring

Anders Holm Klitgaard
Odense

Lene Sigh Knudsen
Brabrand

Elly Koch
Hjørring

Bente Kragh
Aarhus

Merete Krarup
Roslev

Tue Krarup-Pedersen
Aarhus

Anja Kristensen
Aarhus

Knud Hanefelt Kristensen
Herning

Finn Kvorning
Varde

Earle Labor
Shreveport, La.

Maggi Lykke Larsen
Beder

Shirley and Knud Larsen
Brabrand

Karen M. Lauridsen
Aarhus

Jørgen Lauritsen
Ringkøbing

René Lauritsen
Aarhus

Peter A. Lindhardt
Pernille Holm Møller
Aarhus

Marianne Lüttichau
Copenhagen

Ian Lukins
Ugelbølle

Karen E.B. Lund
Aarhus

Tina Lund
Aarhus

Birgitte Lyngholm
Skive

Svend Madsen
Skive

Carmen Maier
Ebeltoft

Lone Mailandt
Aarhus

Trine Malchow-Møller
Aarhus

Inger Gammelby Meiborg
Aarhus

Kjeld Mejndor
Randers

Kirsten Busck Mellor
Langaa

Ole Michelsen
Aarhus

Susanne Midtiby
Skødstrup

Dorte Mikkelsen
Viby J.

Sylvia Mikkelsen
Højbjerg

Hans Elgaard Mogensen
Aarhus

Lisbet S. Mogensen
Stockholm

Lucy and Lee Morgan
Shreveport, La.

Henrik Mossin
Hundested

Mathilde Møldrup
Aarhus

Bo Nake
Varde

Bodil Hohwü Nielsen
Aarhus

Gudrun Rauer Nielsen
Fanø

Mads Nielsen
Næstved

Lisbeth Nissen
Haderslev

Alastair Niven
Buckinghamshire

Troels Nymann
Tarm

Hanne-Lis Nyskov
Ebeltoft

Alice Schou Nørgaard
Maarslet

Anne-Birgit Odgaard
Thisted

Morten Berg Olesen
Aalborg

Stine Wium Olesen
Esbjerg

Astrid Regine Olsen
Frederikshavn

Flemming Olsen
Lyngby

Gary Ottosen
Aarhus

Gunhild Otzen
Vejle

Louise Otzen
Frederiksberg

Bodil Junker Pedersen
Aarhus

Elisabeth Pedersen
Aarhus

Else Pedersen
Varde

Hanne Kær Pedersen
Aarhus

Helga L. Falkesgaard Pedersen
Frederiksberg

John Allan Pedersen
Dybvad

K. Kjærsgaard Pedersen
Hjørring

Karen Horsdal Pedersen
Aarhus

Kjeld Pedersen
Ulfborg

Lene Pedersen
Aarhus

Peter J. Pedersen
Aarhus

Åse Fogh Pedersen
Tørring

Anne Gerd Petersen
Sønderborg

Malene Holt Petersen
Hobro

Per Serritslev Petersen
Aarhus

Birger Petterson
Skjern

Luise Hemmer Pihl
Mørke

Helle Pløger
Brabrand

Gerda Poulsen
Højbjerg

Inger Lomholdt Poulsen
Aarhus

Kirsten Poulsen
Aarhus

Lotte Hammershøj Poulsen
Hinnerup

Marianne Powell
Copenhagen

Kirsten Rahbek
Jelling

Lis Rasmussen
Ballerup

Niels Nørlund Rasmussen
Lystrup

Poul Agnar Rasmussen
Thisted

Steen Hedegaard Rasmussen
Aasiaat

Ulla Rasmussen
Randers

Gerd Kjærholm Redon
St. Germain-en-Laye

Jørgen Reelsbo
Viby J.

Hans Chr. Risgaard
Randers

Gunner Roed
Thisted

Anker Rosenskjold
Frederikshavn

Annette W. Rousing
Aarhus

Ellen Rønhede
Vestervig

Lene Saksager
Rønde

Lars Ole Sauerberg
Odense

Frauke Schaumburg
Odense

Henriette Schaumburg-Müller
Aarhus

Michael Josiah Anthony Shaw
Galten

Tania Sheikh
Aarhus

Catharina Siemerling
Ebeltoft

Michael Skovmand
Hanne Glavind
Hornslet

Terkel Skårup
Copenhagen

David Slater
Ørsted

Inge Ærenlund Sloth
Aarhus

Sanne Kristine Späth
Aarhus

Anne-Marie Stefansson
Grenaa

Jesper Strøm
Aarhus

Frode Søby
Aabyhøj

Bente Beck Sørensen
Skive

Bodil Sørensen
Aarhus

Frede Sørensen
Dronninglund

George Lyhne Sørensen
Skørping

Henrik Enemark Sørensen
Aarhus

Inga M.R. Sørensen
Værløse

Margit and Knud Sørensen
Højbjerg

Marina Kofoed Sørensen
Aarhus

Hanne Tang
Frederiksberg

Jane Winum Thomsen
Risskov

Stinne Creutz Thomsen
Aarhus

Anja Teresa Thyssen
Aarhus

Poul Tornøe
Copenhagen

Anna Trosborg
Aarhus

Gudmund Tybjerg
Haderslev

Torben Vestergaard
Aalborg

Gitte Vittrup
Frederiksberg

Henny Wad
Esbjerg

Søren Wad
Aarhus

Gitte Wallmann
Risskov

Richard Webb
Aarhus

Jette and Karl-Heinz Westarp
Haarup

Allan Føgh Westphall
Brabrand

Inge Wilhelmsen
Hjørring

Inge Windeballe
Egaa

Kathleen Yates
Rønde

Tania Young
Viby J.

Finn Zacho-Petersen
Randers

Marie-Louise Østblom
Ry

Claus Bratt Østergaard
Holte

Frede Østergaard
Rønde

Inger Østergaard
Birkerød

Index